AMERICAN INDIAN LIVES

EDITED BY JAY MILLER

★

Mourning Dove

A Salishan Autobiography

University of Nebraska Press

Lincoln & London

First Bison Book printing: 1994

Library of Congress Cataloging
in Publication Data
Mourning Dove, 1888–1936.
Mourning Dove: a Salishan
autobiography / edited by Jay Miller.
p.   cm. – (American Indian lives)
Bibliography: p.   Includes index.
ISBN 0-8032-3119-9 (alkaline paper)
ISBN 978-0-8032-8207-0 (pbk)
1. Mourning Dove, 1888–1936.
2. Salishan Indians – Biography.
3. Salishan Indians – Women.
4. Salishan Indians –
Social life and customs.
I. Miller, Jay, 1947–   II. Title.
III. Series.
E99.S21M68   1990
979.7′004979 – dc20
89-14780   CIP

♾

Contents

List of Illustrations, vii

Acknowledgments, ix

Introduction, xi

★

I. A WOMAN'S WORLD

1. My Life, 3

2. Spiritual Training, 34

3. Courtship and Marriage, 49

4. The Dutiful Wife, 60

5. Baby Care, 70

6. Charming Affections, 79

7. Widowhood, 91

★

II. SEASONAL ACTIVITIES

8. The Fishery
at Kettle Falls, 99

9. Fall Hunting, 114

10. Winter Dancing, 123

11. The Seancing Rite, 130

12. The Sweatlodge
Diety, 136

Contents

III. OKANOGAN HISTORY

13. Tribal
Backgrounds, 145

14. The Big Snow
and Flood Rampage of
1892–1893, 157

15. Early Farming, 167

16. The Invasions of Miners
and Settlers, 177

★

APPENDIX

The Red Cross and the
Okanogans, 189

★

Notes, 193

Glossary of
Colville-Okanogan
Terms, 235

References, 241

Index, 255

Illustrations

1.
Mourning Dove
in youth and maturity, xviii

2.
The school at Pia, xxii

3.
Reconstruction of
St. Paul Mission at
Kettle Falls, 9

4.
The Catholic church
at Pia, 21

5.
Tanning a hide, 108

6.
Roasting and drying salmon, 110

7.
Fishing at a weir, 110

8.
Sanpoil artifacts, 111

9.
Making a tule mat, 111

10.
Debris caught in a tree
from flooding, 165

Acknowledgments

This manuscript came to my attention five years after I began working with the confederated tribes of the Colville Reservation. For almost a decade now I have been learning from these elders, and their wonderful wisdom is unabated. Thanks to Mourning Dove, many new vistas have opened for us.

Among the Colvilles, help has come from so many quarters that I will not be able to thank everyone here. But I would like to single out Isabel Friedlander La Course Arcasa, Julianne Timentwa and her sons Jim and Leslie, the late Herman Friedlander and his wife, Maude, T. B. and Pearl Charlie, Emily Peone, Jerome Miller, Shirley Palmer, Suzanne Morgan, Lucy Covington, Andrew Joseph, Melvin La Course, Nettie Francis, Christine Sam, Nancy Judge, Laura Scoble, Agnes Nanamkin Friedlander, Matilde and Adam Bearcub, Sue Matt, and Mary Miller Marchand and family. Special thanks also go to the Fredin family: Adeline, Larry, Christine, and Laurie. Charles Quintasket and Mary Lemury provided kind and generous help, along with necessary corrections, as the elders of Mourning Dove's family.

For help with technical or academic concerns, I am obligated to Dale Kinkade, Anthony Mattina, Donald Parman, Vi and Don Hilbert, Joanne Miller Hooker, Gary Gibbs, Glenn, Dot, Kether, and Keith Williams, Ann Schuh, Donna Steinburn, and the Chesnin-Bernsteins: Harry, Noah, Zachary, Sara, and Ann. Catherine Schrump and Alan Stay referred me to important citations. In Chicago, Mike, Esther, Ben, and Dan Lieber gave me a home. Others of my families—Millers, Toulouses, and Dunns—provided helpful insights into my work that they probably never imagined. C. B. Blue Clark deserves a special note of thanks for his many kindnesses and timely help with files from the National Archives. A. LaVonne Brown Ruoff has taught me much about the craft of editing.

My friends rallied to my aid during a brief visit to Seattle to locate important documents in May 1986. For their efforts, cars, and meals, I am most grateful.

For their earlier care and attention to the manuscript, my greatest appreciation goes to Erna Gunther, a friend of many years who did not live to see the work completed, and to Gerry Guie and her late husband, Dean, who stored the manuscript for fifty years.

Timely help was graciously provided by Gary Lundell at the University of Washington Archives, Joyce Justice at the Federal Archives and Records Center in Seattle, Sister Rita Bergimini at the Sisters of Providence Archives in West Seattle, and by the able staff, particularly Charles Cullen, Fred Hoxie, John Aubrey, Richard H. Brown, Ruth Hamilton, and Violet Brown, at the Newberry Library in Chicago, my haven both as a fellow and as editor/assistant director of the D'Arcy McNickle Center for the History of the American Indian. The American Philosophical Society kindly permitted the use of illustrations by Karneecher from their Boas collection. They do not, however, own the originals, and efforts to track them down or to find the artist's relatives or heirs have been unsuccessful.

Introduction

MOURNING DOVE was the pen name of Christine Quintas-ket, a remarkable woman from the Colville Confederated Tribes of eastern Washington State.[1] Now best known as the first Native American woman to publish a novel, she was a regional celebrity throughout the Inland Northwest during her lifetime. As such she led two lives—a public one as Mourning Dove and a private one as a woman struggling to make ends meet. Her public life as a writer is all the more astounding because her formal education was scant, her command of Standard English was faulty, and her companions were sometimes unsupportive.

Her private life was difficult. Primarily a seasonal laborer, she moved with the jobs and never had a stable home where she could write at leisure. Instead, after backbreaking days in the orchards and fields, she would write for most of the night in a tent or cabin. Despite great hardship, both financial and emotional, she persisted in her goal of producing stories that gave Indians a sympathetic hearing.

Sympathy was not something she often experienced. When her only novel seemed near release, local newspapers made public her ambitions. Her neighbors, both white and Indian, grew suspicious and even hostile. When she later became politically active, some white reservation officals were critical of her, striking at her most heartfelt aspiration: they denied her literary ability. An agency farmer (a federal employee hired to turn Indian fishers and hunters into yeomen farmers) said she had not written the novel but only allowed her name to appear on the work of a white man. While it is true that the novel was produced in collaboration with white editors, she provided the initial copy, discussed changes, and approved the result.

Mourning Dove determined she would do something on her own, and this autobiography is the outcome. Writing in anger and haste, she produced the collection of rough pages and chapters that were edited into this book. In the meantime she managed to have the agency farmer removed from his post and demanded other agency reforms. Despite such distractions, she worked hard at her writing and for her people. Eventually the accumulated stress and overwork took their toll and she died in 1936, at about age fifty. Her efforts survive, establishing her place in Native American literature and in the literary history of the Northwest.

Little has been recorded about her life. What is available includes fictions she created to protect her privacy. Intent on being a novelist, Christine often wove such fictions, usually quite plausible, into her work. Certainly there are several points where her manuscript is not strictly accurate. Although this might be unintentional, since she worked from memory, it is clear that she went to considerable effort to disguise and shuffle events so as to distance her writing from her family, both to shelter them from public scrutiny and to avoid criticism of her literary ambitions. She is remembered with much affection by her family and friends on the Colville Reservation, the only people who knew that she was both Mourning Dove and Christine Quintasket. In public letters she used other first and last names.

By her own account, Christine was born in a canoe while her mother was crossing the Kootenay River in Idaho, and her first clothing was the steersman's shirt. This entry foreshadowed her life of constant motion and independent activity. She said the year of her birth was 1888, but her schoolmates (born about that time) remember her as older and bigger than themselves. Therefore 1885 may be more likely.

Although her parents, Joseph and Lucy, held respected places in traditional society, they lacked the wealth and formal education valued by whites. Without material resources, Christine realized that education was vital to achieving her goal. Although her first stay at the Goodwin Catholic Mission near Kettle Falls was traumatic enough to make her deathly ill, she returned to school several times in her life.

When she was approved for a patent in fee simple for her allotted land on 14 March 1921 (at the time, Colville superintendent O. C. Upchurch wrote, "She is intelligent and industrious, and as capable of handling her affairs as the average white woman in the community"), she listed her schooling as Colville Mission, four years; Fort Spokane, one year; Fort Shaw, three years; and Calgary College, two years.[2]

The 1894 census records show her at Goodwin Mission school. She was lonely and was punished for speaking only Salishan, and she became ill after a few months. She went back to the mission from 1897 through 1899, when she made her first communion. Federal funds were cut for Indians at the mission in 1899, so these students then went to school at the Fort Spokane agency after 1900. The loss of government funds for Indian religious schools followed from the Browning Rule of 1896, stipulating that "schools of the federal government be filled before Indian students be allowed to enroll in church-oriented institutions."[3] Christine was at school when her mother, Lucy, died in 1902, supposedly the victim of sorcery performed on a dried black toad with its mouth propped open and its body skewered. The neighbor woman suspected of this crime drowned in a shallow puddle four months later after an alcoholic binge at a Vernon, British Columbia, hop-picking camp.

Lucy was born at Kettle Falls, an important upper Columbia salmon fishery in the territory of her Colvile tribe. (The Colvile tribe with one *l* is but one of the many tribes on the Colville Reservation.) Lucy's father, whose name is unknown, was from the Trout Lake band of the Arrow Lakes or Lakes tribe, and her mother, Maria, was the daughter of the Colvile chief at the falls. Later Maria

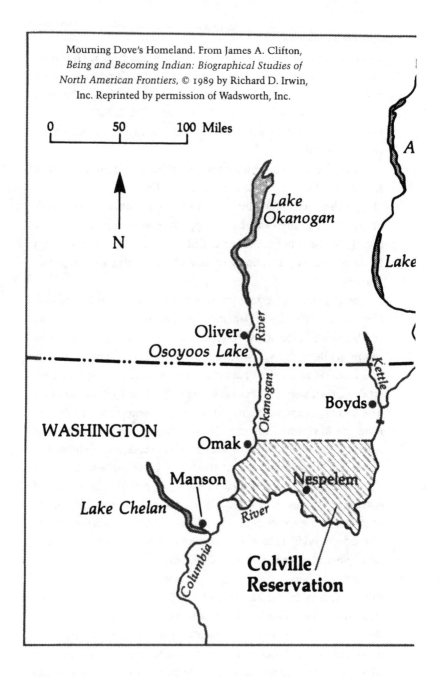

Mourning Dove's Homeland. From James A. Clifton,
*Being and Becoming Indian: Biographical Studies of
North American Frontiers,* © 1989 by Richard D. Irwin,
Inc. Reprinted by permission of Wadsworth, Inc.

0   50   100 Miles

N

*Lake
Okanogan*

Lake

A

Oliver
Osoyoos Lake

River

Okanogan

Kettle

Boyds

WASHINGTON

Omak

Manson

Nespelem

Lake Chelan

River

Columbia

**Colville
Reservation**

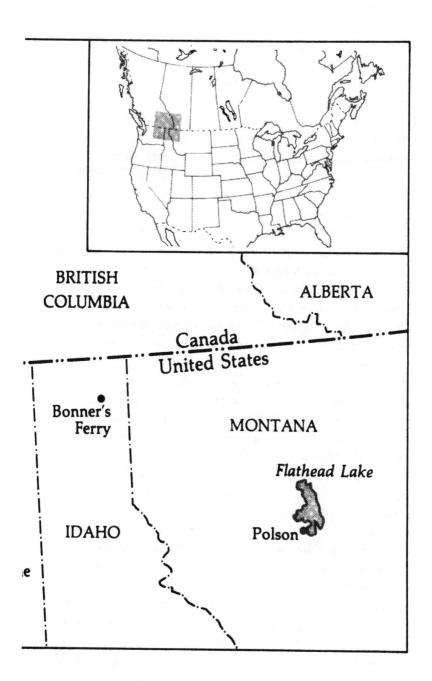

took her family to live among the Kootenays at Tobacco Plains because she was opposed to the flogging of criminals instituted by the new chief.

Christine's father, Joseph, was an orphan whose mother was a Nicola, an Athapaskan-speaking tribe living among the Okanagans. Mourning Dove claimed his father was a Scot, but his other children and the census records deny this. Evidently Christine provided a white ancestor to appeal to her readers. This may also explain why she kept her writings away from her father. She said it was because he was old and did not understand such things; but since he was an orphan she could imagine her grandfather as she wished.

As in any native family, close relations extended beyond blood kin. When Christine found Teequalt or Long Theresa, an old woman wandering aimlessly and waiting to die, her mother welcomed the stranger into the family and made special accommodations to her traditional life-style. Thereafter Teequalt took over Christine's pubertal and spiritual training. When her father worked as a hauler, he brought home Jimmy Ryan, a white orphan who became a son. Jimmy helped the family learn English and taught the children to read from his penny-dreadful novels. Mourning Dove said that Jimmy taught her the "Mysteries" of books, although her mother often scolded her for wasting time reading.

Though she died in 1902, Lucy is listed on the census through 1905, when the name of a second wife preempts hers. In 1904 Joseph married Cecelia, a woman a little older than Christine, and their first daughter was born in 1905. Before this Christine had managed the household. Now free to return to school, she entered Fort Shaw Indian school near Great Falls, Montana, which closed in 1910. While in Montana, she saw much of her grandmother, Maria, who died that same year. At the school Christine met Hector McLeod, a Flathead. According to the census, they were married in 1909 and lived at Polson, at the southern tip of Flathead Lake. There Christine witnessed the 1908 roundup of the last free-ranging bison herd, and it had such a profound impact on her that she based her first novel on it.

Within a few years Christine was estranged from Hector, after a stormy marriage. Hector could be violent and abusive, but he was also intelligent and generous. Family members recall a photograph of Christine, wearing a big hat, and Hector standing on the observation platform of the Oriental Limited, which was taking them to Milwaukee for their honeymoon. Throughout his life Hector was involved with bootleggers and gamblers. In later years he wore a hook in place of his right arm, shot off by a bootlegger in St. Ignatius. He was shot to death while playing cards in Shurz, Nevada, on 23 April 1937.[4]

By 1912 Christine was living in Portland, where she began her novel and took Mourning Dove as her pen name. She initially called herself Morning Dove, both as a sign of the dawning of her career and to commemorate the ever-faithful wife of Salmon, in Colville legend, who welcomes his return each spring. During a visit to a Spokane museum at the end of 1921, however, she saw a mounted bird with the label "mourning dove," which added tragic overtones to her pen name. Sometimes she used Hu-mi-shu-ma, her spelling of the onomatopoetic Okanogan name of this bird. In Portland, away from family, she had time to write. Her efforts seem to have been framed by her reaction to *The Brand*, a novel set among the Flatheads.[5] Mourning Dove's work had a similar plot but a more sympathetic viewpoint. The result discouraged her; she thought it flawed and hid it away in a trunk.

Determined to improve her skills, she enrolled in a Calgary business school from about 1913 through 1915 to learn typing and basic writing. According to an informative newspaper article,

she showed steady high grades. She also showed a dignity that rebuffed the snubs and cruel remarks. . . . It was in these lonely years that she commenced to write down her thoughts. She

1. Mourning Dove in youth and maturity. Editor's
collection.

wrote long journals of her experiences and her thoughts and dreams for the two races. She saw herself as the voice of her people in the wilderness of continued misunderstanding, trying to bring the two races closer together.

Her notes finally evolved into a novel about a young Indian agent who used an Indian maiden's love lightly. There was much bitterness and pathos in this amateur book which she hid in the bottom of her trunk.

After her course in Calgary, Hu-mi-shu-ma became a teacher on the [Inkameep] Indian reserve at Oliver, B.C.[6]

At the Walla Walla Frontier Days celebration, probably in 1915, she met Lucullus Virgil McWhorter, a Yakima businessman and Indian-rights advocate, who was so impressed by her that he charged her, in a letter dated 29 November 1915, with primary responsibility for preserving Salish traditions. He described his vision for her—"a future of renown: a name that will live through the ages." They kept up a steady correspondence until she died. Her letters (now in the McWhorter Collection, Holland Library, Washington State University) are signed variously as Christal, Christina, or Catherine, along with McLeod or Galler, when she did not sign as Mourning Dove. Yet, throughout her life, among the Colvilles she was known as Christine Quintasket.

In 1916 she was back in Polson keeping house for an unnamed family with six children, complaining of "headaches" and "no stamina." The next year she contracted pneumonia and inflammatory rheumatism. Although she seemed near death, she gradually recovered after an aunt doctored her with herbs and native treatments.

In an important interview (19 April 1916) in the *Spokesman Review*, the Spokane-based newspaper of the Inland Northwest, Christine spoke in anticipation of the sale of her novel, revealing many of her hopes and aspirations. Unfortunately, delays were to postpone publication for another decade.

An early passion for learning came to her and in spite of the fact that at 14 she was only in the third grade of the Colville public schools, she disputed vigorously with relatives over her desire to continue her education. Un-Indianlike, her womanly spirit refused to be broken by the dominance of the male; she left her home and pursued the fond fancy of her heart. At Fort Spokane, and at Fort Shaw, Mont., she continued her studies. She was, in the graded Colville schools, much larger than the white girls; her relatives thought she knew enough. In succeeding years she acquired a full grammar school education and then went to Calgary, Alberta, where she took a business school course, mastering shorthand, typewriting, and bookkeeping.

In the same article, Christine makes the clearest statement of her lifelong goal as a writer: "It is all wrong, this saying that Indians do not feel as deeply as whites. We do feel, and by and by some of us are going to be able to make our feelings appreciated, and then will the true Indian character be revealed." Espousing the importance of expressing these feelings, especially to a literate audience, she adds that education is also the common ground between herself and her father's second wife and family: "But my stepmother is enthusiastically interested in [her children's] education. She gave an acre and a sixtieth to the white school district supervisors, and now a schoolhouse stands on land that was hers by government allotment and hers are the only Indian children that go to school in it. All the rest are white."

About 1917 or 1918, Christine was a teacher on the Inkameep Okanagan reserve near Oliver, British Columbia. She continued writing and used some of her salary to buy a typewriter. She enjoyed telling her family that the previous teacher was an American black man who had all the Indian children talking as if they were on a southern plantation. Because her sister was married to a brother of

2. The second Larson schoolhouse was built on land
donated by Mourning Dove's stepmother. The hilltop in
the rear is Pia, its name a native designation for this area.
Photo taken in 1988, editor's collection.

the reserve chief, Christine expanded her role as teacher to provide
advice and writing skills for the local band leaders.

In 1919 she married Fred Galler, a Colville of Wenatchi and
pioneer white ancestry, who was tolerant of her career. Although
there were fights and separations, especially when Fred drank or did
things Christine considered "low life," they stayed together and
often worked as migrant laborers. Fred is recalled today as a kind
man who worked hard but had little ambition.

The couple lived in East Omak on the Colville Reservation. Now
that she was back among her people, her interest changed from
fiction to folklore. From their first meeting, McWhorter had encouraged Mourning Dove to collect and write down traditional stories,
which were fast disappearing in their original Salish versions. Initially she was reluctant to take time away from her writing for these
"folklores," as she always called them, but soon she enjoyed it.

With the novel *Cogewea* (1927) finally published, fifteen years after she completed the draft, McWhorter turned the editing of the Indian legends over to his friend Heister Dean Guie, who worked for the Yakima town newspaper. Guie was married to Geraldine Coffin, who may have influenced Mourning Dove, during her stay as their house guest, by talking about her own experiences as one of the first students in the anthropology program at the University of Washington.

McWhorter remained involved in the editing project. Letters between Guie and Mourning Dove passed through him for comment and interpretation. McWhorter was concerned that Indian themes and concerns be highlighted, whereas Mourning Dove wanted to express her knowledge and literary talents. Guie strived for consistency, sometimes straining the collaboration. He asked endless questions about the pattern number (three or five), species name translations, spellings, and other details. Mourning Dove expressed frustration and sometimes anger in her responses, arguing strongly for her own view. Guie did, however, insist that they write for a popular audience. By abbreviating and bowdlerizing the stories, he thought, they would produce suitable bedtime reading for children. Though Mourning Dove recorded tales mentioning incest, transvestism, and infanticide, these were ignored by mutual agreement.[7]

All three of the collaborators, who shared a concern for modesty and propriety, approved these omissions, but Mourning Dove went even further and removed morals and "just-so" explanations from some of the stories so they could not be ridiculed by whites. The accounts of how things came to be as they are and episodes likely to suggest superstition to a white audience were deleted, though such alterations made the stories unrecognizable to her own family and other Colville elders. This is perplexing because her letters reveal that Mourning Dove herself subscribed to superstitions about the number thirteen, Fridays, snakes, and the dark. Choosing to ignore these must have been a deliberate decision on her part.

Ironically, some incidents were included that would have shocked the three collaborators if they had analyzed Salish cultures. Thus the fog that surrounds Coyote during his escapes is not a metaphor for the unexplainable,[8] but an expression of the symbolic equation of fog and semen. Similarly, the liquid Coyote used to insult a bison skull is not spit but urine.

When she was aware of such features of traditional culture, Mourning Dove considered them "ugly" and actively suppressed references to them. By consciously calling her work fiction, she could omit material or cast it in the best way to appeal to a general audience. She invented military traits foreign to Plateau cultures, probably because whites expected Indians to be warriors. When discussing religion, she skipped over the seasonal feasts thanking each food for ripening and instead concentrated on the dramatic public rituals most like Judeo-Christian ones.

Other discrepancies may have been inadvertent. Her dates and species names are not reliable. Pia, the name for the area near her family's homestead, refers to the red-tailed hawk, not the eagle as she said in letters. She knew it was a raptor but was unsure just which one. Yet she was curious enough to correct her mistake, probably after an educational visit to a museum where birds were on display, like the one that taught her how to spell "mourning dove."

She had a definite female bias. Her reference to Sweatlodge as the wife of the Creator differs from available literature and from modern elders on the Colville Reservation. Often she gives a specifically female practice as an example of the general one. Her feminism extended to a stated rejection of marriage.

Throughout her life Mourning Dove was under considerable stress because she often acted contrary to approved female behavior. She also experienced the emotional strain of living in a large family and a close community and weathering rocky marriages. The deaths of her mother, grandmother, and beloved elders left scars, and constant overwork made her vulnerable to disease. Disagreements with husbands, neighbors, and officials also took their toll. She was constantly made aware that she led a life different from other people's expectations. Her writing about subjects that could be sensitive, such as traditional beliefs or practices mocked by non-Indians, aroused the suspicion of fellow natives and some whites. She worked out her frustrations in her writing, including letters to newspapers, which are mentioned in her correspondence with McWhorter but have not yet been located.

For Christine, the name Mourning Dove came to symbolize freedom and escape. She protected it by using it only with outsiders. Most of her professional activities she performed as Christine Galler, deliberately hiding the Quintasket family name from outsiders. Throughout her public career she used her married names, although most Colvilles knew her by her maiden name.

With some reluctance she took up public speaking, addressing the Omak Commercial Club about fishing rights on 11 April 1930, the Campfire Girls during their Indian Year on 10 February 1930, and the Brewster Women's Christian Temperance Union on 29 January 1935. She was active in the Wild Sunflower Club, promoting native crafts and traditions, and was one of nine 1928 charter members of the Eagle Feather Club, whose motto was "one for all, all for one" and who were interested in social welfare and betterment for Indians. As a member, she successfully intervened on behalf of girls in trouble with the law, getting them released in her custody.

Throughout her lifetime, Mourning Dove was also active in reservation politics. A special concern of hers was having the Biles-Coleman Company in East Omak fulfill its agreement to hire Indian workers in return for being allowed to set up their lumber mill on the reservation side of the Okanogan River. In addition, during the early 1930s she was outspoken in the movement to cut the number of agency personnel. It was in this context that she worked to have the agency farmer who disparaged her literary efforts removed from office. Her contribution also included several drafts of her own autobiography. School staff, clergy, elders, and her family rallied to her political standard. In 1935 she was elected the first woman on the Colville council.

All these efforts taxed her strength. She complained constantly of a "nevrous" (her spelling) disposition, which only got worse. She became disoriented and was taken on 30 July 1936 to the state hospital at Medical Lake, where she died at 10:15 P.M. on 8 August of "exhaustion from manic depressive psychosis." The death certificate listed her occupation as housewife and writer. She died childless, without debt and without savings.

Mourning Dove had bought a plot in a local white cemetery. After a life devoted to providing a bridge between Indian and white, she decided to leave the reservation. Her concern that marriage would obscure her own identity was justified: Fred paid for her funeral and a marker that says only "Mrs. Fred Galler." Across the Okanogan River on the Colville Reservation, her family and spiritual heirs still honor her memory.

THE COLVILLE RESERVATION

The Colville Confederated Tribes, mostly Interior Salishans, occupy a reservation bounded on the west by the Okanogan River and on the east and south by the Columbia, now flooded behind Grand Coulee Dam and Chief Joseph Dam. The northern boundary was the Canadian border until the North Half was taken away in 1892. As a "legally dedicated land base," including or neighboring ancestral territories, the reservation provides strong continuity between these Native Americans and their unbroken traditions.

Aboriginally the Columbia River was the lifeline connecting many tribes, including those now known as Interior Salishans. The lower Columbia was occupied by Chinookan communities near its mouth and Sahaptian ones upriver. The Chinooks were devastated and dispersed by European diseases by 1830, and the Sahaptians, as a consequence of an 1855 treaty, were forced to relocate to the Yakima Reservation in Washington or to the Warm Springs and Umatilla reservations in Oregon. The divide between Sahaptians and Salishans was Priest Rapids on the Columbia.

Upriver from there, the Salishans living along tributaries were the (Moses) Columbians (whose main village was at Vantage), Peskwaws (called Wenatchis by Sahaptians), Entiats, Chelans, Methows, Okanogans, Nespelems, Sanpoils, Colviles, and (Arrow) Lakes, who were mostly in modern Canada.[9] Canadian neighbors were the Kootenays and the Fraser River Salishans. Salishan tribes to the west were the Spokans, Kalispels, Flatheads, and Coeur d'Alenes.

Two dialect chains (interlinked speech communities) make up Interior Salish, with the Methows as the buffer between them. The chains are distinguished by differences in vocabulary and inflection. In speech, a predominant vowel can be heard. Among the Columbians-Peskwaws-Entiats-Chelans it is *ay*, while the Okanogans-Nespelems-Sanpoils-Colviles-Lakes use *aa* and the Methows *ii*. To avoid confusing the Colville Reservation and the tribe of the same name at Kettle Falls, to which Mourning Dove's maternal line belonged, I will spell the tribal name Colvile. Also, the Okanogans, without their consent or approval (as they say), are now divided by an international border into American or River Okanogans and Canadian or Lake Okanagans. I will call them both Okanogans unless they need to be distinguished.

The plight of the Colville Reservation during the 1960s attracted several scholars, who added to earlier research.[10] All of them have noted that the dominant Plateau values, pacifism and gender equality, allowed Colville women to flourish. Changes brought on by the horse, fur traders, and missionaries intensified rather than diminished earlier practices.

Reconstructed aboriginal patterns provide a baseline for understanding Colville traditions. These tribal groups shifted seasonally between winter villages along the Columbia, at confluences with its tributaries, and summer camps at resource-harvesting locations. Villages were situated near firewood, fresh water, and sheltering terrain.

Certain families were always known for their leadership abilities, both civil and religious. Their men and women acquired powers of varying strengths from sacred sites visited generation after generation. Men and women had different roles and careers in a statistical, but not an absolute, sense. Generally, men led in the public arena and women in the domestic, but crossover was possible. While men were often concerned with practical considerations, women looked after the general welfare. For example, at marriage a bride began keeping a calendrical ball of string to record details of family history. Like Mourning Dove, Plateau women were the recorders and conveyers of tradition. Changes introduced by horses and the fur trade only made women wealthier and more influential, provided they already had proper supernatural sanction. One writer notes that "women who obtained a spirit helper found themselves in competitive positions with males and new doors opened to them."[11]

The horse greatly increased the Indians' mobility. The adoption of guns and the trappings of equestrian nomadism gave some eastern Plateau tribes the look of Plains Indians, on horseback in the feather headdresses and beaded buckskins of popular media image. Some groups, like the Sanpoils and Nespelems, kept their Plateau orientation and acquired only a few horses; others, like the Columbians, used large horse herds to hunt bison in the Northern Plains and developed a growing confederacy to protect these interests. While men were away, women, particularly senior ones, took on more responsibilities, and their social, domestic, and political importance grew as groups of males took long trips to the Plains to hunt bison.[12]

Although pacifism was an important value for Plateau tribes, they often had to defend themselves from Plains raiders. Once fur traders became established on the Plateau, they discouraged warfare so the natives could devote all their energy to pelts and trading. Some communities left traditional use areas and moved to newly established trading posts. After the traders came the missionaries, who also worked to end overt hostilities but in doing so inadvertently helped increase the covert use of sorcery.

Thus aboriginal beliefs and institutions have been perpetuated, though now they are fitted into an overall Catholic context. Guardian spirits, vision quests, shamanism, sorcery, and rituals reflecting a basic belief in power (*shumix*) remain entrenched.[13] In part this was encouraged by the Jesuit missionaries' tolerance toward beliefs not directly in conflict with Catholic doctrine. Although Mourning Dove believed in the superiority of Catholicism and though many Plateau tribes were preconditioned toward it by converted Iroquois traders, Jesuits also had the advantage of being the only missionaries in the area between 1847 and 1858, since the 1855 Treaty War enabled the army to move all Protestant missionary families out of the war zone. The Jesuits and a few Oblates stayed, either at their missions or in native camps, strengthening the impression that they were dedicated and self-sacrificing. Because many of them were foreign-born, in contrast to the American Protestant missionaries, natives further identified them with their own interests rather than those of the American enemy.

With the end of the war, settlers moved into the region to stay. Although tensions were minimized by concentrating natives onto reservations, the Salishans continued to roam free because they were never forced to sign treaties. Chief Moses (Split-Sun) of the Columbians kept his people dispersed and concealed for their own safety. Also, natives lacked the numbers to retaliate after the depopulation caused by smallpox and other epidemics such as those of 1832 and 1854–55. Alcohol also took its toll.

Eventually these Interior Salishans were assigned to two reservations by presidential executive order. The Sanpoils, whose particularly conservative and inhospitable stance toward the government was encouraged by their prophet Kolaskin, became the nucleus for the Colville Reservation. Ulysses S. Grant signed the order in 1872, then removed the eastern third of the reservation by making the Columbia River its eastern boundary. This deprived these tribes of prime farmland and the fishery at Kettle Falls, which was permanently lost when it was flooded behind Grand Coulee Dam in 1939. Moses, on behalf of members of the Columbian Confederacy, was given a reservation in 1879 to the west of Colville, in the territory of the Methows, but he surrendered it for financial considerations in 1883 and moved with most of his followers to the Colville agency. Moses invited Chief Joseph and the Wallowa Nez Perces, returning from imprisonment in Indian Territory in 1885, to join him at Nespelem.[14] The Northern Half of the Colville Reservation was lost in 1892, and by terms of the 1905 McLaughlin Agreement the reduced reservation, or Southern Half, was allotted in eighty-acre plots for each enrolled member.[15] Mineral entry, allowing outsiders to make mining claims on the remaining reservation lands, was legislated for 1896, and the unallotted land was opened for homesteading in 1900. All these events are emotionally reported in Mourning Dove's final chapters and discussed in my added notes.

Much of recent Colville history has been a fight for survival and economic stability. In one of her last letters, Mourning Dove wrote to McWhorter about her disappointment that the Colvilles did not approve their own constitution under the Indian Reorganization (Wheeler-Howard) Act and other reforms advocated by John Collier. A constitution was approved by the Colvilles on 28 May 1937 and revised on 26 February 1938. Mourning Dove was spared the bitter confrontations over the attempt to terminate federal responsibility for her reservation.[16]

The Colvilles continued to achieve a measure of success by white standards until the Bureau of Indian Affairs tried to terminate the reservation under House Resolution 7190 of 1955. A 1960 Stanford report urged the liquidation of the Colville Reservation and the dispersal of the assets among the members. Mercifully, this did not happen; its consequences would have been catastrophic. Members of the reservation rallied and fought off the attack, halting disaster, though many are still bitter toward those enrolled Colvilles who advocated termination.

A renewed tribal council has implemented a deliberate strategy of building upon traditional values of flexibility and resourcefulness to develop economic programs encouraging timber sales, mining, and industry.

Salishan adaptational specialties continue. As one observer has noted, the Interior Salish have typically relied on the encampment type of gathering, such as the powwow, in preference to the feasts sponsored by the Sahaptians.[17] The advantage of the Salish pattern is that it brings people together for longer periods of closer interaction, helping to make the Salish dominant in the modern politics of the Plateau.

Today Colville is a reservation with an effective leadership and a complex diversity of people.[18] Catholics remain in the majority, but shamans, Shakers, and Protestants are also in evidence. Far from disappearing, the traditions recorded by Mourning Dove continue to thrive, both in her own family and in others; but they are mostly translated into English with a Catholic cast. Her efforts to transfer traditions from oral to written modes, with some editorial changes, were but a hint of the larger transformations all Colvilles have been undergoing.

THE AUTOBIOGRAPHY

The assortment of pages making up the manuscript for this book came to me in 1981. When Dean Guie died, his wife, Gerry, found the pages in their attic, put away until Dean's retirement would allow him leisure to edit them. They were not more stories, as he imagined, but drafts of Mourning Dove's autobiography. She had first given the material to McWhorter; but while living with the Guies the fall before *Coyote Stories* went to press, she retrieved the pages from McWhorter and left them with the Guies. Since Dean was a newspaper editor already enthusiastic about reworking her material, Mourning Dove undoubtedly hoped for a speedy revision. It did not happen. The pages were put away, and a few years later Mourning Dove died. At some point Dean did rewrite the chapter on babies, but nothing further was done with it.

Concerned that a publication result from the drafts but hampered by leg braces and a partial paralysis, Gerry turned the pages over to Erna Gunther, a legend in Northwest scholarship who had been Gerry's professor and was a friend of many years. Gunther typed out versions of the incidents and chapters but eventually returned the drafts to Gerry. In 1981, at Gunther's insistence, Gerry mailed a selection of pages to the University of Washington Press, where the editors asked me to review it because of my ties with Colville elders. I was both impressed and vexed by the submission. It was the most sustained discussion of Interior Salish life by an insider that I had ever seen, full of historical and ethnographic gems, but badly disjointed and ungrammatical.

Intrigued, I made contact with Gerry Guie, then went to visit her in Yakima. There I saw the whole text, arranged in twenty folders in a long box. Each folder held many pages related to the same topic. There were discolored sheets from Mourning Dove's original—full of typos, strikeovers, crossouts, and double-sided pages; yellow sheets typed by Gunther; and odds and ends of scraps and carbons from both Mourning Dove and Gunther. I started with Mourning Dove's originals, which I took back to Seattle with me. There I immediately photocopied them and began sorting. Often the type and location of page numbers was the best clue to a chapter sequence. A connected narrative revealed the topic, then an opening page could be sought. A few chapters were complete, although random pages always helped round out the account. Most frustrating were the sheets typed on both sides, usually dealing with different subjects.

I later returned to Yakima and picked up the rest of the pages. Once I had assembled the original chapters, Gunther's revisions helped me to fill in gaps where pages were missing. I sorted the pages into connected text, carbon copies, and variant accounts. Eventually I identified chapters and arranged them into a "master text." These chapters fell into three areas: female activities, seasonal activities, and incidents from recent history. The bulk of the remaining pages related to Mourning Dove's own life, and I created the first chapter from them.

Page headings suggest that Mourning Dove was working on two versions of the same events. "Tipi Life" was a descriptive ethnography of the Okanogans and Colviles, while "Educating the Indian" was based on her personal experiences and those of her people. There was more of the personal version, which was also more interesting, so I made it the basis for the master text of this book. "Tipi Life" is the more intriguing title because it both pays homage to *The American Indian Tepee*, edited by McWhorter and Rev. Red Fox Skiuhushu before they had a bitter falling-out, and challenges a comment made in *The Brand* in which the greenhorn heroine speculates that a tipi is "something good to eat" and the shady Indian agent replies, "Your appetite will be gone when you see or even smell one."[19]

Mourning Dove's unfinished drafts allow a glimpse at her compositional style, but it is clear that she intended her efforts to be edited. Unsure about spelling and usage, she was never comfortable with English, and some of her phrasings can be difficult to understand unless one is familiar with Colville English idiom. The printed text therefore represents my sense of her work.

Over the years I have helped Colville elders who wanted to leave a record of stories or wisdom. After they wrote out their material, we went over it line by line and word by word. This gave me the experience to edit Mourning Dove's writings. Her family has also encouraged me to make her effort as correct as it could be, and they helped me struggle with some obscure passages.

I rewrote each sentence to achieve agreement of subject and verb, a uniform past tense, and appropriate use of pronouns. Since pronouns in Interior Salish do not recognize gender, "he" and "she" tend to be used interchangeably in Salish-influenced English. That occasionally happens in Mourning Dove's writing, but the context indicates that she generally intended to follow the traditional English practice of using "he" to refer to men or to persons of unspecified sex and "she" to refer to girls and women, although she commonly used "he or she" for children and for shamans. None of these translations reflects accurately the sense of the Salish pronoun, which is more like "one" or "this" or "that" than like the generalized "he."

In rewriting I attempted to apply standard English conventions of syntax, spelling, and grammar while retaining Mourning Dove's words. Whenever possible I kept her paragraphing. Gaps in the master text were filled out with passages from the other versions. My editorial additions are enclosed in brackets.

Throughout, the editing has had an anthropological bias. I have imposed consistency while trying to retain examples of all her usages. For all its unfulfilled literary possibilities, the autobiography does represent a personal ethnography of lasting value. Her descriptions are detailed, and her sense of history is unique.

I chose certain synonyms over others for more frequent use. Although Mourning Dove used both "sweat house" and "sweat lodge," and both "native" and "primitive," I have predominantly used "lodge" and "native" to accord with both academic and reservation usage. Sweatlodge is also in her chapter title. The terms "tipi" (in place of her "teepee" and "tepee") and "taboo" (in place of her "tabu") are the proper terms for distinguishing Native American practices from those of the rest of the world. The spelling "tabu" refers specifically to Polynesian belief. The Colville/Colvile contrast distinguishes the multitribal reservation and its members from the namesake tribe centered at Kettle Falls and helps specify when material relates to Mourning Dove's maternal line. Thus, while her mother's family were Colvile leaders and her father was from the Okanagans, both families were legally Colvilles. One of

Mourning Dove's favorite words is "till," but it was edited out of her publications, where "until" is used sparingly. Since she approved of the published term, I have generally used "until" and have given it its full text frequency.

The manuscript had been printed out and I was checking historical sources and visiting elders when Erna Gunther died. Her books and papers came to the University of Washington Archives in 1985 and 1986. I was allowed to examine each delivery to search for missing pages. As more and more were found, it became apparent that the missing sections had been misfiled rather than destroyed. Text fragments filled gaps in a few chapters, and a continuous narrative added the whole of chapter 7 on widowhood, closing out the female life cycle. A few sections were helped by a page or two in the McWhorter Collection.

Among the Gunther papers is a lucid twenty-page account of the three accidents that taught Mourning Dove to pay attention to her elders. While it further indicates how rough the overall drafts were, it also shows that with time and effort she could write polished prose. Allowing for such hindsight, however, we need to consider two of the most difficult paragraphs in the master text. The very first paragraph was written this way in the version used:

There is two things that I am most grateful for in my life. First that I was born a descendent of the genuine American, the Indian—and that by birth happened in the year of 1888. In that year the Indians of my tribe the Swhy-ayl-puh (Colviles) were in the cycle of history of readjustment as to living conditions. They were in a pathetic state of turmoil in trying to learn how to till the soil for a living. This was done in a very small and crude scale. It was no easy manner for the aboriginal stock that was accustomed to making a living in a different method for untold centuries by bow and arrow route, to handle the plow and sow seed for food.

Elsewhere Mourning Dove's descriptions are run together, almost jumbled, like this one of clothing, which appears in chapter 4
of this book.

> The clothing of the family is usually made of deer skins
> tanned, or furs of small animals like the rabbit skin is used for
> babies in winter months to keep them snug and warm. Coyote
> skins make the jackets of the older people when tanned with
> the fur on by tying the rear end around the neck and tying it
> under the arms and down in front to keep their shoulders
> warm.

Finally, her obituaries suggest that the last chapters in this autobiography represent what survives of her "History of the Okanogan." It is fitting, therefore, that they provide her finale, at least for
now. Her letters refer to a trunk full of her literary efforts and
mementos, so there is some hope that other works by her may be
found.

CONCLUSION

With the persistence of a crusader, Mourning Dove intended to
change things by her writing. Her chief nemesis was the stereotype
of the stoic Indian. Hence her work abounds in emotional and
melodramatic incidents. The hurt and trauma in her own life contributed to this, as did her early reading of penny dreadfuls. As she
knew only too well, natives do indeed "feel as deeply as whites."

These factors must have played a large part in her decision to
write her autobiography. Other works may be included, but more
than likely all of them draw upon her own life experiences.

Native Americans had many sources for autobiography, all rely-
ing on the experience of individuals living within a close community. Among these, H. David Brumble (1968) lists coup tales, stories
of prowess in hunting and warfare, self-examinations, self-vindica-
tions, didactic narratives, and tales about the personal acquisition
of supernatural power through religious inspiration. A. LaVonne

Brown Ruoff, working from prose accounts, also notes the influence of popular literature, such as spiritual confessions, missionary reminiscences, and slave narratives.[20] Other sources were stories of captivity or the lives of famous and legendary characters, almost all of them men. As written statements, native autobiographies have always involved collaboration, with those engaged having different goals in mind. Some provide ethnographic data and context, others enhance an author's image or serve as literary exercises.

As Gretchen Bataille and Kay Sands point out, the English tradition of autobiography celebrates individuality and creativity within a confessional form.[21] Further, as Elaine Showalter has observed, some women began to write as compensation for loneliness and suffering, sharing with other women to foster intense feelings of female solidarity:

> For women in England, the female subculture came first through a shared and increasingly secretive and ritualized physical experience. Puberty, menstruation, sexual initiation, pregnancy, childbirth, and menopause—the entire female sexual life cycle—constituted a habit of living that had to be concealed. . . .
>
> The training of Victorian girls in repression, concealment, and self-censorship was deeply inhibiting especially for those who wanted to write.[22]

In America, autobiography celebrated the intangibles of self-worth, the getting of knowledge and wisdom, the fostering of virtue, and the various strategies for success. The American woman grappled with her condition—its trials, tribulations, and triumphs. According to Nina Baym, "her dilemma, simply, was mistreatment, unfairness, disadvantage, and powerlessness, recurrent injustices occasioned by her status as female and child." In novels of the time, solutions "all involve the heroine's accepting herself as a female while rejecting the equation of female with permanent child."[23]

Among the Salish, autobiography involved the oral recitation of

the deeds of past generations of people who held the same hereditary name. Thus the momentary deeds of an individual were sub-
sumed within those of prior namesakes, providing the same kinds
of moral lessons as legends and sagas. The emphasis is on the
communal and the conventional, not the unique. Everyone is part of
a larger whole, although the totality is organized by gender, age, and
ability. If life has evolved as a punctuated equilibrium, Native
American men have provided the punctuation and women the continuity. From this biological perspective, many of the observations
about female authorship apply universally because of the experiences common to women.

Although she espoused fiction as her vehicle, Mourning Dove
wrote about events as she chose and arranged them from her own
experience. True fiction, however, relies on imagination. Her appeal
to a white ancestry, denied by her family and the tribal census,
indicates how strongly she saw herself as a mediator between Indian
and white. What Robert Bone, despite some criticism of his approach, has observed for black authors also applies here: "Above all
else, melodrama is a literature of social aspiration." For Mourning
Dove, however, this aspiration was motivated by a desire to equalize
her status in native and white societies. To do so she chose a means
aptly suited to the two contexts: discipline and creativity are highly
valued by both. She came to share in the larger tradition of women
writers who, as Baym writes, "saw cultivation of the mind as the
great key to freedom, the means by which women, learning to think
about their situation, could learn how to master it. Like Benjamin
Franklin before them and Malcolm X after them, they saw literacy
as the foundation of liberation."[24]

Within the native context, Mourning Dove was the inverse of
Frances Slocum, the Lost Sister of the Wyoming. A Quaker girl
captured by the Delawares, Slocum married a Miami chief and
insisted on staying with the Miamis her entire life. White writers
found her problematic, a baffling woman born white but grown
native in heart and soul.[25] The enigma was that Slocum was wealthy

by white standards yet remained Indian. The materialist aim is to strive, achieve, and change in the interests of wealth, but Indians do none of these in terms understandable to Euro-Americans.

It is just this paradox that Mourning Dove evoked with her awkward dramatics. She and her family achieved moderate success by constant effort, despite continual difficulties; nevertheless, they shared their bounty with others. Somehow hardships were endured and the community survived as members participated in an endlessly invigorating experience emphasizing human values.

I. A WOMAN'S WORLD

★

CHAPTER I

My Life

THERE are two things I am most grateful for in my life. The first is that I was born a descendant of the genuine Americans, the Indians; the second, that my birth happened in the year 1888. In that year the Indians of my tribe, the Colvile (Swhy-ayl-puh), were well into the cycle of history involving their readjustment in living conditions. They were in a pathetic state of turmoil caused by trying to learn how to till the soil for a living, which was being done on a very small and crude scale. It was no easy matter for members of this aboriginal stock, accustomed to making a different livelihood (by the bow and arrow), to handle the plow and sow seed for food. Yet I was born long enough ago to have known people who lived in the ancient way before everything started to change.[1]

The vast forests that our Indian forebears had jealously guarded from white invasion lay in ruins. The wildlife, staple food for natives, was slowly and surely vanishing each year; all the game was disappearing.

The first invaders were the fur traders selling firearms to the Indians of the Northwest, who enthusiastically adopted their use. Together with their white neighbors, they destroyed their ancestral heritage by killing the wild game of the forest, the livelihood of their past.

The appeal of cheap beads and bright cloth was too much of a lure for the innocent Indians of that period. They were enticed to hunt and to overkill game to such an extent that they eventually had to get food elsewhere.

My father, Joseph Quintasket (originally T-quin-task-et, meaning Dark Cloud), was born about 1864 in a kwat-zee (pit dwelling) in the upper or Lake Okanagan community of En-hwx-kwas-t'nun (Arrow Scraper), located a short distance south of present Kelowna, British Columbia, on the east side of Lake Okanagan.[2] Arrow Scraper was a winter village, visited in 1842 by the famous Father De Smet, who blessed the ground and left a cross standing where, twenty years later, Father Pandosy built a church.[3] Although the village belonged to the Okanagan, many of the Nicola, called En-koh-tu-me-whoh in the Okanogan language, spent the winters there too.

Father's mother was a Nicola Indian, with a strain of Okanagan [Canadian side of Okanogans] in her family. His father was a white man, a Scot named Andrew, who at one time was in the employ of the Hudson's Bay Company. When Father was nine years old, his mother died in a Colvile Indian camp near Pinkney City (the earlier name for the present town of Colville) where they were visiting. His mother's husband died two months later, leaving him an orphan.[4] He never returned to live with the Lake Okanagan. He grew up without any school education, but he learned to speak broken English and to read figures on price tags and money. He also learned some French while boarding with a family. As a grown man, he served as a tribal policeman under Major Anderson, Indian agent of the Colville Reservation.[5]

Father was always respected, known for his openhanded hospitality to the hungry and the needy. His home was at Pia, also called Kelly Hill, near Boyds, Washington, where he raised cattle and chickens—a contented farmer into his old age.

Father's mother's mother was Pah-tah-heet-sa, a famous Nicola medicine woman. Quite frequently this old woman would make up a pack of dried venison and salmon and go to visit her two daughters, both of whom married among the Okanagan. One day the people at her village were getting ready to go over the Nicola Trail, which was infested with mean cougars and grizzly bears. The old woman recalled that this trail had huckleberry bushes that would be about ripe with the luxurious food. She hurried ahead of all the armed warriors, who led the women and children to protect them from attack by wild animals.

When this brave woman drew near the berry patch, she saw a grizzly feeding. This did not stop her. She took her digging stick of dogwood and prepared to fight if the bear meant to charge at her, which the bear did not hesitate to do. With a howl that would have frozen the blood of any coward, it charged. She threw off her pack and held her stick to challenge the brute, saying, "You are a mean animal and I am a mean woman. Let us fight this out to see who will get the berry patch."

The bear did not answer her but opened its mouth wide and came at a leap. She watched for her chance and drove the sharp stick into the animal's mouth. The bear fell back in pain, then jumped at her, even more angry. The fight went on long enough that the warriors approached, not expecting to see such a sight. When they drew their arrows to shoot, she commanded them, "Don't shoot. Wait! We are fighting this to the finish. He is a mean animal and I am a mean woman. We will see who is the strongest and conqueror in this battle."

The woman roared in imitation of the angry bear and drove her stick again into the wide, wide mouth. Every time it charged, this would drive it back. The people watched the fight until the sun lay low in the western sky. Only then did the grizzly walk away, broken and bleeding. The old woman had only a few scratches.

She picked up her basket and gathered the berries she had won, while the people stood in wonderment. She died very old when she and her buckskin horse rolled down a steep embankment near

Oroville. She and the horse drowned and were both buried on the bank of the Similkameen River in an unmarked grave. Thus ended a brave, mean woman.

My mother, Lucy Stui-kin (Sna'itckstŵ), was a full-blood. She was born about 1868 at Kettle Falls, which we call Swah-netk-qhu, meaning Big Falls or Big Water, also our name for the Columbia River. Her father was Stui-kin (Beaver Head) of the Trout Lake (Sin-na-aich-kis-tu) band of the Arrow Lakes people, with a strain of Kootenay ancestry.[6] Her mother was Soma-how-atqhu (She Got Her Power From Water), youngest daughter of Head Chief See-whelh-ken of the People of the Falls (Swhy-ayl-puh), the true Colvile tribe, also known by the white name of Maria. She came to visit when I was a girl.

It was summer, and we saw two horsemen galloping toward our tipi at Pia. I was riding the pinto my uncle Louie Stui-kin had given me. It was fat, with glossy hair in black, yellow, and white. To please me, Father kept him saddled until I was in bed each night. That way he was always ready to ride. I recognized one of the riders as Andrew, my mother's cousin, whom we always called uncle out of respect. Among Indians, cousins are considered the same as brothers and sisters. Andrew was a hard rider; his mount was foaming when he stopped and jumped off. He called me over and gave me a coin, saying "Kee-ten (my pet name), I want to borrow your horse." I looked at his own panting horse and shook my head. I loved my pinto and did not want him abused. Uncle laughed and offered more coins. Eventually he gave me all the coins he had before I consented because Mother scolded me, "Kee-ten, let your uncle have your pony."

Andrew took a rope and went toward the pinto. Resenting the approach of a stranger, my pony walked off, never letting Uncle get close. Angry, Andrew took the lasso off his mount and tried for the pinto, who dodged away. Other riders joined in, but my pony would not be caught. Finally they gave up in disgust, and my horse started to feed. When Mother heard, she made me go after him. I went up the hillside to where he was nibbling new grass, but he kept turning his head so I could not grab the broken reins.

I reverted to my original method of catching him. I got down on all fours and pretended I was a dog, barking at him. He stood back to watch me, and I caught him. When I got him back to camp, Uncle gave me another coin. This was the first money I ever earned, proving I was a very proud wage laborer with a talent.

Later that same day, my sister Sulee and I were watching for my pony to come back.[7] Our toys were buckskin dolls, dishes made from broken bottles in pretty colors, and fresh flowers. We were playing quietly because I had gotten into the bag of sugar and eaten so much that I felt sick. Mother gave me bear grease to eat, and I felt like I was going to die for a little while. In the distance we saw an old woman approaching with a large pack on her back. When it became clear she was coming to our tipi, I ran to tell Mother about the visitor. She was tanning hides down by the creek. Mother scolded me, "Do not be so inquisitive, staring at people when they honor us as guests. Be patient, and all will be revealed to us in due time. Now sit by the door and wait for her to arrive." Sister and I went to our play area near the door. The oldest and least-regarded robes were piled there and covered with fir boughs so children and dogs could play without doing harm. We secretly watched the woman come closer.

Then the door flap was suddenly thrown back, and a large shawl-covered pack was thrown into the tipi. Mother used a poker to stop it from rolling into the fire. Then the visitor entered, stooping low through the oval doorway. As she stood up Mother cried out just one word, "toom" (Mother).[8] She lowered her head, and tears slowly ran down her cheeks. Grandmother did the same, for they had not seen each other since my grandfather had been buried years before. He had accidentally shot himself while on a hunting trip.

Grandmother came to visit us from her home in Tobacco Plains, the main Kootenay camp in British Columbia.[9] She was rich in robes, horses, and trade goods, so the pack became a source of countless surprises after she finished her greetings and handshakes. She handed out gifts, saying, "I saved all of these things for you. Here are shawls, handkerchiefs, beads, bright cloth for dresses, and a wonderful cape." All of us got something special, but I got the cape. It was velvet, tight along the back, decorated with blue and purple brocade, and trimmed with jet beads on silk tassels. For years I wore it only to church, but I was so proud and vain about it that I am sure I broke many commandments doing so. When the girls my age were watching, I would whirl around to show it off and make the beads jingle to attract their attention.

When I was learning to talk, I called my grandmother by the baby name of Patee. When she arrived she took me into her lap, smoothed my tangled hair, and crooned. She asked if I still remembered calling her Patee. Ever after, until she died in 1910, I called her that. I loved her greatly. Her dignity and low, musical voice showed that she was the daughter of a chief. She was plump, straight as an arrow, and had gray-white hair in two braids, a slightly square chin, pretty but worn teeth, long fingers, and small feet. I could wear her moccasins until I was eleven. She would only dress in buckskin and eat native foods. If she could get shoes small enough, she wore them to keep her feet dry.

When her father, Chief See-whehl-ken, died his nephew Kinkanawah succeeded him. Of his three daughters, the oldest sister married Major Galibeth [Galbraith], an Englishman at Fort Steele, British Columbia, and the second one married an English soldier at Fort Colville named Shuttleworth, who in later years fell heir to a lordship but courageously turned it down to stay with his children at Merritt, British Columbia.[10] My grandmother would marry only a native, and Stui-kin gave many horses for her. All their children died except my mother [?].

I remember when I first met Chief Kinkanawah at Kettle Falls. He lived in one of the log cabins on the west side of the little draw near Goodwin Mission. Mother took us to see him. The cabin was dark, with one dirty window. He sat among blankets and furs near

3. The St. Paul Mission at Kettle Falls, as reconstructed in
1939. Photo taken in 1988, editor's collection.

the fireplace. Mother shook hands and nudged me to greet my
granduncle. The chief took my hand and looked into my face.
Laughing in a teasing way, he said, "So this is Kee-ten. My what an
ugly little girl. Small nose and eyes like a coyote. Your grandmother
was a beauty, the favorite daughter of my uncle, the chief. Everyone
adored her. Your grandfather [gave] many ponies and prime robes to
her parents to [gain] her as his wife. She was worth it. She is a
priceless woman."

The chief dropped my hand out of his long, tapered fingers and
wiped tears from his eyes. His hollow laughter was at the expense of
my feelings about being ugly. His laughing helped to hide his real
feelings in front of my parents. He was then an old man, but he still
led with authority.

Father and Mother were married in St. Paul's Church, near the
Kettle Falls fishery.[11] The church was on the east side of the Columbia, almost overlooking old Fort Colville. The first church was a
small log cabin built in the 1840s by Father Ravalli, a Jesuit. Later it

9

was replaced, with the help of some Indians, in 1856, by a building of hand-hewn logs and a floor of whipsawed lumber, pegged down. There was not a nail or a piece of iron anywhere in the church. This is where my parents were married. Later a frame church was erected at Goodwin Mission, and the log one was abandoned. Years later it burned down, but the ruins can still be seen.

I was their oldest child, born in the Moon of Leaves (April) in the year 1888.[12] I was born near the present site of Bonner's Ferry, Idaho, while my mother and grandmother were in a canoe crossing the Kootenay River. My family was traveling with my mother's brother, Louie Stui-kin, who ran a pack train between Walla Walla, Washington Territory, and Fort Steele, British Columbia, carrying supplies to the mining district. My father was working for him at this time, and they were heading back to Walla Walla. By the time they had reached the Kootenay, my birth was expected momentarily, but the men did not want to stop. My grandmother had insisted on camping on the other side because it had better horse pasture. My father helped to swim the horses, and my mother and her mother started over in a canoe with a Kootenay named Swansen, a name given to him by the fur traders. He paddled hard, but I came into the world before he could beach the canoe. They had brought clothing for a newborn, but it was left on a packhorse on the other side of the river, with our other gear. The Kootenay man kindly pulled off his plaid shirt and lent it to my grandmother to swaddle me. Thus my first clothing was a man's shirt, and my parents always felt that this led me to act more like a boy, a tomboy, who liked to play more with the boys than with the girls.

I was the oldest of seven children, and five were living at the time of Mother's death in 1902. Until I was four years old I had all the attention given to an only child. The care lavished on me by my parents, my doting grandmother, and other relations surely spoiled me. I had everything I wanted: toys, dogs, tame ground squirrels and chipmunks. My whims were many and, as I have been told, I always got my way about things. If anyone rebuked me I would throw myself down, scream, and kick until I was humored. This willfulness only amused my parents, and I had everything my own way. This changed when my parents had other children. When I was three a brother had been born, but he died. When I was over four, my sister Sulee was born.

I did not like it when all the affection that had been bestowed upon me now was heaped upon the bundle in the papoose cradle. So vivid is my recollection of unhappiness that to this day whenever I see a child being neglected in the excitement and pleasure of caring for a new baby my sympathy goes out to him or her. I understand the feeling of loneliness and hurt too often overlooked by impatient elders.

A few days after her birth, according to tribal custom, Sulee was named Mook-mook-t'ku-nalx (Snow Dress) after our mother's grandmother, the wife of Chief See-whehl-ken. Later she was christened Julia by Father De Rouge. We soon modified Julia to Sulee.

For a long time I believed the words of the old woman who was midwife when Sulee arrived. She told me, "I found her under the robes" as she held up the crying infant for me to view. I was standing at the doorway of the tipi, where I had been commanded to stay that cold, midwinter afternoon.

If that woman could find a baby under the robes I could too, I thought, and for many days I tried. I would throw back the robes and gaudy blankets, and then my mother would scold me for jumbling the bedclothes. She would smile faintly when I explained that I was hunting for a new baby.

Although our children seldom receive physical punishment, it was my lot to be spanked many times before I realized that there was room for more than one child on my mother's lap and that I must show respect for my little sister. I naturally turned to my father for affection, and he, with his generous, understanding nature, encouraged my love and confidence. We became very close to each other.

Being born an Indian gave me the advantage over the average

Caucasian who became interested in Indian subjects. My nationality gave me the opportunity to know authentically, from personal experience, a fraction of the real, ancient Indian life that existed before the present generation, which is too busy learning from the white man's books to study ancestral history. [Alas,] the average Indian of today does not know anything about tribal history from as recently as a century ago.

I speak the Indian language of my own tribe better than I do the adopted lingo of the English-Americans. I had the opportunity to learn the legends, religion, customs, and theories of my people thoroughly. No foreigner could possibly penetrate or research these because of the effort needed to overcome the shy reluctance of the Indian when it comes to giving information to whites. I have been most fortunate in having the actual experience of living the real Indian life within a tipi and of learning the ancient Indian teachings passed on to children, which the present generation of Indians has largely had the misfortune to regard as only historical customs rather than current beliefs.

I have always had a good memory, and so I learned these teachings most carefully. My earliest childhood recollections involve learning to obey the wisdom of my elders. Three memories stand out particularly clearly.

In the first, my mother's voice comes to me as a hazy, uncontrolled "brain of thought." She is using the agitated tone of our dialect. "Put your head down! Put your head down!" But I was unable to obey her commanding voice. The horse I was riding was running wild, and a large tree limb was coming at me. My tiny fingers gripped the saddle horn, and I kept staring straight ahead over the ears of my pony. Moments before, I had been slowly following after my mother, going through the woods searching for huckleberries. Then things became a rush and the limb was coming closer and closer. It would not get out of the way! It pushed against the pony's head and then, with an awful swish, swept me over the rump onto the ground. Oh, how it hurt, and how I cried.

Mother picked me up and wiped the blood from my nose and mouth. "Kee-ten," she spoke my name gently, "have you no ears?" She touched one of them. "Your ears are made to listen through. You must listen to your elders. If you do not mind when they speak, you will always get hurt."

I think I was about four when this happened, the first of three times that were so painfully unpleasant because of my own disobedience and willfulness.

The second instance was even more frightening. Two Kootenay girls were taking care of me. We were playing by a stream, and I thought it was great fun to run away from them and wade into the water, paying no heed to their calls. They had to come after me to lift me to the bank. Finally either they got tired of retrieving me or I managed to slip away and waded into deeper water. Then the current threw me down and rolled me over and over. I was gasping and choking before the older of the girls managed to pull me out. I never tried to run into the water again, and to this day I am afraid of it.

Many years afterward, I asked my father the name of that stream. After thinking for some time, he remembered it was Fort Steele Creek in British Columbia. So I made a special trip there to see where I was almost drowned. I expected to find a large, roaring creek, if not a river. I was quite surprised to see that it was a very small stream, hardly ankle deep and singing softly over small, smooth-worn stones!

My people are noted for their skill at swimming and diving, and I, but for that terrifying childhood experience, might have become a good swimmer—especially if one accepts omens as having any meaning. After all, I was born on the water while crossing the Kootenay River.

That immersion in Fort Steele Creek was a severe punishment for disobedience, but it took a third painful lesson to teach me that older persons should be listened to, always.

One day I was running around and around the outside of our tipi. "Do not run around the tipi," my mother said. "You might fall and get hurt." But I had to run around just once more. And I fell. My face landed on one of the small pegs that pinned and stretched the canvas to the ground. The peg stuck into the middle of my nose—broke it, I guess—and flattened it so that my nose never grew into a pleasant shape. I still carry the scar, and I have developed a great admiration for lovely, nicely chiseled noses so unlike my own.

After that time I was more obedient, others tell me, and I paid careful attention to the words of my parents and older persons. This manuscript is one result of such careful attention to what they were willing to share with me for my benefit and now for yours.

My own spiritual, moral, and traditional training was supervised by a woman called Teequalt, whom we came to adopt as a grandmother. She was my tutor during her later years.

I had came upon an old woman sitting all by herself. I came up to her full of eagerness. Seeing me, she gathered up her heavy load and got to her feet with the help of a cane. In a loud tone she scolded me, on the verge of sobbing, "Leave me alone. I am walking, walking until I die. Nobody wants me." She waved me away and cried, "Leave me alone." She left our trail and wandered into the chokecherry thicket on the hillside.[13]

I stood there embarrassed. I just could not understand why this woman wanted to die when the land was beautiful, covered with flowers in many hues and shapes. The songs of the meadowlarks mingled with the robins scolding from the treetops, where their nests were. Crickets added their own tunes. It was wonderful to be alive and inhale the clear spring air. My childish mind saw the large world as all happiness. But this woman was sad, weeping and wanting to walk until she died.

Abruptly, I turned on my heel and ran uphill to tell Mother. Reaching the door, almost out of breath, I said, "Mother (toom), I have found a new grandmother, and she wants to die." This so startled Mother that she almost dropped the new baby she was lacing into the cradleboard. Without a pause, she handed me the baby and went swiftly down the trail to find the old woman. She did find her and offered her our home for as long as she wanted to stay. Thereafter Teequalt was always with us, and we stayed closer to home because she could not travel very far.

She was a wonderful storyteller.[14] She was twelve when she first heard of the new people (whites) coming into our country in boats (bateaux) instead of canoes. When my parents went for game or berries, we children took care of her. We prepared meals according to her instructions, then we would sit at her feet and listen to her wonderful stories.

With our adopted grandmother, we became like the other children. Our own grandmother lived far off, and we had always envied other children who were blessed by having elders in their home.

She was a great teacher, remembering many of the old ways then out of custom. Before whites came, there was no smallpox. When it first came, many died from it because they did not know how to take care of it.

According to her story, "There were many people in those days; game was bountiful in the forests, and fish filled the streams. We were happy because we had plenty to eat. Sometimes we had trouble with raiding tribes, but not often. Our warriors found pleasure in fighting them back. They killed and brought back scalps to earn an honored name as an enemy killer. The pleasure of killing did not end until the Black Gowns came, preaching that their God forbids war.[15]

"It was early in the fall when some people came back from the west, where there is a big saltwater lake. They had gone to trade furs for shells and got a sickness that was very bad. We called it "breaking out" (smallpox). Most of these traders died on the way home, but a few made it, fearing that they had been diseased by a hostile shaman.

"A few days after they reached home, everyone started getting sick. All were frightened and called on the wisest shaman to doctor them, but they died anyway. Shamans also died. Some tried to use the sweat lodge, but when they jumped into the cold water after sweating, they got worse and died faster. The dead were left in tipis when survivors moved away. Dogs and coyotes ate their flesh. Sometimes only a small baby survived, starving at the breast of its dead mother. Many of the old and weak survived, however, because they went to bed and kept warm while the strong and healthy died.

"Both of my parents died, leaving me alone with my old grandmother surrounded by the dead. Grandmother tried to bury people, but there were too many. There was plenty of food stored in the lodges, so we ate well. We were alone until the following spring when survivors began to drift back."

While Teequalt was with us, our old neighbor Ka-at-qhu [Big beside Water; known as Big Lip] died, shortly after her old husband. Father told me, "Kee-ten, since none of her grandchildren took her name, you will have to be called Ka-at-qhu. Your lips are small enough that this name will not be a deterrent to you." After this, the people called me Ka-at-qhu for a long time.[16] I was proud of the name; it made me feel grown up. I began to imagine being an adult and earning money to buy things for my struggling parents. I would have many ponies and cattle, beautiful robes, and bright red dresses with ruffles. When Mother scolded me for getting into mischief, which was often, I dreamed of a home of my own where I could have all the grandmothers I wanted to tell me stories. I never imagined the many hardships and shattered dreams my life had in store.

I carried the name Ka-at-qhu for a long time, although my parents still called me Kee-ten. Some years later, a woman shaman of the Okanogan came to visit my parents. One day she prepared my mother's sweat lodge for herself. I helped her carry wood and water from the creek. This pleased her, and she said, "I am going to give you my name before I die. I want somebody worthy of the name Ha-ah-pecha (Striped Blanket) to have it. I want a strong woman to carry this honorable name from my ancestors." To this day I am not sure whether she was referring to my strong arms or staunch character. Her offer startled me, but I did not question her. The old people said she had great powers, and I was afraid of offending her. I carried her name for many years, and many old Okanogan still use it when they see me. This honors the wonderful woman who cured so many of them. She never gave me her great powers, or at least I never had the sensation that she did.

The first home I remember was a tipi (swool-hu). The cover—of long strips of unbleached muslin that my mother had arranged on a level spot and sewed together by hand—was stretched snugly around a conical framework of peeled poles and "buttoned" down the front with wooden pins. The bottom was pegged to the ground with sharpened stakes, and the door was a flap that opened outward. Smoke flaps or ears, each one supported by a pole shoved into a corner pocket, provided an adjustable flue. When a change in the wind made the tipi smoky inside, my mother would go out and shift the ear poles until the fire drew nicely again.

Before the people had muslin or canvas for manufacturing tipi covers, sewn tule mats or buffalo hides were used. The tule-mat tents were considered the most ancient style. One layer of lapped mats was enough for the summertime, and two to four layers kept out the snow and cold in winter.

This type of home was very convenient for the Indians because they moved about so much in olden times.[17] Folded into a compact bundle, this cover was carried on a packhorse, lashed on top of the load. Poles did not usually have to be taken along, since in our country they were available at most camping places.

The left side of our tipi was where my father and mother customarily sat and slept, and the right side was for the children. The oldest and dirtiest robes covered this spot, where I played with my pets without interference from my elders. It might be likened to a child's play corner or nursery in a white home.

We slept with our feet toward the fire in the center. Every morning Mother took the bedding outside and shook it, then she folded the robes and blankets before placing them near the wall. Just inside the doorway, on each side, we kept our food, cooking utensils, water pails, and some firewood.

The rear section of the tipi was reserved for visitors, and the floor there was covered with the best robes. We had a beautiful tanned buffalo robe that always was spread for our guests to sit upon. The women who came to call generally refused this place of honor, but the men who came as visitors invariably sat there and leaned back on the painted rawhide parfleches stacked along the back. We stored clothing, preserved foods, and other odds and ends in these. The parfleches were distributed against the bottom of the tipi wall in such a way that they shut out drafts.

My mother was noted for the number and quality of her parfleches, many of which she bought from the Kootenay, who were said to make especially good ones. All were painted with pretty designs in red, black, blue, green, and yellow.[18] The paints were prepared from certain plants and finely powdered mineral earths. The Okanogan and Colvile used to buy a very good red earth paint from the Similkameen Indians. Large quantities of this paint were obtained at Vermillion in the Upper Similkameen Valley of British Columbia.

In order to take the paint, the rawhide had to be moistened thoroughly. The designs then were outlined with a pointed stick or a sharp awl, and while the hide was still damp the paint was applied with a special flat, narrow paint stick or with a finger. Sometimes dry paint was used and other times it was mixed with water to make a thick paste. After the hide and painted designs were thoroughly dry, animal fat or oil was smeared over the surface, making a nice gloss. The best parfleches were made from buffalo hides with the hair removed. After the wild buffalo were all killed off, parfleches were manufactured from the skins of domestic cattle.

White people often called these stiff rawhide containers "Indian trunks." Our name for them is pen-pen-nox, meaning "folded at the ends." This most appropriately describes the oblong parfleche, whose ends fold over the top and meet in the middle, where they are fastened with thongs. The square type of bag was a doubled piece of rawhide laced up the sides and had a triangular flap like that of an envelope folded over the top. Their construction duplicates that of our modern envelope, only the folds were tied, not glued. The lacings often were left long to form decorative fringes. These "trunks" were ideally adapted for transporting on horses.

When Sulee and I were children, the family did not remain long in any one place in the summertime. We traveled with other families in search of food to be preserved for winter use. These expeditions sometimes took us far into the mountains where there were many grizzly bears and cougars, but my mother and the other women never seemed to be afraid of meeting these dangerous animals. Some of our trips were only into the lower mountains, where deer were plentiful. Often we went to Okanogan country to gather bitterroot (spit-lum), which grew abundantly on the sagebrush flats close to the Okanogan River.[19] The women dug up this plant with pointed dogwood digging sticks, called pee-cha. The points often were hardened by charring. Digging sticks used in hard ground were almost straight, while those used in soft ground were curved. The handles for both were crossbars made of elk horn. In recent years the wooden sticks have been replaced by sharp-pointed iron rods.

The flowers of the bitterroot plant are dainty and attractive, in various shades of pink. The plants grow low to the ground on rocky slopes and gravel flats. The thin, twisted roots are dug when the plant is in bud. They are peeled immediately while they remain moist. The inner white rinds are dried on racks. When they are fully dried, they keep a long time. While the root is very bitter and unpalatable when raw, it is healthful and nutritious after it is cooked. It is boiled by itself or mixed with serviceberries.

Until I was old enough to manage a pony, I rode behind Mother's saddle. She tied me to her with a strong cord that went around my waist, and if I fell asleep or started to slide off, she would slap my legs to wake me. Sulee also rode with us, strapped in her cradleboard hanging from the saddle pommel.

Women and children followed the packhorses, and the men rode ahead to watch for game animals and also to protect us from grizzly bears. In the days of tribal wars, this order of march was necessary for the safety of the family, and it may have been the origin of the custom of an Indian man walking a few steps in advance of the women and others. This frequently amuses whites, but some of their own customs seem just as odd or foolish to the oldtime Indians.[20]

I loved the free life of moving from one camping place to another all summer long.

One trip that my parents seldom failed to make each year was from the Colvile winter village at Kettle Falls to S'oo-yoos Lake, British Columbia, in the country of the Upper Okanagan. Some Chinese men had settled in this area to placer mine for gold and had taken native wives. Chesaw was named for one of them. The well-trodden trail took us over the pass of Deadman Creek (so called because an Indian killed a miner there; later it was known as Boulder Creek) up Kettle River to Midway, British Columbia, which the Indians called In-kla-whin-whe-ten (Battling Place), where the Shuswap had a big fight with the Colvile and Okanogan; across the divide at Mock-tsin (Knoll between a Divide), where stood the stone maiden called En-am-tues (Sitting on the Summit) known from ancient legend; and down the sagebrush slopes to the narrows of S'oo-yoos (Osoyoos Lake, as the whites know it), where the trail crossed toward the Nicola country and continued westward to the shores of the Pacific (In-sil-whu-eet-qu).[21]

At this point the lake narrowed almost to its center, and the water was shallow enough for a horseman to ford safely. It was an oldtime wintering place of the Upper Okanagan.

The dog salmon (kee-su) spawned at the narrows in September, and the people from the Colvile country joined with the Okanogan in reaping the salmon harvest for winter food. The men speared or gaffed the salmon, and the women cleaned and sliced the fish before stretching the fillets flat with dry cedar skewers to hold the pieces in shape while they were drying on racks set up in the shade. It usually

4. The Catholic church at Pia, still a spiritual center for
the Lakes community among the Colvilles.
Photo taken in 1988, editor's collection.

required a week to dry the salmon at that time of the year. Sometimes Mother hastened the curing with a tiny willow fire that sent
up a thread of pungent smoke. We would not leave for home until we
had enough dried salmon to make heavy loads for our packhorses.
We always took more salmon than we needed for ourselves, since we
had to provide plenty to feed hungry relatives and people who came
to visit us.

All our supplies and stored food were taken to our winter settlements. My family usually stayed at Pia (Kelly Hill), but one year my
parents decided they would come back to the lowlands for the
winter and avoid the use of snowshoes. They decided to stay at the
old campground at Kettle Falls, across from where the Kettle River
branches off from the Columbia. This location was sheltered from
the north wind, and firewood was more available there.

We left our fall camp, and Father rode among the large pack train of horses and ponies that were all loaded with food, clothing, and camping gear. He drove them toward the winter camp while my sister and I rode with our mother toward the back.

When we reached the Kettle River, our horses forded easily through the low water of late fall. On the other side, on a bench, a short distance above the bank of the Columbia, we found the winter quarters already well populated by people coming from all directions.[22] This was one of the important winter grounds of the Colvile.

My parents selected a spot on the edge of the encampment, and while my father hobbled our horses in the night pasture, Mother cut some long, straight trees, cleaned them for use as poles, and tied them together at one end. My father leveled the surface of the ground with the blade of his ax, laid out the canvas covering, and with Mother's help set up the conical framework of lodgepoles by arranging their bases in a circle. Mother arranged the other poles against this tripod before Father covered all of them with our canvas tipi, adding long strips of tule mats for insulation. Mother placed bark around the outside to block drafts, while Father covered the bottom with bark and fir boughs. He took the dirt he had removed while leveling the ground and placed it all around the bottom of the tent to seal up the lodge. With this, my parents created a large and comfortable winter home, warm and cozy with only a small fire in the center of the room to keep it toasty.

My mother took a rope and went upstream, where she gathered a large load of fir boughs and carried them back in a great big heap on her back. These she carefully placed end to end all around the fireplace, to save our bedding from getting soiled. Our beds had extra fir boughs, making them higher. She bordered each bed with poles to keep the boughs from spreading and thinning out our mattresses.

After my parents finished the new winter lodge, they built a high scaffold beside it to store our provisions out of reach of the countless village dogs. These "razor-back" animals were mongrel types that were usually considered absolutely worthless except as guards. An

Indian dog was seldom taught to bite strangers. They saw so many people every day that they were not really dangerous like dogs that have been isolated with their masters on some backwoods farm. Their bark was truly much worse than their bite. Their greatest pleasure came in barking at other village dogs, sometimes howling like coyotes or wolves. They were only half-fed by their owners, to train them to look after their own welfare and continue the much admired craft of hunting.

Our food scaffold was well loaded and we were comfortable in our winter home when Father left us to go to Pia to look after our ponies in the pasture there. He intended to move them before the snow got any deeper. He returned the same evening with his sleek, fat herd. He hobbled the older horses and turned them loose in front of our tipi after leading them to water. I clearly remember that he smiled while looking at them, feeling the satisfaction of owning a herd of nicely colored ponies. One horse was especially pretty, with black markings and a brown tint on a white background. I wanted this horse and asked Father for it. The horses were then wandering in front of our camp, grazing on the occasional blade of grass that peeped above the new snow, which was not as deep as the snow we left behind in the mountains.

My father laughed at me for wanting a horse when I was still too much of a coward to ride by myself. The memory of my fall from the horse caused by the tree limb was still fresh. Yet I had asked, and before my father's gaze left the horses that evening, he gave me a little buckskin pony for my own. I ran into the tipi to give the good news to my mother and to brag to Sulee, but she was not old enough to understand my thrill. I had often played with the ponies alone and with my cousins, but now I had one of my own.

My mother and grandmother made dolls of buckskin stuffed with deer hair, with red seeds for eyes and wisps of horse tail glued on the head for hair, but dolls never appealed to me. I preferred playing with the bows and arrows my father made for me or listening to old men tell stories of warfare and horrible bloodshed.[23] Most of all, I loved my dogs. The village was full of them. They were very ordinary, mongrels really, but to me they were wonderful, faithful creatures who would follow me everywhere on my play hunts for deer and along imaginary war trails.

For more excitement, we played with calves and horses. Boys would chase a calf that was wild and had never been tied before. They would try to ride it, but the back was often wet from sweat, and there was no mane to hold on to. Sometimes they would try to ride a colt. If it became tired and panting, then I could often stay on its back for a short period. When the boys were weary of the animals, they showed off to Sulee and me, together with other children who came to the barn or corral to watch. They would jump over rails to show off their physical agility. I stood in admiration until the boys began to tease me to join them. I tried to jump the rail but missed and was thrown to the ground, bruising my shins. I choked back tears, afraid my cousins would call me an old woman or a crybaby. For many days afterward, however, I practiced until I could briefly ride the colt and calf or beat boys at the footrace and broad jump. The animals grew accustomed to me, and my muscles were hard and strong by the time I had my own pony. Sulee and I would ride double around the ranch.

These lovely interludes devoted to play, camping, food preparation, and living in the old way changed when I grew up. We had to adapt to the modern world and the sacred teachings of the Catholic church.[24] My own childhood enjoyments were abruptly halted when I was sent to mission school.

Although Mother continued persistently to give me my ancient education with the help of my native teacher, she was also a fanatically religious Catholic. We never missed mass or church unless it was absolutely necessary. If church was not scheduled at the little mission below our cabin, then we "pilgrimed" to Goodwin Mission to attend church. Winter and summer, she never failed to make her confession and communion on the first Friday of every month. To her mind, and that of many of the early converts, the word of the priest was law. She strictly observed anything that the pioneer Father De Rouge so much as hinted at. On the other hand, my father was considered a "slacker" or a black sheep of the flock. He attended church only occasionally and without the devotion of my mother.

Goodwin was originally called Grove School when founded in 1865, but my people were very reluctant to part with their children.[25] Only ten came that first year, three boys and seven girls. These were James Bernard, Joseph Seymour, Alex Quetasket (Black Cloud), Mary Rose Joseph, Bridgett Edwards, Jennie Page, Louise Pichette, Agatha Pichette, Rosila Seymour, and a girl called Mary Ann.

During one of our monthly trips to Goodwin for the first Friday service, we met Father De Rouge on the big steps of the church, where he had come outside to mingle with his beloved Indian congregation.

The good [Jesuit] priest came forward and shook hands with Mother, spying me behind her wide skirts. He looked right at me and asked if I had made my first communion. He had a way of jumbling up words from several Indian languages he had learned so that his words sounded childish, but I dared not chuckle at his comment. Instead, I shook my head in answer to his question. He looked at mother reproachfully and, shaking his head, said, "Tut, Tut, Lucy. You must let your child go to school with the good sisters to learn her religion so that she can make her first communion like other children of her age." Mother tried to make a protest, saying she needed me at home to care for the babies. But Father De Rouge could seldom be enticed to change his mind. He always had a very strict, ruling hand with the Indians. His word was much respected by the natives of the Colville Reservation.

He shook his finger at Mother and said, "Tut, Tut, Lucy. I command you." Then, pointing at the cross atop the bell tower of the church, he continued, "Your church commands that your child

must go to school to learn her religion and the laws of the church."
In obedience, Mother promised to send me to the mission for the fall
term of 1898.

I had known Father De Rouge all my life. He had been a station-
ary superior at the Goodwin Mission until the arrival of Father
Carnia [Caruana], whom the Indians called T-quit-na-wiss (Large
Stomach), since the new priest had plenty of abdominal carriage.[26]
After that De Rouge became a traveling priest, covering all the
territory of the Colville Reservation and beyond. He taught the
Indians their prayers and erected the first little cabins that served as
chapels until they were later remodeled into larger frame churches.
These early church locations included Ellisford, St. Mary's Mission
on Omak Creek, Nespelem, Keller, and Inchelium.[27] These last four
compose the modern districts of the Colville Reservation. Earlier
these districts all had their share of the faithful work of the self-
sacrificing Father Etienne (Stephen) De Rouge.[28]

He was the descendant of a rich and influential French count, but
he rejected his claim to this title to fulfill his mission among his
beloved Colville. Many times he would stop by our cabin home at
Pia to visit with the family. He traveled astride his cayuse leading a
pack animal loaded with the sacred belongings needed to say
mass.[29] This gave him the convenience of holding services in any
Indian tipi or cabin where night would overtake him. He was never
too busy to answer a call for help, rushing in the night to visit the
sick or administer the last sacraments to poor, dying natives. His
life was thoroughly wrapped up in his chosen work. He spent every
penny he could get from his rich family and from small Indian
contributions to aid the needy.

It was through his influence and encouragement that the Indians
gradually discontinued their ancient customs and were more willing to send their children to school at Goodwin. He later erected a
fine and roomy school at St. Mary's Mission, after he had permanently established other churches that were maintained either by
traveling priests or by one permanently settled in the location to

teach the Indians and provide an example. This boarding school, built with his own money and contributions from Catholic whites in the East, remains a successful monument to his life's work.

After Father De Rouge settled in the Okanogan, his successors were two young priests, Father Caldi and Father Edward Griva.[30] Both of them were of the sacrificing type of Jesuit like De Rouge. Father Caldi was named by the Indians Sal-ista, perhaps a more convenient way of pronouncing his name in their dialect.

Mother fulfilled her pledge to Father De Rouge in the fall of 1898 when I was about eleven. I was eager to learn more English and do more reading. I first went to Goodwin Mission school in 1895, but I did not stay long.

When my father told me I had better start at school, I was scared. It took much coaxing, and buying me candy and nuts along with other luxuries at the log store at Marcus, before I consented to go.

Father was holding my hand when we went through the big white gates into the clean yard of the school. A high whitewashed fence enclosed all the huge buildings, which looked so uninviting. I hated to stay but promised Father I would not get lonesome. I walked at his side as he briskly entered a building to meet a woman in a long black skirt, with a roll of stiff white, oval cloth around her pale face. I looked away from her lovely, tapered fingers. I loved my mother's careworn hands better.

Since I could not understand English, I could not comprehend the conversation between Father and the kind woman in black. Later I learned she was the superior at the school. When my father was ready to leave, I screamed, kicked, and clung to him, begging to go home. This had always worked before, but now his eyes grew dim and he gently handed me to the sister and shamelessly ran out the door. When the sister tried to calm me, I screamed all the louder and kicked her. She picked me up off the floor and marched me into a dark closet under the long stairway to scream as loud as I could. She left me to sob myself to sleep. This cured my temper.

I was too young to understand. I did not know English, and the other girls were forbidden to speak any native language.[31] I was very much alone. Most of the time I played with wooden blocks and the youngest girls. I did not attend much school.

Each morning the children got up and dressed to attend church before breakfast. We walked in a double row along the path that climbed the slope to the large church, where my parents came for feast days. We entered the church from the west side door as the boys entered from the east one. The few adults came through the front double doors. There was also a small school chapel that we used when the weather was too bad to march outside.

Our dormitory had three rows of single iron beds, covered every day with white spreads and stiff-starched pillow shams that we folded each night and laid on a small stand beside the bed. Every Sunday night we were issued spotlessly clean nighties. This was the first nightgown I ever wore. Previously, I had slept in all my clothes.

Our dining hall, called the refectory, looked big to me, perhaps because I was used to eating in a cramped space. I was afraid of falling off the chair and always waited for others to sit first. The tables were lined up close to the walls, and the sister in charge had her table in the center, where she served our food on white enamel plates. We brought them up to her empty and carried them back full. Then we all waited until she rang the bell to begin eating.

The school ran strictly. We never talked during meals without permission, given only on Sunday or special holidays. Otherwise there was silence—a terrible silent silence. I was used to the freedom of the forest, and it was hard to learn this strict discipline. I was punished many times before I learned.

I stayed at the mission for less than a year because I took ill and father had to come and take me to the family camp at Kettle Falls. People were catching late salmon and eel. I returned to the mission again until my mother died in 1902 and I went home to care for my siblings.

After a few days of eating and relishing the fish my father caught, I was well enough to try to ride the new pony my parents gave me on my return. He was a surefooted buckskin cayuse with a black mane and tail. I at once named him Pep-pa-la-wh, (Cream Color) for his markings. He was the wildest little pony to catch, so after he was brought down from the hills, I kept him staked close to our camp until he became more gentle. I would climb on large stumps or rocks to get on him, helped along by the saddle strings.

My second stay at the school was less traumatic. I was anxious to learn more English and read. The school had been enlarged, with much larger buildings adjoining the old ones. The old chicken yard was moved farther away from the hospital windows. There was a fine white modern building, with a full veranda along the front, for the white students who paid fifteen dollars a month to board there. Although they were next door, we never met them; it was as if we lived in different worlds. They had their own playroom, refectory, classrooms, and dormitory. We only saw them in church, when they filed in ahead of us and sat in front of the guardian sisters. Our own teachers sat on long benches behind our rows. The only white girls we got to know were the charity orphans who boarded with us.

The paying boarders got school tuition, books, meals, and free music lessons for their money. This price was so low that many white families around Marcus, Meyers Falls, Colville, and Chewelah sent their children to Goodwin. Native children only went as far as the lower grades, but some had the privilege of attending more academic grades in the classroom of the white girls. Only two girls ever did this, and they were both white charity cases. Some Indian children studied music free, learning piano and organ. We all learned to sing church hymns. Eva, the chunky little daughter of Bridgett Lemere, became a fine organist and choir leader at the Pia Mission. She had a beautiful voice, and her fingers flew over the keys so lightly that the sacred music would ring through the building. Her sister Annie was a few years older than I and became my chum. I stayed away from the girls my own age because my whole life was spent around older people, except for my sisters.

Annie was beautiful and slightly built. We sympathized with

29

each other because we could not sing like Eva or play an instrument. She was kind, gentle, and understanding. We often shared little secrets with each other. She stood up for me against the older girls. Four years before, I had no defender at the school.

I was very interested in my work. With the knowledge Jimmy Ryan [cf. Chap. 16] had taught me from his yellowback novels, I passed first grade during the first semester. After my promotion the sisters had no second reader, so I had to study out of the third-year one. My marks were so good in all classes but grammar, which I never could understand, that I graduated at third level. I worked hard on catechism, which Mother had taught me in the native language. When I passed, I made my first communion in the big church, with many younger girls, including Eva and Annie Lemere. Our white dresses and shoes were supplied by the sisters. We wore flowing veils with flowered wreaths to hold them in place. It was Easter morning of 1899. We filed back to the convent, and the sisters gave us a big banquet with many goodies. It was a memorable day, and I thoroughly believed in the Catholic creed. I honored it as much as my native tutor had taught me to revere the ancient traditions of my forebears. I saw no difference between them and never questioned the priest.

I was so enthusiastic that I promised the sisters and girls I would come back in the fall. We were dismissed in June on the feast of Corpus Christi, always a big event in our year.

I never got back to Goodwin, however. Mother had a son, christened Johnny, whom I had to take care of because the duties of the ranch took much of her time. I began secretly to read Jimmy's books. My parents scolded and rebuked me many times because they thought reading was an excuse for being idle. There was much work to be done around the cabin and in the fields.

One day I heard about the Tonasket Indian School, where the Pierre children went to school. I begged Mother to go, but she replied in agitated tones, "Do you want to know too much, and be like the other schoolgirls around here? They come home from school and have no shame for their good character. That is all girls learn in government schools—running around and exposing their bodies." I ran outside into the rosebushes and cried in bitter humiliation. I wanted to go to school and learn the Mysteries of books. My meager education was just enough to make out the simplest words. Jimmy Ryan was only a little better, but he could speak English well.

In the past our interaction with different tribes was generally through intermarriage among important families and through religious events held most often during the winter under the direction of shamans (Indian doctors). Often the religious relations were not as cordial as the marital ones, because there was always a great deal of envy and antagonism among the shamans.

A powerful shaman once asked me to dress in my best clothes and paint my face before dancing at a gathering. His intention was to use my beauty as a young girl to attract the envy of other shamans so he could kill them. Knowing this, I refused and suffered the consequences. I was ill by the time I reached home and was diagnosed as having double pneumonia, but no doctor, white or Indian, could cure me.[32] My old granduncle was finally called out of retirement. He had me placed with my head pointing south for one day, then had me turned toward the north for the next. He decided the evil shaman had shot two tiny eagle wing feathers into my system. He asked my family if they wanted the other shaman killed or just punished by having his power taken away. Being good, compassionate Christians, they asked only that he lose his power. This was done.

Fifteen years later, after I was married, an old Wenatchi shaman and his wife asked my husband, Fred Galler, to drive them into Similkameen territory.[33] Since it was my new car, I went along on the trip while the Indian doctor made a lot of money. When the season of Winter Dancing began and the spirits were strongest, the local Similkameen doctors tried to find a way to hurt the old man. As they sent their spirits south, they flew over our home while Fred and I were asleep. One was a Dwarf and the other a Bluejay. I dreamed of their passing and took ill. This was enough to warn the old man, who cured me as thanks. Both Catholicism and shamanism have been part of the beliefs and experiences of my entire life.

Together these were part of my childhood experiences and made me resolve to help my people record their traditions and gain all the rights they are entitled to. My memories as a child remain with me yet, influencing all that I do, say, or think.

I can picture myself then. I was usually ragged and dirty faced, and my hair always seemed to be in a tangle, although I know Mother combed it frequently and oiled it with bear grease so my tresses would grow long and silky. In mild weather I seldom wore moccasins, and my clothing was merely a straight, long slip that had the mean habit of wrapping around my legs when I ran fast. I cannot remember that I ever wore underclothing. The slip was usually made of cast-off blue denim or old flour sacks printed with large, faded letters, but letters and writing were of no interest to me then. In the cold months, whenever the ice got too sharp for my bare feet, I wore moccasins and a shawl fashioned from a blanket. The shawl was cut square and folded crosswise, then crisscrossed over my chest, wound around my waist, and knotted in back.

I was always a dreamer about my future and that of my people. I used to climb to the tops of trees or onto large rocks to gaze into the rich valley where we lived and imagine myself a grown woman with a wonderful personality combining truth, honesty, and determination to do right.[34] At night I would lie awake in the tule-covered tipi and build "air castles" of future bounty while my tired parents took their well-deserved rest. Some nights I was a dashing leader of my broken people. Other nights I was going to be wealthy with many cattle and ponies grazing on knee-high bunchgrass along the hillsides, as it was forty years ago.

Whatever I dreamed or imagined, I always bore in mind the teachings of my parents that truthfulness and honesty must be the objective in future life. This was the measure of a successful person. It was the foundation of all my teachings as a child.

★

CHAPTER 2

Spiritual Training

THE TRADITIONAL importance of the native doctor among our people gave parents an enticement for sending their children out into the forest each night to hunt for a supernatural spirit and become accomplished shamans. An Indian doctor, with the knowledge of spirit guardians and animal guides, had greater influence among the natives than did the chief, [especially] if he was a good medicine man with one or more powerful spirits. This profession gave him influence over the people because they feared him for possible witchcraft. He was paid large sums for services rendered to those who were ill. He was usually a rich man with many young wives. While such powers could also be earned by a woman, her powers were never equal to those of an influential man. It is an accepted fact that the woman in Indian life was never up to standards equal to those of a man. Whether this originated during the caveman period or was a natural consequence of the greater strength of the man I leave to the reader to decide.

Children were encouraged to develop strict discipline and a high regard for sharing. When a girl picked her first berries and dug her first roots, they were given away to an elder so she would share her future success. When a child carried water for the home, an elder would give compliments, pretending to taste meat in water carried by a boy or berries in that of a girl. The child was encouraged not to be lazy and to grow straight like a sapling.[1]

Parents never lost the love and honor of their children because any severe punishment was done by a special "child whipper." He was usually a homely old man without a home. He went around gathering red willow [switches] and tying them around his waist. Then he visited homes to whip disobedient children. Sometimes he did this just for his own amusement. All children were afraid of him. Parents made him welcome and gave him food and small gifts.

Grandparents were always kind and indulgent, teaching morality through stories and example. They instilled the need for willpower and concern for others.

Children, at the early age of six or seven, were continually sent out each night to hunt for a guardian spirit to enable them to be shamans. Both boys and girls were obliged to undertake this search.

First a child was sent out for water to a spring or a creek close to the tipi. He or she was given a little basket and was expected to return with water for the parents or the spiritual teacher to prove that the destination was reached and the child was not playing "hooky." This first lesson was intended to make the child familiar with darkness and brave enough to overcome a fear of ghosts.[2]

As children grew older they were sent a little farther away each night until they graduated from short to long distances, when the teacher or parents gave them something special to take along on these night journeys. The article might be a small piece of fur from the medicine bag of a shaman or a bone from some animal that was the guiding spirit of a shaman. The child took this to some designated spot chosen by the tutor and left it there or had to sleep with it there all night. Sometimes the place was a sweat house or the skeleton of a dead animal, in the hope that the child would receive a vision of the animal spirit associated with the entrusted skin or bone. On some occasions this exercise, directed by a tutor, was intended to prepare the child to inherit the guide of the shaman after his death.[3] The child was always instructed never to run away from any [apparition in] animal form that chose to speak to him or her while on these expeditions hunting for knowledge.

It was supposed that lost spirits were roving about everywhere in the invisible air, waiting for children to find them if they searched long and patiently enough.[4] The Sweatlodge spirit was the most powerful for someone to find, as traditional teachings specify that "it" is part of the Great Spirit, who changed his wife and mate [?] into this ribbed conical shape. No other guiding spirit could ever overcome this power because "it" had five special strengths: wood for ribs, fire for heat, stones for stamina, earth for support, and water for cleansing. In all, it was a symbol of combined strengths, much more than the abode of any animal or spirit. The power of any individual supernatural could be easily found and devoured by Sweatlodge, according to Indian theory.

A child might find these supernatural powers almost anyplace: water, cliffs, forest, mountains, remains of lightning-struck trees, animal carcasses, old campfires, or the sweat lodge itself. The spirits were supposed to appear to a child when they were impressed by the dedication and lured by the purity of the persistent seeker.

[The spirit's] appearance came to a child in a vision, in the form of an animal or an object that spoke about how the spirit would help him or her in future life, especially when needed during times of distress. It sang its spiritual song for the child to memorize and use when calling upon the spirit guardian as an adult. Such a vision did not always come to a child while awake. Sometimes it came while the child was asleep beside the token he or she had been given.

Parents usually knew when children had found a spirit because they acted in a dreamy, hazy mood upon their return to the tipi. They did not play, preferring to sit around in deep thought. The visionary was not questioned by the elders, because children were not supposed to tell the secret or it would break the charm of their connection with some form of power and the spirit would be lost. If a child attempted to tell a parent or tutor, the adult quickly reminded the youngster of the duty not to reveal what was found or heard on the hunt [quest].

Finding a spirit gave a child a future career in medicine, with the ability to cure the sick or to foresee things that would happen to others, like accident, sickness, or death in the family. The power included the ability to keep such an accident from happening, since the guardian spirit warned him or her during sleep before such a thing could happen. It also specified in dreams and visions what to do to overcome personal sickness or how to protect against an attempt by another shaman to kill you to get your spirit powers. Such death and alienation of powers could occur only if the rival had stronger power to begin with. Thus, if a child found only one spirit, he or she was much more easily overcome by another, more experienced shaman. The more spirits a child found, the greater future success, influence, and importance that person would have, and the greater his or her resistance against other shamans.[5] He or she could better protect self and family, cure others, and acquire many riches and ponies as compensation.

Indian theory holds that each spirit has the same strengths as its animal counterpart, as judged by close observation of nature and the outcome of actual fights, in "real" life, between such animals or shamans with their powers.

Parents always impressed on their children the motto: "Obedience in listening to the words of wise elders makes a successful medicine person." While the power and the guidance for a career came from a spirit, it was the elders, learned in these tribal traditions, who provided the fine points of usage and established the social context for approved practice.[6]

Another warning often repeated with the advice of a tutor emphasized the importance of the family for an individual. Elders said: "The orphan has no education, schooling, or advice to become a great person."

It was thus only a natural necessity that parents should send their children out into the night to hunt for this secret knowledge to make themselves great and powerful. This training, for all its hardships, continued until puberty, when particularly strenuous work was added to the regime to give the child energy and stamina for a long life.

A boy reached this age when his voice began to change and he got lazy, preferring to sleep late in the mornings and yawning through the day. Then parents would exchange knowing glances with each other and remark, "su-le-whoo-mah" (puberty). With that one word, training became more intense and determined. A mother always had new moccasins ready for her son or daughter at this time.

A girl always started her fast at the first sign of menstruation, usually at an age between twelve and fifteen. She was regarded as immediately contaminated and not allowed to come in contact with her family for ten days. When she did return, she had to take several sweat baths and put on a complete change of clothing. The discarded clothing was tied in a bundle and put in the fork of a tree near the menstrual tipi.

In the old days, no village was complete without such shelters reserved especially for the women during their periods.[7] They were usually located downstream so as not to pollute the water used for cooking and drinking. Men absolutely shunned the women at this time. They were believed to cause ill luck and sickness to any man who came in contact with them.

Fasting youths had to bathe each morning at the first streak of dawn. While in this solitary retirement, they dried off with spiny fir boughs to become strong and healthy.

A girl prayed about motherhood at this time. Although she had to stay away from the sweat lodge and from hunting, fishing, and gambling gear, she could pick berries and dig up roots. She could not pick herbs or make love potions. She stayed away from camp, but if she had to go there, she never went behind a tipi or stepped near the head of a bed. If she came near someone already ill, she might make that person die.

Boys prayed to be successful hunters and warriors. They prayed to the rising sun to be lucky in war, gambling, and love. They asked for many wives and ponies. They wanted fearless bravery before the enemy. A boy practiced bravery by shooting arrows at stumps, rocks, or anything else. He took part in ʳham battles.

If youths wanted to become doctors, they went through great hardships to receive a vision. Like everyone else, they were very careful never to walk behind a shaman.

On the tenth day a boy returned home, a graduate of forest schooling. He took his place among adults as a man, able to join war parties, speak in council, and marry.

The girl was purified when she returned and stayed in her parents' tipi, thereafter rigidly chaperoned. She was wrapped in a virgin's cape so men could not see her body.[8] She had two capes, one for everyday and another for periods of menstruation. Most capes were made of fur or buckskin, but girls from important families wore capes woven of mountain goat [wool]. After puberty, a girl was also laced into snug bloomers, which came off only when her mother or chaperon was there, such as for her morning bath.

I well remember my own introduction to womanhood because I took the trauma so badly.[9]

Ever since I was seven years old, my parents, my adopted grandmother Teequalt, and other relatives had coached me to hunt for the spiritual blessings of a medicine woman. I followed the rules and never was afraid to go after water or run other errands at night, the time to search for a vision to accomplish my goal. I used to get up at dawn and bathe in cold water. At first I resented this, but I grew to like it afterward. I remember that my feet would stick to the ice when I got out of the hole chopped into the stream where we took our morning baths during winter. People used to bathtubs and plenty of hot water might think this terrible, but it is a refreshing sensation. Getting out, the water feels warm against the frigid air, creating a sensation that penetrates the body and makes a person feel like running and jumping. It is a great preventive against the common cold; usually a person taking this daily bath is always healthy and long-lived.

When my mother and Teequalt began to anticipate my puberty, they became more serious in their instructions. I was told to bathe and take on more responsibilities around the house. I was also made to run uphill without stopping until I reached the top of each of the little round knolls close to our home. This was intended to strengthen my lungs and increase my wind power. The old lady (Teequalt) who was my tutor sat in the shade pretending to watch me do my exercises, but I believe that she could not have seen me from where she sat. Only my mother had a clear view of me at those distances, and she never failed to call out if I stumbled and failed to reach the top of a hill without stopping.

From then on, I had to carry all the water in the house. If I stopped to pout, I was ordered to run rather than walk to the spring with my small pails. This was to give me energy for my lifework, my teacher explained. I began to have many small chores to do whenever I was not in training. I carried all the firewood, worked beside my father in the fields, and went to round up the horses each day before my breakfast and daily cold-water bath. Deep in my heart, I felt that my parents were being most cruel to me. Their pampering had suddenly stopped, and they lacked any consideration or mercy. When alone I used to grieve, often on long hikes when I could secretly sob aloud. One day, however, my mother commented that my eyes looked red, as if I had been crying. After that I was much more careful to bathe my face in cold water before returning home after crying in sympathy for myself. I always retained my love for my tutor, for she never scolded me, always seeking instead to urge me on and assure me that all the hardship was for my own future benefit. My mother was different, for she would sometimes threaten me if I refused to mind the tutor and the teachings I was then learning to observe so carefully.

I well remember how I used to envy Sulee and my new sister

Keleta as they slept peacefully each morning while I was rudely awakened to take my daily cold bath before the sun rose. While my sisters continued to play at will, I was obliged to do many duties about the tipi and cabin. It seemed that I had to learn something new every day. I now had to become competent to cook, sew, and help tan hides. Of course I could not quite understand it all and only later learned to forgive my sisters their youth and freedom until their times came to learn the serious and arduous duties of a woman.

I remember vividly the first sewing I did for myself. It was an apron already cut out for me. Mother gave me her needle case and had me wrap up my finger so I could wear her big thimble. I already had a sense of what sewing involved, so I made my first stitches very carefully. These were evenly spaced until I grew tired and made them long and uneven. Then I was obliged to rip them all out and sew up the seam again. I did this several times over the next two days, amid many tears, until I had a pretty pink apron with figures on it. Through it all, my mother and teacher seemed aloof to the depth of my childish sorrow.

My eating was carefully watched, and I was never allowed to fill up at meals as I had previously. I could never eat at the table when company was present and had to wait to eat anything at all until after they had left. Many times only scraps of meat and gristle would be left on the deer bones by our elderly guests. Even with their worn-down teeth, there was seldom very much food on the bones.

One day some surveyors were passing our cabin, led by the half-breed interpreter Charlie Brown, who stopped to ask my mother if she would permit me to baby-sit with his children while Mrs. Brown did the weekly wash. Their camp was at the little mission, directly across the ravine from the small church. Mother readily agreed, because Charlie was her first cousin and she was always partial to her relatives.

I got on my pony and rode down the hill to the camp of the survey crew supervised by Mr. Clair Hunt. Between there and the church, however, I began to have giddy fainting spells. My head swam, and I almost fell off my horse. I got off and led him through a small grove of trees almost in sight of the camp. There, in the privacy of that grove, I learned that I had reached the age of maturity. I had previously been told by Teequalt and my mother to be on the watch for this distasteful arrival, and I began mostly to dread it. They emphasized the necessity of telling them at once. I sat down on a big boulder beside the road and cried, because I could not help but dread telling my mother about the event.

I walked home leading my pony, letting him occasionally browse along the way on green bunchgrass growing beside the wagon road. I was lingering purposely to be alone in my sorrow.

I was then just twelve years old. Up to this time I had played with other children and boys whenever I had time free from helping my mother and attending to lessons given by my native teacher. Many times I could play most of the day with the baby strapped on my back while my mother was busy tanning deerskins, cooking, cleaning, and doing other chores. I would wander alone through the hills, spying on the birds. I used a long stick with berries on the end to feed baby birds in nests. I did not want to leave behind any human odors. I loved my freedom.

When I finally reached home that day, I was heartbroken by the time I told my mother. She had me release my pony immediately and stay away from him until I was no longer confined. A menstruating woman could ruin a horse, making it lose its luster or hair, according to our ancient beliefs, becoming a wretched, lazy mount. Teequalt said that women were never allowed near war and hunting ponies in the old days.

Mother stopped tanning and began to prepare me for my last ordeal of searching for spiritual guidance. She combed my hair and braided it tightly into two knots beside my ears. When I reached up to feel my hair she said, "Do not touch your hair, you are unclean. You will stop its growth. Use a stick when you want to scratch your scalp." She folded my braids and tied them with buckskin thongs so they would not come loose during my ten days of solitary fasting. Then she washed my face and painted it with a mixture of vermilion earth and tallow. I was given a little buckskin bag with an extra pair of moccasins, bear grease for cream, some red face paint, and a bow-wood comb in a fan shape, which had its own buckskin sack. A buckskin cape was tied at my neck. She dressed me warmly, tied a small woolen shawl around my shoulders, and put new moccasins on my feet. I was ready.

I was ready to spend ten days in the mountain wilderness as a young woman. This was my last preparation for a future as a renowned medicine woman.

It was almost noon when I was leaving. Father came home for lunch. He objected at once, and my parents argued. Father said I had looked for a power for years and had never got anything. Now it was too late. He said our ancient customs were foolish, exposing children to cold and perhaps ruining their health. The modern world required that Indians be more like whites. Medicine women were no longer needed; the agency doctor was better qualified to treat the sick.

I stood waiting at the door, faintly hoping that Father would get the best of my mother just this once. Mother did not say very much, but I could sense the disgust behind her stoicism. She waited for Father to finish. Then she waved her hand at me to leave. I closed the rough-hewn door and started walking toward the mountains.

I was hungry, being accustomed to three regular meals a day. I picked some wild sunflower stalks, peeled them, and enjoyed the familiar flavor.

When I got to the base of the mountain, I picked up two stones and put them inside my dress above the belt. I went quickly up the slope without stopping until I was almost at the top. As I had been taught, I loosened my belt and let the first stone drop, saying "When I have children, that is the way they will come, with me on the run." I dropped the second stone at the top and said, "This is the way the afterbirth of the child will come. I will never have trouble bearing my children."

I continued to follow the teachings. When I washed my face in the creek, I would use fir boughs to dry off so my hands did not touch my face. Otherwise I would wrinkle early in life. I blew a breath toward the rising sun and whispered, "May the Great Spirit protect my youth for many years to come." I rubbed my hands and feet with the green boughs, blowing first to the sun and then to my fingertips and toes, praying they would remain small and unwrinkled.

I never touched my hair with my hands, only with the comb. I would groom myself each dawn beside mountain streams and greet the rising sun either by sitting and looking toward it or by standing with arms extended in deep prayer. I prayed for future success, always ending with, "May the Great Spirit and Creator spare my life from accidents, illness, deformity, and laziness. Bless me with a long and prosperous life. Make me, dear God of the Heavens, to be honest and strong in character, to face life with an honorable, truthful, and strong will, without fearing man or beast."

Frequently I would kneel on a mountainside and pray to the God that Father De Rouge had told us about. I never realized a difference between worshiping our Universal God and the God of Moses and Mount Sinai. My young mind believed in both sects. Perhaps if the priest had known how deeply rooted the puberty fast is in our religion, he would have made an effort to stop it. There were many things the natives practiced that the priests had no knowledge of. People still believed in the old ways, and no one was criticized for sending their children out alone; instead they were honored for doing so. During my childhood, people were just beginning to think that the custom was foolish. Later, Jesuit and white teachings mostly won out.

In ancient belief, the education of a child was never complete without this final ten-day fast. Yet my fasts had brought no results.

When the snow began to fall, I was introduced to a new method of training away from home.

One cold evening Teequalt took her hemp medicine bag and removed small, well-worn animal bones. She placed them on her palm and sang in low tones. Sulee and I sat beside her, watching in awed silence. We had been taught to reverence the ways of our native shamans. When her secret song was done, Teequalt turned in my direction and said, "When I was a small girl like you, I found the spirit of this bird one night, while I was searching far into the mountains of our country. Tonight I am giving you this spirit. You are young. The trail of life is before you. Your moccasins may have to walk over stony ground and you may need a guardian."

After a pause she continued, "If you are not afraid tonight, you will see a vision of this power I earned when I was a little girl like you. It is the power of Eagle, chief of birds." Then she gave me the leg bones of an eagle, decorated with fluffy feathers from the breast and the tips of the wing and tail.

Unsure what I should do, I thanked her and went into the cabin to confer with my mother. She immediately got out warm clothing and a new pair of moccasins. From the other side of the box heater, Father raised his objections again. This time Mother responded right away, "The old lady has given her the sacred medicine bones to take out tonight." Father said, "If she were a boy, her future would depend on such undertakings, but she is a girl and will marry soon. She does not need a power to cook and tan hides. Let her alone."

Mother went on, "Women are known to make good doctors. We need them every bit as much as warriors." Meanwhile, she continued to dress me warmly.

Their argument was mild, and Mother held out. After a few awkward moments of silence, Father started to talk to Jimmy Ryan in broken English. I could not understand them.

Mother sent me out that night to the highest peaks north of our place, where eagles nested on the cliffs. As I left my small dog followed me around the big hillside, along the trail that led to our spring, where I scooped up water between my palms and took a long drink before going on. In the dark, I had difficulty following the horse trail to where the stock was watered.

I must have gone two miles before I lost sight of the dim kerosene light from our lone window. Before then, I stopped every so often to see if my family was still awake. I had no fear. I had learned that darkness could not hurt me. I gave no thought to animals. I knew there were no bears in the lowlands, and cougars rarely attacked humans. In fact they are cowardly and attack only when someone is not watching for them. As members of the cat family, they would be afraid of my dog. He ran around as I walked along, chasing things I could not identify.

I slipped on rocks, got tangled in thickets, and tore my shawl on wild rosebushes. When I reached the deep ravine of Toulou Creek, I could not locate the crossing that my father used when he hauled logs for the cabin and the hundreds of cedar rails for the fence. He made a wide swath to drive his team through. I followed the creek, thinking I was high enough to save my feet from getting wet.

Finally, I took off my moccasins, waded across, and put them back on. I went up the steep incline to the bluffs where the eagles nested.

Toward morning I was on the edge directly above a nesting ledge. I stood there and tried to locate the light of home, but it was completely dark. Even the cabins near the church were hidden. An owl hooted back in the thickets of the ravine and was answered by its mate. Occasionally crickets broke the silence as I stood waiting for the eagles to speak to me and give me their spiritual guardianship. My legs grew numb, so I sat under a tree, waiting patiently and fingering the leg bones and downy feathers. My dog rested beside me and would press his cold nose against my hands, settled on my lap. This kept me awake, although I got terribly sleepy.

I did doze but was rudely awakened when my dog jumped up to chase a curious chipmunk. I saw a light streak of gray toward the east. The tree squirrels started their scolding in the treetops. As the dawn came, I could plainly see our cabin in the center of the Pia foothills. The eagles were soon circling overhead, staying well away from me. If they did speak to me, they were too far away to hear. I was afraid to go home, so I waited all day there. As the sun dipped low in the evening, my hunger drove me homeward.

I was too young to lie or invent a story, so I told the truth. My parents were disappointed. My tutor said my dog kept me from having a vision because I was not truly alone. After this I was obliged to hunt by myself, which made these trips very lonely.

Once an old pony had died over the ridge from a big sidehill. Teequalt sent me to sleep all night beside the carcass, which had rotted to the extent that it swarmed with good-sized maggots. The stench kept me from getting too close. Coyotes howled close by, trying to reach their food, but I was not afraid. Wolves had formerly been a danger, but they were extinct, along with the red and black foxes taken by the fur trade. As usual, I came home in the morning without success.

My tutor and my mother consoled me. They urged me to use the sweat lodge and to sleep at places where there were pictographs. These were specially designated spots of great power.[10] Lightning-struck trees were also suggested, because the power of thunder is greater than any in the Animal Kingdom. I wanted a power to cure, but my teacher said that I would need many spirits to be able to resist other doctors when they tried to steal my power.

At least I was not lazy or an orphan, because they are said never to become great.

When summer came I went out again and had a strange experience. I went down by the river and walked very carefully through the tall grass under the cottonwoods, fearing to step on a rattlesnake. Suddenly a dog came at me with menace. I felt a sensation as if cold water was thrown on me, and the dog got even larger, with a swirl of fire around him. He began to sing. I became very fearful and was about to faint when I thought to pray to God. The dog vanished.

When I felt able, I ran home without regard to the rattlers infesting that country.

I paid a boy a dollar to find and kill the dog. Several years later the dog came to me in a dream and said that if I had followed his song and dance, I would have become a great doctor, able to cure the sick and have good luck. If I did not accept him, he would go to a little boy with a pack of dogs as his power. I knew the boy. When I awoke, I decided to choose the Christian God. The dog left me for good. The little boy died shortly afterward, and I went to his funeral. Perhaps he had no right to the "ghost spirits" of my ancestors. This dog had been one of my grandmother's powers, and I was probably meant to inherit it.

★

CHAPTER 3

Courtship and Marriage

AFTER a girl returned from the isolation of the menstrual hut, [the culmination of] her intensive spiritual training, she was looked upon as a woman of value. Her mother put a cape around her shoulders and tied it at the neck. This was never removed when she was in public. It was called the virgin cape and signified that she was unmarried. These capes varied in length. Some were to the knee so that they fully covered her form when she was sitting down. Others were to the ankle and used when she was traveling with people to prevent her accidentally showing her legs to a man, who could ["touch her with his eyes"]. The daughter of a chief usually wore a cape woven of mountain sheep wool with black bars, about ten inches long, woven prominently into the front to show her membership in the chiefly class. Each bar indicated a chief in her ancestry, something like the way an English coat of arms is divided to show different noble branches of the family. Every girl had at least two capes, one for the unclean period of menstruation and the other for the rest of the time at home.[1]

These virgins also wore an undergarment or bloomers of heavy buckskin, carefully fitted to their form. It laced up the sides with buckskin cords and was tied at each side of the waist. It was never removed without the consent of and in the presence of a girl's mother or chaperon.

The chaperon was a grandmother or some elderly woman relative who watched the girl day and night. She always slept next to the girl's bed and kept a big stick to chase away dogs and other [nocturnal] intruders. She also used the stick to stir the fire occasionally at night so there would still be embers in the morning to rekindle it. With only flint and steel to make a fire, relighting the fire was a tedious labor.

The girl never went to bed until all the men in the family had done so, for fear that they might accidentally see her uncovered and cause her to be very ashamed, particularly before her older brothers. After her chaperon had built up the fire, she was up before dawn and began the day by taking a cold bath or swim. Otherwise she never went outside her father's tent during the day. Instead, she was expected to sit on her heels with her back to the door, never speaking to any men who happened to visit there. She was allowed to speak to women if she used low tones and they were alone in the tipi. She kept herself busy by weaving, sewing, and decorating items such as moccasins and clothing with porcupine quills.

When the family was traveling, she was in the rear of the group of women and children moving behind the men.[2] Her chaperon maintained a watchful eye on her. She carried her own belongings, such as clothing, bedding, and personal articles, bundled into a large pack on her back. After we came to own horses, she rode behind with the other virgins and chaperons, their gear loaded on their mounts or packhorses.

The reason for all this care was that a girl who guarded her chastity was considered valuable in the eyes of our warriors [men]. A man would willingly give many ponies and robes to her parents for such a wife. Hence parents jealously guarded the character of their daughters, keeping them pure, clean, and above the gossiping tongues of the old women of the village, who were always ready with cruel criticism that could damage the honor and reputation of a girl and her family if given a chance to do so.[3]

If a man wanted a girl to be his wife, he did not go directly to her and begin courting, because she was very well chaperoned. He first came to visit her parents on the pretext of a social call, returning several times if he felt welcomed and encouraged. He gave the father presents of robes and ponies. A few days later he came back and gave other gifts to the grandparents, chaperon, and other near relatives with influence on the girl.[4] Finally, he sent his mother or other close female relative to ask the father of the girl for her to be his wife.

Usually there was a great deal of consultation among the relatives until all were satisfied with the match. Then the parents gave their consent. Sometimes the chief of the tribe was consulted alone by the mother or chaperon, or they took the wife of the chief into their confidence to ask the advice of her husband on the alliance. For the marriage of important people, the whole community had to reach a satisfied consensus.

Everyone was concerned with the character of the groom and the quality of his family before they reached an agreement. Usually the girl had the final right to approve or reject this man; however, her parents felt they knew what was best for her and the family. Sometimes they would force a marriage the bride did not want or like, but if she had been properly raised and knew her place in society, she went along with the wisdom of her elders.

Parents decided when a girl was available for marriage. A commoner was usually married early, before age twenty, because she became a burden to her poor parents due to the extra work of feeding both her and the chaperon, who received no compensation other than food and clothing. The daughter of a chief (a princess [?]) usually married around twenty because her parents could afford to take care of her longer. It was rare that she married older because then she was close to bringing shame on the family by becoming an old maid or unwanted woman. Her life [as a spinster] was unbearable and unhappy. To escape this inferior mark of status, she usually married sooner than she would otherwise.

A girl of common stock, poor family, or cowardly clan married into the lower strata.[5] Only seldom did she marry into the family of a chief or distinguished warrior, and then only because of unusual beauty, ability in weaving or decoration, or modest and chaste character unstained by gossip. While her family might be poor, they were nonetheless honest and upstanding, much given to hard work. In this manner she provided the ideal type of wife for a chief, one from an honest family with conscientious work habits. The wife of a chief with foresight selected such a girl so as to secure a good life mate for her son and an industrious daughter-in-law to do the housework in the tipi where she was the supreme adviser.

While the girl was chaperoned, elopement was all but impossible. Rarely, a romantic couple would find a way, but they had to leave their home country and travel as far as their ponies could carry them. They had either to find a refuge by joining a subtribe of their homeland or move to a tribe of strangers. They could go home only after the birth of the first child, who provided them with an excuse for forgiveness from the grandparents. If the wife was deserted shortly after the elopement, she would seldom come home because of her shame. Eventually, if she married a stranger, she could return to her community as an "honest" woman.

Frequently the friendship of two families would lead them to contract a marriage between their babies so that they would be expected to marry when they grew up. During childhood the future spouses were reminded of the promises of their families, who were always exchanging gifts. The parents of the boy usually gave the most gifts. If either child died before the marriage, a younger child was offered; otherwise the other family was released from the promise and the gift exchange was discontinued.

When I was a child, this custom of giving gifts between in-laws had become a fragmentary practice. I was involved in such a transaction only once.

When I was eleven, an Okanagan boy named Pierre Paul came to visit my parents at Pia. He was then eighteen, old enough to marry, and came leading a beautiful buckskin horse bred from heavier stock than the smaller cayuses we were used to. The horse was cream-colored with a white mane and tail. It was a favorite of mine, and I used to love to ride it when Father would permit me. It was a valuable present admired by everyone. Pierre stayed in our home for about three weeks. I liked him because he was never too busy to play with us children, to make me horses of willow, and to help me ride the calves in the barnyard. By then I had learned to ride bucking colts and calves so as to outdo the sons of my Aunt Mary who had teased me so badly. They were older and considered budding expert riders.

His family was very influential, rich in ponies and good land overlooking Osoyoos Lake. After he left, Aunt Mary explained to me how I was related to him, much to my surprise. His parents and mine had contracted a child marriage between us while we were still babies because our parents were such good friends. A decade later, his mother had sent him over one hundred miles across the Colville Reservation to see if I was old enough to marry him and fulfill the promised contract. The buckskin was intended to carry me back home as his wife.

Pierre Paul never approached the subject of our marriage while he played with me or coached me to stay on the bucking animals. Both he and my parents thought I was still too young. I had yet to reach puberty, and this saved me the embarrassment of being married before I was a woman or of having a husband I did not care for or even know. I really only liked Pierre as a big brother, because he always took my part in childhood fights with my cousins.

During that summer mother and I would go into Marcus to shop and to pick up pretty pieces of broken glass behind the saloons. Mother would try to prepare me for marriage, but these little confidence talks only increased my hatred for all men in general. I decided I would never marry. I began to grow unhappy again, trying to imagine a way out. But I had to keep my thoughts to myself because I was afraid of the scolding and rebuke I would get from my parents and native tutor. So I kept my secret in my breast.

The only girl chum I could dare to confide my secret dread to was Annie Lemere, who had married just after we had returned from the mission school. Her parents had made a choice for her. She married the oldest son of Joe and Rosila [Rosalee] Seymour [Seymore], our neighbors. Eneas Seymour was the catch of the season. Many were the Indian girls who would shyly glance toward his clean-cut features, hair trimmed in the latest mode, and well-tailored suits of dark material. He had been educated at the Goodwin Mission school for boys.

Annie looked beautiful in her light-blue silk dress, made by her mother. Her hat was a light cream-colored leghorn, with long black velvet streamers that waved playfully behind her back as she left the Pia church steps. She squeezed my fingers when I passed her following my own mother. Annie seemed happy with her parents' choice, although she had to learn to ignore the flashing eyes of the other jealous girls.

As is the custom, the bride went to live with her mother-in-law. This is not the ending expected for a beautiful story of young love, but it is authentic to our lifeways.

My contracted marriage never took place, and any promises ended the following winter when Pierre accidentally froze to death while hunting.

After he died, I had a very different sort of marriage proposal the next summer, an experience I cannot forget.

An old man with much personal property came by one day to find us children playing on an old saddle strapped across a fence rail. He watched us for a while, even going so far as to ride the hobbyhorse, before he abruptly told me that my mother had just accepted his proposal of marriage for me. I was dumbfounded and shamefully burst into tears. I had a fear and disgust of him. I begged him not to marry me against my will before I had the chance to go back to learn more at the mission. To my surprise, he promised that he would wait until I was ready for marriage and had more schooling. I thanked him for extending the time for our engagement.

I never married him because Father came to my rescue when I confided in him that I hated the thought of marriage. Mother continued to insist that I should marry as soon as I came of puberty age, to save me from disgracing the family and myself because of my wayward ways of acting like a tomboy and riding calves.

A marriage was seldom conducted in public unless the girl was a princess. Then the ceremony took place with the whole village as witnesses, resting comfortably in a circle under the shade of the council lodge or a sunshade of boughs. A marriage between commoners was held in the tipi home of the bride, with just their families gathered together for the occasion.

The groom arrived on the day of the marriage with his family, who set up camp next to that of the bride. At the proper time, he walked into the lodge of the girl with his relatives following, and all of them sat on one side. The girl and her family sat across the fire from them.

For an important marriage the chief presided, aided by his wife. He passed a pipe around the room so each could share a smoke in common. In this way the families were publicly united to banish any past or future disagreements and thus stood as "one united." The chief then gave the couple an oration of his advice, pointing out the good characteristics of each, and then offered his congratulations to them for a happy future.[6]

The father of the girl took her by the hand and led her to meet the groom at the back of the tent or middle rear of the gathering. In this manner he gave his daughter in marriage to the man. The husband then removed the virgin's cape from his wife's shoulders so all could now view her form. This declared them married for all to see.[7] They then sat upon the finest robes with their most prominent guests.

Food was then provided by both sets of parents, a wedding feast shared by everyone to rejoice in the uniting of the two families.

The first night the couple slept at the home of the bride. The husband removed the buckskin bloomers worn by the girl, and the work of the chaperon was finished.

The next day the couple left to live at the camp of the husband's people, often moving into his parents' home. A newly married couple usually did not live alone until they had children, making their old home too small for all of them. Yet if the groom was of poor family, they might move in with the family of the bride and stay there for several years until they had collected enough material to set up their own household.[8]

When a bride moved in with her mother-in-law, she took over all the hard work of the tipi. The older woman retired from heavy work, content to sit, rest, or sleep while the daughter-in-law worked continuously. If the new bride was inclined to be lazy or was unwilling to get up mornings after the old woman called, the mother-in-law would beat her legs and feet. A new wife seldom talked back to her in-laws. Sometimes her sisters-in-law also abused her in an overbearing way, but her husband usually would not come to her rescue because ancient teachings held that she had to learn her own place in the new family.

If a man tired of a woman soon after marriage or left her for another woman, she might continue to live with his parents if she had made a place for herself, faithfully doing all the housework and food preparation in the hope that her husband would return to her some day. Next to the dog, the native woman had no equal in taking abuse from "her man." On other occasions a woman who was abandoned would return to her own parents to stay until she was ready to remarry. Then she would appear in public with her face decorated with red paint to challenge [encourage] another marriage proposal. A woman who was abandoned was considered lawfully divorced and thus honorably entitled to another husband.

If she truly loved the man and felt ashamed at the desertion, she might hang herself from a tree branch, throw herself into the river, or plunge onto a sharp weapon. Her suicide would be blamed on her abandoner.[9]

A woman who committed adultery disgraced her family and was either lawfully killed by a male relative, who shot her with an arrow, or offered the chance to commit suicide to save her family from adverse criticism, reproach, or gossip. Her "feelings" were never considered, only the lawful resentment of her community.

An Indian woman would have only one husband at a time, and if she married too many times she was marked by lost decency and became known as "Mrs. Many Husbands."

If a woman had been previously married, a man courted her in a different way. He might visit her family several times without speaking directly to her. He would look at her beauty and watch her skills at cooking, cleaning, and sewing. If he was satisfied, he took some small pebbles and threw them near her when no one else was paying attention. If she was in favor of him, she tossed some pebbles back to him to encourage the proposal. Then he left and held conferences with his own relatives. Meanwhile, she was doing the same with her close kin. If everyone agreed, the man then went to wait for her at the place where her camp got water. When she came, he would quietly ask for the marriage. If she accepted, he walked into her tipi just before bedtime and sat on her bed. If she allowed this, that was a public declaration of their marriage. Everyone else in the tipi gave each other an understanding look and offered congratulations and advice for their future happiness.

A husband could have as many wives as he could support, so polygamy was a mark of wealth.[10] These wives seldom lived together in one tipi; each usually had her own home. Often the youngest was the favorite who lived with his parents so that his mother could keep a watchful eye on her and also have a strong helper. Other wives had separate homes or lived with relatives, receiving meat and visits from the husband in turn. In return, each made him moccasins, clothing, and other artistic gifts as a dutiful wife. She showed these to the co-wives, who advised and helped each other as the need arose. As long as all were satisfied with their influential status as the lawful wives of an important man, all went smoothly.

When a man died, his wife mourned for a period of at least one year. A longer period of mourning meant that she truly loved him and held him with regard in her heart. She did not look after her appearance, remaining unkempt in old clothing till she was ready to remarry. Whenever she appeared in public wearing good clothing and red face paint, men knew she was ready to marry again. Often a dead husband's brother or another close male relative had first claim on the status of husband so as to perpetuate the alliance between the two families. If such a man wanted his former sister-in-law, he came forward and proposed; otherwise he made himself scarce so the woman could arrange another marriage.[11]

If a woman decided she did not want to be the wife of a man who held such a "mortgage right" to her, she went to him and asked permission to marry someone of her own choice. Such a personal request was usually granted. Sometimes mutual consent was involved, and both people found themselves at liberty to choose the spouse each wanted.

If a woman married someone else without asking permission of the "mortgage-holder," however, her former in-laws had the right to duel with the new husband, fighting with either bow and arrows, a long spear, or a rough-and-tumble wrestling match with a stone knife, the opponents slashing each other until one of them was badly wounded or killed. The best man would win the woman, who followed him out of fear or gratitude that she was loved or wanted strongly enough that men would fight over her.

Much of this devotion, concern, and love was missed by white people, who often failed to understand the native perspective. A man never openly showed affection to a woman in public unless he intended to make light and sport of her character. Even though legally married to a woman, he never showed the true feeling of his heart, as a white man does in kissing and embracing a woman. An Indian who did this would shame the woman and call her character into serious question. It was told that in primitive times an Indian man never kissed a woman in any lovemaking. He did embrace her close to his heart in his affections, but never in a physical sense unless they were quite alone. A faithful woman was satisfied that her spouse loved her by the very nature of his stoicism.

CHAPTER 4

★

The Dutiful Wife

WHEN an Indian girl married at a wedding feast and moved in with the parents of her husband, she began to learn in earnest how to cook, do housework, and care for a family of her own. She learned all the occupations appropriate to a woman, such as basket weaving, sewing, tanning, skin decoration, and child care. Her future status was judged by how carefully and well she did these tasks, so her in-laws were often harsh with her at the beginning of her learning period. If her husband's mother was dead, the couple initially went to live with an aunt or other older female relative. A woman learned crafts as she was growing up, but cooking was mostly learned after marriage when she started housekeeping.

Her first morning in the tipi of her in-laws marked the start of intensive training in the domestic activities that would determine her standing for the rest of her life. Her mother-in-law was first up to stir the coals or build the fire for a new day. Then she shook the new bride awake to have her take a cold bath and bring back a basketful of water for the morning meal. If the bride appeared to be at all lazy or refused to rise cheerfully, her mother-in-law used the firestick on her feet and shins, saying, "Get up and take care of your husband's food and clothing. If you do not, you will always be poor."

If the bride still failed to leave her warm bed, the older woman would hit her feet even harder and say in a more serious tone, "If you wished to sleep long in your bed, why did you take my son to ruin his life by having a lazy wife, a weight on all his efforts? You do not deserve his support. He will soon leave you for another woman. A man does not like to have a lazy wife when other women are willing to work for him and his parents. You will be called "woman thrown away" when my son leaves you.

This usually had the result of bringing the new wife around to do the bidding of the mother-in-law to save herself the embarrassment of being left by her husband for another more dutiful woman. She avoided the predicament of having people laugh at her and call her "grass widow" or "woman thrown away."

From that day, the new wife took up the duties of the tipi home while the older woman left the life thread to the new drudge and slave of the household. This was the major tragedy in the life of a woman, cut off from the pampering help and loyalty of her parental ties and living with a man who did not take her side against his own relatives for fear of being criticized for spoiling his wife.

The mother-in-law was relieved of heavy duties and spent her time at more leisurely activities like basket making, skin decoration, and advising the family. She remained the supreme head of the family, ruling her husband, son, daughter-in-law, and children when they arrived. Her wisdom guided the household. Her dreams and visions were always given due consideration. She advised and enforced all the numerous taboos required for first pregnancy. She had responsibility for the care and tutoring of the grandchildren when they were old enough to understand.

Of course the compensation for the hard work of the young woman was that in time she herself became a mother-in-law, held in reverence and respect by her family and in awe by the wives of her sons. Respect for the mother-in-law continued even as her words were given less weight because her brain became clouded with age. For as long as she was alive, she was given the tenderest and choicest morsels of meat by the family.

Women had responsibility for camp life, everything from manufacturing the tents from tules and skins to setting these up in the locations chosen at each of the seasonal camps. The winter site was the one considered permanent and the one people identified with. During the other seasons people moved freely among the anciently established campsites, gathering food to be stored for the winter.

The household articles were few and rather crudely made for want of a wide range of material to manufacture them. A family might have a few baskets or woven kettles for cooking and carrying water for the home. Eating implements were a few spoons, made from mountain sheep horn, large enough to cover the palm of the hand.

The horns were soaked in hot water until they were soft enough to cut and shape on round stones to form the bowl. They were tied tightly in place on the curved stone with buckskin cords, leaving the untouched portion as the handle. These spoons, serving as both ladle and soup bowl, were used in turn by the family members while eating. Usually men had their own special spoons while women and children had another type to save the men from eating food from the same container the women used.

The only other eating implements were stone or metal knives used at table and for housework such as cutting up buckskins or sinews, much as we now use scissors, and scraping bone or horn. A man always had his own special hunting knife, used to gut his kills and to cut his food during meals. Men and women kept their knives separate so as to avoid offending the animals hunted or the fish caught.

Sometimes sharpened sticks were whittled for use much as we now use a fork to pick up food while eating. Mostly everyone used the fingers while eating all manner of food, for then everyone could share together from the same dishes.

The tablecloth was matting made of tules or of grass and hemp fibers. Sometimes these table coverings were made of flat cedar slats laced together with hemp cord to make a long strip that was rolled out inside the lodge for food to be placed upon. Their size depended on the space available. For a tipi, the mat was about three feet wide and four to five feet long so it was easily placed over the area of a bed or sitting place.

Cooking usually involved boiling food in a water-filled basket by placing heated rocks in it and stirring them rapidly so as not to scorch the inside. A woman changed the stones several times during this cooking process, but it took only a short time to have the water boiling and the meat tender enough to eat. As each rock cooled off, she lifted it out with forked sticks. She used other stick tongs to lift out the food and place it on matting to drain. These tongs were easy to wash and were left outside to dry between meals.

Some meat was broiled by spreading it out, pushing a sharpened stick through both ends, and sticking it in the ground angled toward the fire to cook until it was brown and juicy.

Except for children, who had their meals prepared for them by a mother, grandmother, or sister, every member of a family wanting to eat would cook some meat on a stick placed at their usual locations beside the fire. Each place was marked by a mat or weaving belonging to that person. A family meal was eaten around a mat or woven cedar strip placed on the most open spot in the tipi, usually the mother's sleeping place. Children were given pieces of dried meat to chew on during their play. If a hunter made a kill during the day, he would usually build a fire and roast a snack for himself. For big meals or feasts with guests, cedar strips or matting were placed opposite the doorway in the place of honor. The family ate according to their supply, more when they had plenty and less when they had to ration.

Every family had one good heavy meal a day, usually in the evening when the hunters had returned home with fresh meat and the women had prepared new or stored provisions. There was no set time, but people were hungry by sunset. Women seldom ate anything until after they returned from root digging or berry picking around noon. Often they had only a light lunch. Men frequently had a morning meal consisting of small pieces of dried meat or a few berries to give them strength for hunting, fishing, or the heavy construction of traps and weirs.

Family clothing was usually made of tanned deerskin, but the fur of small animals such as rabbits was used for baby clothes during the winter to keep them warm and snug. Coyote skins were used for the jackets of older people, tanned with the fur left on. The skin was tied with the rear end around the back of the neck and shoulders, and the legs were doubled under the arms and across the front to keep the shoulders warm. A dress required two doeskins, trimmed at the neck, with the forelegs sewn together as sleeves. The sides were laced or sewn together, and an uneven hem was cut with a stone knife. Dresses were trimmed with porcupine quills dyed with herbs or earths for color, in different shades to suit the taste of the individual. The quills were flattened by pressing them between smooth stones and sewn on with sinew thread taken from the backbone of a deer, which was dried, shredded, and twisted to a needlelike point that was pushed through holes made with the help of a sharpened deer-shinbone awl. A very artistic designer made beautiful clothing decorated in many shades.[1] Decoration was highly prized on adults' clothing, children's gear, and a baby's cradleboard. A wife with a decorative knack was much regarded by the community and brought fame to her husband and family. Such finery was not used daily, but only for occasions such as council meetings, social get-togethers accompanied by gambling, feasting, or games, and religious gatherings.

Colville made baskets of cedar roots and grasses, but these could not compare with those with beautiful designs made by the Klickitat and other lower Columbia River tribes, or by tribes of Canada like the Shuswap and Thompson.[2] Hence they were obliged to trade with these others for better baskets for holding water and decorating a feast table. They traded buckskins decorated with quillwork and other personal items in exchange for these highly prized, evenly woven, and tightly made baskets.

The Colville traded with coastal people for shells, baskets, and seafood. The shells were used as clothing decoration, earrings, necklaces, and bracelets. A large seashell was used as a pendant at the front of a gown, attached to a long buckskin string to keep it in place. All these imports were considered valuable because they were rare to my people and had traveled a long way before they reached Kettle Falls.

An Indian woman led a life of drudgery the year round, performing many and various duties. When the spring Buttercup Moon arrived in the month at present called March, she went hunting for the "famine food" [the wild balsamroot we call the] Indian sunflower.[3] It was the first fresh food a family had after a winter of living on preserved foods. It has saved many families from starvation. A woman gathered these shoots as soon as the ground thawed enough for her to use her digging stick on the tender white sprouts. She proudly brought them home to her husband and family to improve their diet.

In the Moon of Leaves (April), the bitterroot or rock rose grew, and the roots were dug when the flower was still in the bud stage.[4] They were eaten with soup or dried and preserved for the winter. Women, alone or in groups, would spend their time digging these roots from rocky knolls and sidehills. This food was very good for curing stomach upset caused by eating too much meat during the winter. It gave balance to the diet and was much relished by all of us.

In High Water Moon (June) the serviceberries grew in abundance, and women took their picking baskets into the hills. The berries were eaten fresh or spread on mats to become sun dried before being laced up in fiber sacks for storage. People were willing to travel far to pick them. In July and August they moved camp to gather, dry, and store chokecherries.

The summer was spent alternating between berry picking in the hills and taking salmon in the rivers. When the salmon ran in the Columbia and its tributaries, a family divided up for different tasks.

The husband speared, netted, and trapped the fish while the wife was busy cutting them up in thin slices and curing them on drying racks in the sun.

When it came time for the fall hunt, the woman had to work especially hard to prepare her family for this journey, seeing that all their clothes were clean and ready, carried in parfleches and in pack saddles, after we had horses. Many things needed to be taken along for the comfort of her husband and family, but space also had to be made for the dried meat they would bring back.

When a man killed game and brought it to the camp, his wife cut up the meat for drying. Sometimes he would leave the deer where it was killed and tell her its location in the mountains. She might have to make several trips to the spot to carry it all back. In this case she could only begin to cut and prepare the meat at night, because her day was spent carrying it. Her time was very full because she also had to look after her children and keep her husband in moccasins, since he wore out many pairs during his long daily hikes in the mountains. A tipi wife had very little time for herself. She also had to allow time to clean and scrape off the hides so they would be relatively clean and light to bring home for future tanning, adding to her drudgery.

All this work made her old long before her time. If a husband needed anything, it was his wife who got it for him. In addition, her children, in-laws, and relatives all thought she was the one to do all the hard work to make their own lot that much easier. She did not complain because it was expected of her. A woman living with her in-laws was treated almost like a slave taken in warfare from another tribe. She did not know how to refuse a favor asked of her until she had become a mother-in-law with responsibility for all. Then she graduated from hard labor and took to giving advice and encouragement. This was not always the case. Some mothers-in-law were more considerate than others and would help a daughter-in-law to lighten the work or allow her other considerations. If a woman managed to live with her own parents her lot was much easier, but on the whole every tipi wife had to work every day for many years to be able to feed and clothe her family properly.

The winter months were spent by the woman sewing, basket weaving, decorating clothing, and making odds and ends, in addition to repairing things that had become worn and giving attention to the needs of her husband and other members of the household.

The only time she received a vacation was during her menstrual period, when she retired to a hut built away from the encampment. While in the hut, she might tan skins, pick berries, or dig roots for preservation, but food gathered during this time was never eaten by the family until it was cured and laid away for a long period of time.

Among the taboos placed on women were that they not join hunting or war parties while menstruating. A woman could not eat any freshly killed game without impairing the hunter's luck. Among the foods forbidden her were the meat from the head, kidneys, or tenderloin of a deer, any fresh fish, any part of a beaver, or the flesh of a grizzly or other bear. She could not eat the meat of an unborn fawn until she was past menopause. Also, she could touch or cook a deer head only after she had passed this stage in her life. If no old woman was available, then the men had to cook a deer head themselves.

A woman combed her hair every morning after taking a cold bath, usually in a nearby stream or pool of water. She would use the still surface of the water as a crude mirror to apply bear grease as a face cream to soften her skin. Applied to her hair, it made it grow dark and lustrous. She washed her hair once a week with herb tea and massaged her tresses with a syrup made from crushed birch leaves. Her rinse was fresh water mixed with crushed fir boughs, leaving the hair clean, glossy, and ready for bear grease.

An Indian woman would not paint her face every day, for she was kept too busy. Rather, she used a face paint of dull earthen red only for state occasions or social gatherings. She either painted the whole face or placed a streak across the forehead or the cheeks. For more festive events, she added bars or dots according to individual taste. Men decorated with more elaborate designs, using grotesque figures or special patterns to indicate war strengths or spiritual shamanistic powers in the belief (or pretense) that he had been instructed to do so during a dream or vision. A medicine woman might do likewise if her power was sufficiently strong. A common woman without supernatural powers, however, would never do anything of this sort for fear of arousing the criticism of other people or the envy of shamans who would then cause her trouble by stealing her spirit power for themselves.

Regardless of her supernatural contacts, a woman always knew the many uses of various herbs for medicines, for curing childhood ailments like tummyaches, earaches, or toothaches, and for different personal upsets. For example, tanza root boiled to make a green tea settled a baby's digestive organs. Warmed bear grease gave relief from earache, as did the application of a bag of warm sand. Oregon grape roots and tops strengthened the blood in the spring and made the body more hardy. Red willow bark made into a tea cured sores on the face of a child or wounds on an adult. Pine pitch served the same purpose or was diluted in warm water to cure a cold or weak lungs. Another cold cure was a brew of mentholated sagebrush. Hemlock bark and sap strengthened resistance to lung trouble. Princess pine helped clean the blood. Crushed sunflower (balsam) roots were heated to relieve gout in old people. Heated green pine needles were a favorite for invalids or rheumatism sufferers. Wild rhubarb was good for the kidneys.[5]

Before whites arrived there were many fewer diseases, mostly causing stomach and eye discomfort but few fatalities. Tuberculosis and venereal diseases were unknown.[6] Nor were there measles, scarlet fever, smallpox, influenza, and many others. Natives could not cure these with previously proven methods and so began to use white doctors to get results, but only after hundreds had died. Now most of my people recognize two systems of medicine, one effective against our earlier illnesses and sorcery, and the other curing germ-caused diseases from Europe.

What sustained us through all these difficulties was our women working hard and diligently out of love for their families and relatives.[7] What kept them going was the knowledge that everything on the earth has a purpose, every disease an herb to cure it, and every person a mission. This is the Indian theory of existence.

CHAPTER 5

★

Baby Care

THE LIFE of a baby started from the moment of conception. As soon as the mother realized her condition, she began to observe the strict diet and varied taboos required of all parents-to-be. For a first pregnancy, these restrictions were especially severe. She lived under fearsome constraints until ten days after the baby was born. If a woman already had children but it was the first for the husband, the observations were every bit as rigorous. Only after both parents had several children who were alive and healthy were taboos honored with less severity. Parents-to-be were considered very unlucky and generally shunned. They were not allowed to join hunting or war parties, and they could not even drink from the same spring as the rest of the community for fear it would dry up.

A mother-to-be followed a strict program of physical exercise, bathing in cold water before each dawn and praying to the rising sun for health and a safe delivery. She ran everywhere, especially up hills, so the child would not dawdle or be lazy at birth or in later life. She carried two small stones up the hill with her and dropped them just before reaching the top as a symbol for an easy passage. She worked hard all day gathering wood, carrying water, tanning hides, and gathering roots, seeds, and berries. She sat down to sew only if the weather was bad outside. She never slept during the day but rather was the last to bed and the first to rise. The older women in the tipi and camp watched to see that she lived and worked as was expected so her child would be born safely.[1] Otherwise it would develop a large head, making delivery difficult. She needed to keep an even temper so the child would be good-natured and of excellent character.

The parents-to-be spent much time with each other because others avoided them in their special state. In turn, they went out of their way to avoid all hostile shamans, since these were fond of killing mother and child during birth. The mother never passed behind a shaman, even at a distance, because his spirit power might take offense and cause harm. She never laughed at or called attention to anyone misshapen, crippled, handicapped, or enfeebled in any way, to prevent her child from developing the same condition. [Pregnant women] did not look at rabbits so as to prevent a harelip on the infant, or gaze at a corpse lest the child be stillborn or have a helpless body. It was safe for a pregnant woman to attend a funeral only if the father was also there beside her the entire time and they took special precautions.

The father-to-be was careful not to tie or lasso animals to prevent the navel cord from entangling the baby. He did not join hunting or war parties because his luck was not good. The wife never stretched her arms overhead or ate animal innards, for that would also entangle the cord.

In addition to the rabbit, certain other animals were avoided. These included the willow pheasant [grouse], to keep the child from crying until out of breath and convulsing, and the spruce grouse (fool hen), to keep the child from being a moron. No eggs could be eaten because the encasing shell prevented a child with a caul from breaking out. Bear meat was not eaten to prevent giving offense to this powerful being and having it kill the child or attack the parents. Bear could be killed and eaten by the couple only after the pregnancy was over. The woman could never purposely step on blood from a slain animal, and neither parent could beat an animal without injuring the child.

During the sixth month, the wife left her husband's bed and did not return until the child was two months old. She stayed with her mother, or another elderly woman skilled in midwifery moved to her camp and watched over her during this rigorous regime.

When labor pains began, she went to a menstrual hut prepared for this event, continuing to walk around until the contractions were close and severe. By then the midwife had prepared a bed, and the mother lay down. The bed was covered with grass, fir boughs, and sometimes old tule mats. After this all of these were buried to protect the family. They were never burned, since this would dry out the new mother's insides and kill her with a fever. Four stakes were driven into the ground; two of them, about three feet long, were placed at the head of the bed so the woman could grip them as braces during labor, and the others were a foot shorter, two feet apart, at the foot of the bed to brace her soles against while lifting her knees. The midwife waited at the foot of the bed between the bottom stakes and waited for the baby to crown. All of this was done in the strictest modesty, for the woman was always dressed and covered.[2]

If there was time, the woman in labor might have a back brace made of logs to keep her in a sitting position. To moan or cry out caused criticism of her character by other mothers.[3] If the woman got weak and faint, another woman would sit behind her, holding her up and covering her mouth with firm hands so the baby would have only one escape.

When the child arrived, the midwife tied the cord about two inches away from the body and then again three inches beyond that. She cut the cord between these two knots and packed the newborn's navel. When the stump dried up and fell off, it was tied in a little buckskin bag fixed to the cradleboard to ensure the infant's good health. When the child outgrew the board, it was put away and the cord in the bag was buried. It was never burned for the same reason the mother's bedding was not.

Immediately after birth and cord cutting, the newborn was washed and the mouth cleaned before the midwife blew into it. The bath consisted of lukewarm water in a woven basket, with the child rubbed vigorously on the legs and arms to exercise, strengthen, and stretch them. Then it was tightly wrapped up to make it grow tall and straight without bowlegs. The nose was pinched to make it prominent, and the mother massaged it daily for ten days to give it a high, shapely bridge. The corners of the eyes were stretched to ensure large ones. The face was massaged each of the ten days to make it smooth and even featured. This was a prized skill among midwives.[4]

The mother was given a tea of herbs, and her belly was covered with warmed pine boughs to coax out the afterbirth or placenta. Her discharges were absorbed by shredded bark of green willow. When the afterbirth arrived, it and the willow sponges were buried, never burned.

The new mother rested the first day, but thereafter she took care of her own baby. She was in confinement for ten days, drinking tea, massaging the baby, and resting. Women with strong spirit powers would show them off by getting up and leaving the hut before the ten days were finished, but this usually provoked the envy of shamans, who made them get sick or die unless they were truly very powerful. Others who did this lost their health and contracted tuberculosis or other ailments.

The father was also very careful during those ten days. He did not hunt or kill anything, did not tire or tie up a horse, or look at anything deformed. If the child began to seem affected by such an untoward act, he brought a dog into the hut and whipped it before the mother. Sometimes relatives killed a bluejay and skinned off the head and beak. The bird was known for its happiness, so the head was fixed to the cradleboard to laugh off trouble and save the child from going into convulsions and dying.

If the mother did not produce milk, her breasts were heated with warmed, moist sand, or the midwife sucked out [the ducts]. If the mother died, the baby was given to another woman to wet-nurse until it was old enough to be returned to relatives, usually a year later. If there was no wet nurse available, a grandmother might save the infant by having it suck on strips of bear fat and pouring some soup into its mouth. Later, food was chewed up for the baby until the teeth grew in. Animal milk was never given to babies until modern child-care methods were learned.[5]

A child was not named until after the mother left the menstrual hut and life returned to normal. Then the grandparents or some older relative gave the infant a name from those that belonged to the family and had last been used by a deceased ancestor. After children grew up and performed deeds on their own, they took another name referring to a war honor, medicine power, famous action, or success.

Baby clothes were made of soft skins such as rabbit tanned with the fur left on. Diapers were made of buckskin and washed every day, together with cottonwood fiber or milkweed fluff packed into the cradleboard to absorb the wastes. This soft, downy packing was gathered by expectant mothers during the fall and saved in abundance for the new arrival. When it became too soiled for reuse, it was buried. The cradle or baby board also had a hood made of buckskin and rose branches to protect the child, but there was no provision to flatten the skull as some tribes did on the coast.[6] The hood tied securely around the head to keep the ears close in and to make the head round and shapely. For a month the baby was kept tightly bound in the board wrappings and removed only for washing. The board was made either of woven willows or cedar slats laced in a V shape with a rounded top and narrower bottom to better fit the baby's body. The board was made by the father's relatives to welcome the new member, covered with buckskin and sometimes decorated with porcupine quills. After whites came, beads and trinkets were used. Before then the quills were dyed red, blue, and green with plants and earths traded from different sources.

The cradleboard was stuffed with furs and feathers, with a tiny pad for the small of the back, a trifle larger one for the support of the rump, and a third one at the bottom for the feet. The baby was laced inside with legs straight and arms at the sides, with packing between the legs and around the middle. Children became so familiar and comfortable with their boards that they would not sleep unless laced inside. When too big to fit inside any longer, they carried the boards around for security.

The baby was changed morning, noon, and night, when it was transferred from the board used during the day to a soft sleeping sack at night.[7] Strong ties at the top enabled the mother to carry the board on her back, suspend it from her horse, or hang it in a tree to swing in the breeze to lull the infant to sleep. Off the board, the baby never slept alone but always with an older child or a grandparent. When the baby was two months old, the hands were left out of the soft bag at night so the infant could flail if a sleeper inadvertently rolled on it. The struggling little hands gave warning even if it could not cry out.

The infant was not weaned until the mother was again pregnant or other children shamed it into weaning. Some nursed until they were six, perhaps serving as a check on large families in the old days.[8]

A child born out of wedlock was sent either to grandparents, barren relatives, or willing adopters. People never concealed its condition or parentage, so an illegitimate child was expected to lead an unhappy life. In the old days the chaperon system and the importance of chastity until first marriage made this a rare occurrence. A girl usually regarded the honor of her family above all, marrying at about twenty to give new life and branches to the family tree.

If a baby took ill, the mother tried her herb lore to cure it with a weak tea. If this did not help, a shaman was called and he blew his power on the child without touching it. A cure such as this usually involved a high price. If the child cried too much without being sick, the mother fed it the pulverized heart of a fool hen because it made the baby quiet and happy. A mother never allowed a pregnant woman to hold her baby, because the two infants might become jealous and cross. The older child resented the arrival of the new one, and the unborn one envied the care and attention given to the older.

Two babies could never play together until they were old enough to talk to each other in a language understandable to adults. Before this they spoke "baby language," and they might compare their treatment by parents and scheme to die and return to the spirit world.[9]

Babies were nursed whenever it was convenient for mother and child, but they were not encouraged to cry, especially at night when an enemy might locate the camp by the sound. They were encouraged to be quiet and well behaved at all times, for the safety of all. I think this gave our youngsters weak lungs and made them susceptible to white diseases like tuberculosis. Modern homes provide even less fresh air than did our healthy tipis of old.

I saw the wisdom of our birth customs at first hand.

My father was called away unexpectedly shortly before my youngest sister was born. Mother was worried when the baby arrived, and she had to observe the taboos without being sure that Father was doing the same. Greatly concerned, she kept my sister beside her all the time. About five days after she was born, Mother noticed my sister getting red in the face while she was asleep. The red gradually became purple, and foam appeared on her mouth. Mother could not get the baby to wake up, so she cried out to the midwife, who went in search of the head of a blue jay. She did not find one and so substituted shredded green and red willow bark laid on a cloth and warmed by the fire. She placed the baby on this and wrapped her up. This soon broke the spell, and she revived choking and panting. Soon she became normal. That night father returned home, having driven his horse in his hurry so that it was foaming, sweating, and panting. Mother accused him of almost killing his newest child by careless worry but was eventually pleased to have him back and in charge. She always believed the bark wrapping had saved her baby's life.

These taboos were always to be regarded most strictly and seriously, as another story illustrates. In 1900 a young pregnant woman returned to the reservation after getting a white education. She ignored the taboos of our people and even went out of her way to violate them. She especially enjoyed rabbit and purposely ate a meal made from a split deer head. She said she knew better than to follow the old superstitions. When her first child was born, this daughter had an extremely large and pathetic harelip. I saw this woman while I was growing up, and now she is raising beautiful half-breed children, all of whom are normal. In a case like this where normal children were born before and after, it was clear to my people that the violation of the taboos was the reason for the deformed daughter.

When a child outgrew the cradleboard, it was ready to walk unassisted. At night the baby was put to sleep in a swing usually hung over the parents' bed. The swing was made by lapping one end of a folded blanket over a rope or a pole and the other over a parallel one, ten feet away, with the ends folded over both these like an envelope. The weight of the child kept the ends from coming loose.[10] The advantage of this swing was that it swayed end to end rather than side to side so the babe was not likely to fall out. After the cradleboard, a child got very attached to this swing and would not sleep in anything else until past two years of age. Children were drawn away from the swing because they could now walk and desired to play with other children and toys. The swing was easy to put up quickly, either in tree branches or at the back of a tipi. It could be placed high or low depending on need, as when a seated grandmother was baby-sitting.

A spoiled baby might be carried in a shawl or robe even after it was large enough to walk and run. The child had fun pulling on the carrier's hair, earrings, or ornaments. Often an older sister or cousin would have this job, since the mother often had a newborn to attend. In this way Indian girls got the experience they needed to be good and careful mothers. Boys generally had less to do with raising their brothers and sisters, but even they were willing to help out in times of need, just as my father did. Usually a boy who cared for a baby was teased by playmates and made unhappy. A considerate mother tried never to make her children unhappy if she could help it.

When a child was five or six, the old people in the home started the serious teaching, the etiquette of right and wrong.[11] Instruction included legends and family history, tales of bravery, and tribal laws. If a family had no elders, they invited or hired an old person to live with them and give their children a native education. This is the way the poor, homeless elders survived in ancient times.

At seven or eight, instruction became more strenuous. A child had to take a cold bath every morning before breakfast. Father and son went to a different bathing place than a mother and daughter. The former was upstream and the latter was downstream, to avoid contamination. Every day the child ran uphill without pause and learned to swim. They jumped to stretch and strengthen the legs.

Strong discipline was saved for the whipper, who went from camp to camp.[12] Children were taught to make the things they would need in later life. Girls made clothes, and boys made weapons or tools. The first food taken by a child was given away to an elder in the hope of a prayer for long life.

Indian people loved their children above all else, for they were the hope of the future and justification for the trials and tribulations of their parents. They guaranteed the perpetuation of the family and continued the upholding of its honor. They were a special gift from the Creator and the promise of a bright and happy future. They were the focus for much of our time and attention, but they particularly spent time with their grandparents, as these had both the most free time to devote to their care and wisdom to pass on to the next generation. Their parents were in the prime of life and were often too busy working and scouting up food to give them the full attention they deserved. Our most important sense of self and continuity, therefore, came from the very old, who were so kind, gentle, considerate, and wise with us, particularly as children.

★

CHAPTER 6

Charming Affections

T HE MOTHER of my mother was noted for her knowledge of herbs and her skill at making love charms. The Colvile and Okanogan paid her large sums for such love charms. Many asked her to "make medicine" for them, trying to get her secret formulas, but none ever succeeded.

Only to me, her eldest grandchild, did she wish to reveal her secrets, but I refused to learn. How foolish I was! In later years I did want to know about this singular business, but my grandmother was dead by then, and I had to pay in patience, effort, and money for instruction that had once been offered to me free.

I was fourteen when Grandmother attempted to bequeath to me her carefully guarded lore of charms. On the pretext of going for a supply of huckleberries, she took me into the high mountains. She had made me a small birchbark basket to use while picking berries, and she had provided four large cedar-root carrying baskets to fill and hang on our saddles, one on each side of our two horses. I had no idea we were going for any purpose except to pick berries, as Grandmother had not given anyone so much as a hint of her plan. She did not want anyone to know her main reason for the trip, probably because they might follow us to eavesdrop on my training.

A day of riding took us to a meadow just above the timberline. Beyond us was the jagged, snow-patched crest of the Cascade Range.

We made our camp by a small stream, and before sunrise the next morning Grandmother had us bathe in its icy waters. Grandmother put on clean clothing and made me do the same, although I thought it needless since we were so far away from anybody. But I did what I was told, especially since she was a respected elder.

She picked up her digging stick and told me to follow her. We set out walking without the berry baskets. I wondered why we did not take them, particularly because bushes around us were laden with huckleberries. I was hungry and recalled that we had not had breakfast; I began to lag farther and farther behind, picking and eating berries. When she turned to see why I was so slow, Grandmother gave me a vigorous scolding. I did not know, of course, that you were not supposed to eat before undertaking a religious task such as the errand we were making. Her scolding did not stop me from picking berries. I only became more quick and skillful at snatching handfuls of the tart fruit.

Just as the sun was coming up, she halted on a damp spot where a tiny spring bubbled up and dripped into a small pool flanked with yellow flowers of a kind I had never seen before. I was entranced with the lovely, dainty flowers.

Grandmother motioned me forward to stand beside her as she carefully uprooted one of the pretty plants by prying it up with her digging stick and placed it in the palm of her left hand. Straightening up to face the sun, she began to sing her special "song of the herb." Her voice shook with emotion and intensity as drops of perspiration dewed her forehead and upper lip. She sang for perhaps ten minutes before stopping abruptly and lifting the plant for my closer inspection.

"See this plant," she said. "It is valuable, very valuable. It is my inheritance and yours, handed down through our generations. People are willing to pay many ponies to learn this secret. I am showing it to you before I die so that when you get a man he will not throw you away for the love of another woman. Being able to identify and use this plant will enable you to aways keep the affections of your husband."

I averted my head and decided not to hear any of this because I had resolved never to marry. This mention of marriage and husband, instead of arousing romantic thoughts, provoked and repulsed me. I had already experienced the death of the boy I had been betrothed to and was still relieved not to have become an unwilling bride.

Grandmother became sharp with me. "Do not turn your head away. If you do not learn this secret of the herb spirit now, you will be sorry later. Other women always will be stealing your man, and you will become known as a "thrown away woman."

I could stand it no longer and burst into tears. "I do not want to marry, ever. I hate men and will never marry!"

Grandmother tried to tell me about the herb and its strong power. She repeated how to use it, but I did not listen. After a long time she gave up, rebuked me for being foolish, and walked back to camp. It was the first time she was ever cross with me, and I felt very bad.

Ten years passed before I came to appreciate that I had lost something important with my girlish outburst that day in the mountains. It was the spring after my return from school, and I was visiting among the Lake Okanagan of British Columbia. Limited though it was, my schooling had not led me to scorn the ancient beliefs but had stimulated a desire to learn more about them. Above all, it made me realize the vast difference between white and native cultures and to fear for the inevitable destruction of my own. I particularly wanted to delve into the mystery of love charms, both for getting information for the record and for doing some experimenting on my own account. I could not turn to my grandmother because she was dead, but I knew some Lake Okanagan women who might be willing to instruct me for a price.

I made very casual and discreet inquiries of the women, who all pretended to know nothing of love-charm making. One of them, however, whom I shall call Mary, later admitted in strictest privacy that she might be of some help. She was about sixty and was considered to be the best medicine maker in the tribe.

I called on Mary at the tipi she shared with her married daughter. I gave her some tobacco and matches before we talked of everything else but what was uppermost in my mind. I left and came back again a few days later, making her a present of bright cloth and thread. I also left several deer hides for her to tan for me. I paid her liberally for this work, and off and on for several months I came up with odd jobs for her to do and paid her much more than the work was worth.

One day Mary finally said, "I like you and would do something for all your kindness to an old woman like me." This was my chance, and I replied, "My friend, I am poor in the knowledge of herbs and men do not seem to care for me."

She glanced around to be sure we were alone, but even so she whispered. "The herb is valuable and hard to get. But you have been good to me, and my heart goes out to you. I will show you. When the leaves are about to fall and the herb is ready to be picked, I will show you."

Impatiently I waited for Indian summer, and then one golden day I went to see Mary. I found her singing in her sweat lodge, so I undressed and crawled inside. She laughed and whispered to me that I was right on time, for she was then preparing herself for the trip to the mountains. She whispered, "Tomorrow, when the day is young, we will leave the village separately. No one must know we are going together for the herb, not even my daughter. If people see us leave together, they will talk and spoil our success. We will take the trail up Pak-kum-kin (White Top, Mount Baldy).[1] If you see a handkerchief on a tree where the trail forks, you will know I am ahead."

Early the next morning, I saddled my horse and tied two berry baskets to the sides as if I were going berrying. To avoid inquisitive people, I rode out on a trail little used and took the way to the mountain. At the fork in the trail, I found Mary's handkerchief fluttering from a branch. I took it to hide our plans and hurried to catch up. In a short time I came upon her pony and found Mary bathing in the icy waters of a creek. She had me join her to cleanse our bodies in preparation for picking the love plant. After we dressed, we hid our berry baskets in a nearby thicket and resumed the journey. Our travel took the rest of the day, covering thirty miles to the location Mary had in mind. We made our camp high on the slopes of Mount Baldy. The camp was marked by the frame of an old sweat lodge. Even if it had been in good repair, we would not have used it unless we were sure that the person or persons who had built and used it were still alive. To use the lodge of a dead person brought bad luck, perhaps illness and death.

There was not sufficient pliable growth in the area to build a usual sweat house, no willow or serviceberry, so we set up fir boughs and branches like a tipi. Over this conical frame, about four feet high in the center and five feet in diameter, we placed fir boughs, hoping to benefit from their spiritual power as an evergreen. We put more boughs on the floor as a covering.

Mary sang happily the whole time, unworried by the grizzlies, bears, or cougars known to infest the region. As the gloom of night pressed around us, I grew uneasy, thinking that all we had to protect ourselves was my .22 special and Mary's butcher knife. I knew these were very poor weapons against these dangerous animals, but I was showing my lack of faith in our purpose. Mary laughed at my fears when I spoke of them out loud. She said I had to have faith in the spiritual power of our intentions. She reassured me, and the long tiring ride soon put me into a sound sleep.

When the first streak of light appeared the next morning, Mary woke me with a gentle touch. We hurried to make a roaring fire to heat stones for our sweat bath. The air was chilly, so the fire felt good. While the stones heated, we covered the framework with our blankets. Mary said, "Our stones are hot enough." They shone like red coals in the blaze. We removed them with forked sticks and rolled them quickly into the basin just to the left inside the door. We closed the doorway while we went to bathe in the icy stream. Then we crawled into the lodge. I pulled the blanket over the doorway while Mary dipped her hand into the pail of cold water we had brought back with us and sprinkled it over the glowing stones. They sizzled and cracked as the steam shot up and over us. Mary sang her prayer to the Sweatlodge Deity until I learned the words and joined in.

We praised Sweatlodge and gave thanks for past help and favors. When we were sweating from the heat and could stand no more, we crawled out and waded into the stream to splash ourselves. Then we went back to the lodge and prayed again. We went into the stream again. We repeated this several times until we were thoroughly cleansed, both physically and spiritually. At the end we asked Sweatlodge to make our love-charm mission successful. We dressed after bathing and were at last ready to fulfill our venture.

The eastern sky was now warm, and we had only a short walk to the herb ground. As the sun crested the ridge and poured bright light into the woods, we reached a tiny spring just like my grandmother's, but this one had a bed of gay flowers, each with white petals and a yellow center. We were careful not to stand between the sun and the herbs and to keep our shadows off them while Mary sang to them, holding her left palm over her breast and slowly waving her right hand over the flowers. When her song was done, she continued to face the sun, sat down, and used her digging stick to remove one plant gently from the ground.

She addressed the plant, "You are great—the spirit of the earth. I pray for your help. Nothing can overcome your strength. No plant is greater than you. The sun shines upon you, and the brook sings your song with me this day. I beg that my work be a success."

She lifted the herb toward the sun and sang her prayer. "You are great, Sun. You shine upon everything on the earth to make it happy. I pray that my work with the magic herb be successful with your help."

Mary shaved about an inch off the root, from the "south side"

84

that grew nearest to the sun because this had power stronger than any other part of the root. She laid the piece on the ground carefully and replaced it with bits of silk, buckskin, and some small coins tied over the wound with silk threads. She replanted the herb back into the hole she had removed it from, saying, "I pray you to take pity on me. I have cleansed my body to be able to take you and I have paid your root that I have robbed. I ask you for success in getting buckskins, robes, silks, and money easily, that my mouth not go hungry or my body naked. I ask success in this work and pray for your help and favor."

Mary turned to me then and said, "When you are picking this herb, you take it from the place where the flowers are growing together like an encampment of people. The big flower in the center is the chief, and all the others are his children.[2] The plants that have their roots laced together are the ones that love each other. If you intend to separate two lovers and destroy their love, you must separate a pair of entwined plants, like this." She took apart the interlaced roots of two plants and carried the one she designated as the female herb to an aspen sapling. With her butcher knife she sliced the aspen bark, inserting the plant into the slit and pounding it into bitter sapwood. She said, "Your man (speaking the name of a female I knew) will not love you anymore. His heart will be bitter toward you as the sap of the aspen is bitter. All men will hate you with bitterness."

Returning to the herb [bed], she selected another female herb and tied it tightly to a male one, planting this new-made pair with the words, "You two shall always love each other. Nothing will part you but death. I am leaving your welfare in the charge of the chief of these plants." She used the names of a man and a woman known to me, a couple then separated. The husband had abandoned his wife for another woman, so the deserted wife had paid Mary a pony to do this work and bring him back. Not long after, he did return and they have been living happily ever since.

Polytheistic?

Produced plould

According to our old belief, the male plant was the one with flowers, while the female one did not bloom. Perhaps this was because the flowering plant was bigger and more showy.[3]

As we prepared to leave, Mary washed the piece of root she had removed and put it in a buckskin bag. She lifted this to the sun and prayed, "Great Sun, forgive me my deed of this day. Have pity on me and do not let the herb grow angry about my actions." Turning to the flower bed she said, "Great herb spirit, forgive me! You whose body I put against the bitterness of the aspen sap, forgive me. I ask that this evil woman be punished for taking the husband of another. I did not put your body against the bitter sap to insult you. I only followed the teachings of my ancestors. I beg that no ill luck befall me."

During the journey back, Mary gave me further instruction about the herbs and the rules governing their use. Both men and women could pick them. The men usually did it to better their gambling luck or to accumulate riches. Men worked with male plants and women with female ones when only good luck or wealth was being sought. Then it was not necessary to cut a piece from the root. Several plants of the appropriate gender were dug up, tied together with a lock of one's own hair, and replanted with the words, "I place my property with your body. I will be rich in ponies, robes, and money. I will not want for food and clothing while your life grows with me."

Only rarely would someone dig up the chief plant and replant it with a lock of hair, to achieve great wealth or gambling luck.

When love magic was done, the piece of root was always washed and placed in a little bag to keep it from human contamination. Mary was careful to carry the one she took that day in a buckskin bag in her hand, not against her body, until we reached the horses, then she hung it from the saddle horn.

Several different plants were used for love charms, but the rarest and strongest grew only in the high mountains on the edge of snowbanks, glaciers, or alpine springs. They were sought when in full bloom. In the forests at lower elevations, the favorite plants were red and yellow columbine.[4] None of the plants of the low country were thought to be as powerful as those near the timberline. No herb was ever taken until the person had been thoroughly cleansed by three successive days of using the sweat lodge or taking icy baths. Clean clothing was put on after every bath. During the purification treatment, wild rose leaves and fir-bough tips were used to rub the body to remove all impurities and the human smells so repulsive to the spirits of the plants.

Plants were dug only at the first light of sun or just after sunset. The body or its shadow could never block the sun from the herbs. Both sun and herbs were greeted by a song of individual invention and paid with offerings of buckskin, cloth, horsehair, beads, or, recently, coins.

Two weeks after we came back from the mountains, Mary brought over my love charm. It was in a tiny buckskin bag, and I hid it in a fruit jar as she suggested.

Proper love charms always included some animal ingredients pulverized along with a bit of herb root. For my love charm, Mary made a compound of the piece of root mixed with the tip of a black bear's tongue for superior strength, a piece of beaver testes for wisdom, bits of the tongues and wingtips of a pair, male and female, of mourning doves (lovebirds) for enduring love, a piece of hummingbird for beauty and swiftness, a robin tongue and wingtips for constancy, robin and dove eggshells for sympathy, fool-hen heart for gentleness, and male and female green crickets for attraction, since their song is so alluring. She added a pinch of red face paint, mixed these together, and ground them into a fine powder that she put in a buckskin bag.

Such a charm can be used in many different ways to get to someone's heart. It could be secretly sprinkled onto food, mixed in drink or tobacco, or hidden on the person. While this was done, the owner of the charm whispered the words that went with it, giving instructions to the herb and pleading his or her cause with words of love.

The usual method, and the one I used, was to "make medicine," as whites phrase it. When I was ready to put the charm to work, I underwent a thorough cleansing in the vapors of the sweat lodge and the cold waters of a stream for three consecutive days. At sunrise or sunset I went into the water, carrying the charm bag, and sat facing the sun. Praying to make my venture successful, I dipped a wet finger into the contents of the bag. I put my right hand on my left shoulder and my left hand on my right one, then rubbed them down and across my chest until they met over my heart. I prayed, using the name of a man. "You will think of me just as the sun rises, following the trail of the sun. You will come to me with love in your heart."

The owner of a charm had to be very careful with it. It should never come in contact with a dead body, anyone just returned from a funeral, or an unclean woman.[5] The owner had to be purified every time the charm was handled. Once it became contaminated, the owner had bad luck. He or she would get the reverse of what was wished for. The power of a charm could be restored, however, by burying the sack of powder in an anthill for a year.

I was not in love with anyone at the time, nor was I willing to abuse the new power I had been given. I only came to use it after I met a man everyone in the community had been talking about. He was a full-blood Okanagan, a rich bachelor considered the catch of the season. He never showed any interest in women, however, and usually acted bored around females. I did not like him or his ways and so decided to humble him.

I went into the sweat house for three days and made the medicine of the charm. A few days later the man came to see me with love-light in his eyes. He was raised in the traditional teachings, but he dressed like a white in a gray Stetson hat, bright bandana, fancy shirt, pants, and cowboy boots. He was all togged out for courting, and I encouraged his advances. He came back every evening for several days, then one night took me in his arms and asked me to marry him. I did not answer, so he gave me a tight hug. Just then I laughed. This insulted him, and he let me go, but he did not give up hope of persuading me. He kept coming back and became such a nuisance that I asked Mary what I could do to get rid of him. She told me to bathe again with the charm for three days and then ask the herb to let him forget me. I did this, and he stopped coming to see me. Shortly after, he married a pretty Indian girl. He had been a persistent suitor but he followed the old ways, proving to me that Indians never kissed in ancient times. He had never been to school or spent time with whites, so he courted without overt demonstrations of affection. Traditional Indians were much more reserved and dignified in their affections.

My next use of the charm involved an Englishman who was a member of the Royal Northwest Mounted Police. He wore a superior air around my people, so I disliked him. To the amusement of my sister, I took him as my second experiment. I made medicine, and pretty soon Mr. Policeman came riding by the house I was visiting. I watched him secretly from the window. He was too self-important to ask where I lived, so he had to spend several days riding around the village to find me. He came to visit many times. People began to wonder why this Mountie kept coming on the reserve without apparent business. Finally the chief had the native police arrest him and take him to the courthouse, charging him with trespassing on an Okanagan reserve. He refused to explain his reasons for being there, so the chief ordered him off and told him to read the signs posted at each entrance by the Canadian government, forbidding trespass by whites under penalty of a $300 fine.

My sister and I had gone to the courtroom, and she giggled. The man was so ashamed I felt sorry for him, since only my sister and I knew the cause of his embarrassment. As we left the court, a boy rode up to say a cousin of ours had just died.

My sister attended the funeral. The procession to the grave passed along a road near the place where I had buried my charm bag in a glass jar. Later my sister and I realized it was contaminated. We thought it would not be wise to try to use the charm until it had been freed from the taint. So I buried it, sealed in a fruit jar, in an anthill. A year later when I dug it up, it was ruined; the pulverized contents were moldy. The charm was ruined. I was told this was because I buried it in the jar. If I had buried just the bag, the ants would have worked on it and made it pure again. I probably lost the charm because of the way I misused it.

Once in Walla Walla the tables were turned and a man worked a love charm on me.[6] He was a Yakima, gathered with many of us from different tribes for a big celebration. The only language we shared was broken English, but we managed to talk and became friendly. I was taking care of a room of native exhibits, and he would come by to visit. One day he visited, took out a small buckskin bag, and used red paint from it to decorate his face. He called me over to him, as he pulled a small sack with beaded edges out of his shirt. I immediately knew what it was and lost my temper. He held the open bag to my nose to smell it, but I slapped it against his face so that the contents flew out, scattering dust all over. I destroyed, spoiled, and ended his love charm. He left terribly angry because he had probably paid a good horse or two, blankets, or some money for it.

I was now more sure than ever that our ancient Indian wisdom and knowledge was the surest source of safety, salvation, and success in life. The priest preached against love medicine, but even devout Catholics continue to use it. They cannot be shaken in their belief that the spiritual herbs are blessings that God bestowed upon our ancestors centuries ago.

CHAPTER 7

★

Widowhood

SHORTLY after our cabin was completed and we had our tipi moved behind the log house under some birch trees to use as shade from the hot midsummer sun, a neighbor arrived from the little mission below our house to inform us that an old man had died the night before.[1]

His name was In-ya-tink (Walking in Front), one of the last warriors who used to fight against the Kootenay and Blackfeet. He accomplished his name, as a young man, by walking in front of the enemy during a battle to show his bravery.

We knew him and his very aged wife Ka-at-qhu (Big Beside Water). She had an extremely large mouth and was nicknamed Big Lip from her uneven features. This old couple used to tell Sulee and me many stories and legends, and we learned to love them greatly. We missed our grandmother Patee at Fort Steele after we came home that spring. This old couple helped to take her place.

Mother immediately got us ready, and Father laid off his work to join us in visiting the death tipi. We walked down the steep trail that started almost at our cabin doorway. Mother carried blankets for all of us, because we could not expect to return home until after the burial.

As we drew close to the death tipi, covered with old rags and worn tules, we could hear the widow wailing, mourning her dead husband. She was crying aloud, at a steady pace intended to last all day and all night without stopping. We entered and saw her sitting behind the still form stretched out on some tule mats and covered with an old, worn gray blanket.

The aged woman had cut off her own hair close to her neck. The strands lay beside her. Her face was all blackened with wood-fire charcoal, which made her look weird and pathetic, with a large, wrinkled mouth. She was following the tradition of her forebears. From ancient times, when the husband of a Colvile woman died, she cut off her hair unevenly and blackened her face to show her grief. A fickle woman soon washed her face and awaited another man's proposal of marriage. Those who were sincere in their love continued to mourn until the hair grew long enough to braid in plaits hanging to the waist.

Ka-at-qhu performed another old custom that day. She fussed around in her many hemp bags, wailing the whole time, and drew out a buckskin string. She securely tied thong loops around her neck and then around each wrist and ankle. Her limbs were slim and withered. This was her promise not to marry again until the strings wore off and dropped away. She made this vow in public, before the corpse of her husband. This showed there was no room in her heart for the love of another man.

In ancient times a woman usually mourned for a year after the death of her husband. For this entire period, she never washed her face or combed her hair. Her clothing became dirty and ragged, mourning for her dead. This entire time, the men respected her grief and avoided the subject of love and marriage. It would be a great breach of custom and a disgrace for a man to express affection for a widow in mourning. She was dirty and contaminated by the death of her spouse. She passed ill luck to anyone who approached her before her cleansing bath.

If the woman should want to throw off her duty before a year expired, she had to ask the permission of her former in-laws to bathe and clean up. This allowed her to consider marriage proposals. It was quite proper for in-laws to give their consent if orphaned children were involved and in need of food. They also had the right to refuse her.

If the Christianized Indians had listened to Ka-at-qhu that day, the old man would have been buried in the ancient way. She did not want him encased in the wooden coffin that Father and another man had crudely made out of rough, wide, unfinished lumber.

It was the ancient custom to bury the dead wrapped in tanned buckskins and fur robes. The body was placed, in compact form, in a grave lined with spread-out robes, lying on the back with the knees doubled back toward the chest, breaking the hip sockets, placing the arms between the shins and thighs, and doubling back the feet. The body was bound with thongs and sewn into the first robe. Other robes were added, depending on the wealth of the family. The bundle was placed on a high scaffold in the trees for ten days while the family watched and waited to make sure the person did not revive. When there were no certain signs of life, the body was taken to a sandy knoll and buried in a seated position. Some were buried in shale talus slopes under cliffs to prevent intrusion from enemies hunting for scalps.

Most of these ancient customs were discouraged by the Jesuits. In time these ways were discarded for modern methods of worship. Only old people like Ka-at-qhu clung to the ancient ideas.

Shortly after we reached the tipi, other neighbors began arriving, some on foot with children and others on horseback loaded with blankets and tipi coverings. Before night, a camp was set up around the little death hut.

Men erected a big shade of jack pines, where everyone ate food cooked over a big fire, sitting on spread-out tule mats. Most of the food was donated by the visitors.

Every hour or so, day and night, the woman prayer leader would begin Catholic prayers in Kalispel-Spokan. She had been one of the first students at St. Francis Regis Mission. She lived directly across the river from Marcus and spoke fluent English. She was known for her social work among the poor and grieving, seldom missing church or funeral services and adding her clear, beautiful voice to the singing. Hymns were sung in Salish, Chinook Jargon, and Latin.

Three days after the death, the body was placed in the coffin. A shaman came forward and brushed out the casket with rose branches. If this was not done, in a few days the wandering spirit would return and take one of the people into death.

The casket was covered with black cloth and carried to the little cemetery near the church by six old men acting as pallbearers. They never stopped until they reached the side of the grave. If they rested, the spirit would grow angry and kill one of them. Women followed men into the cemetery.

The grave was not dug until just before the coffin arrived, and the hole was half filled with rose branches. The casket was rested on poles set across the opening while prayers and hymns were conducted. Before it was lowered, Chief Aropaghan came forward and spoke of the great deeds of the old man. When he finished, he brushed the coffin with a rose branch. Then he signaled for it to be lowered and covered with dirt by men waiting with shovels. Everyone stepped up to the grave and threw in a handful of dirt, taken from a shovelful held by a man at the foot of the grave. No one left until the grave was filled completely. First women walked out slowly from the left side of the grave, then men from the right. Men and women never mixed together at funerals.[2]

Everyone went back to the man's tipi and shared a funeral feast. Everything in the tipi was spread out on a blanket under the big shade. The chief took up each article and, speaking briefly, gave it to someone. The tipi covering was given away or burned. All was according to ancient custom and the wishes of the widow. This kept the wandering spirit from coming back and endangering the survivors. Nothing remained but the standing gray poles, which were then torn down and burned.

When everything was gone, friends and relatives gave what they could to start a new home for the widow. They also gave her a new tipi.

It was an old custom that when someone of note died a memorial feast was held a year after the funeral feast. The bereaved family spent the year gathering together goods to give away at this burial potlatch. In later years Christians took advantage of modern customs and placed a tombstone on the grave during this memorial.

With her husband gone, Ka-at-qhu failed in health. We visited her often to try to cheer her up, but her sorrow was very deep. She had lived in harmony with that man and raised many children, several of whom were still living. The couple preferred to live by themselves because they rejected many of the new ideas coming into acceptance.

The new tipi was moved closer to the log cabin of a son near the church. She refused to live in the cabin, but her grandchildren brought her food and firewood. She cooked many of her own meals in the tipi.

I used to ride my buckskin down to the tipi every day to check on her needs and health. We grew to love each other. One day she said to me, "When I die, I am leaving you my name." I readily consented. She used to tell me stories by the hour. Frequently Mother would let me stay the night with her. I used to love to have the old lady hold me in her withered arms and tell me stories and history. She had a cute habit of rubbing my matted hair with her fingertips, putting me to sleep too soon to hear the end of her story. She would have to tell it over again.

That winter she fell ill. A son came from Marcus and took her there, where she died. It was too cold and far for us to attend her funeral.

After her death my parents waited until spring, and when no one claimed her name, my mother put up a small feast to celebrate my taking of the name. There were no objections from the relatives and descendants. It had been rightfully given to me. Although she was not a relative, I always called her Grandmother. This was the proper respect term for all old people.

In ancient times it was customary for a person to have many names, by inheritance and by outstanding deeds. A medicine man might take a name when a spirit requested him to do so in a dream or vision. He explained this to his friends.

Before the whites came, we had no surnames. These were given by Jesuits and pioneers for convenience, overcoming the difficulties of pronouncing native words. Some people were named for presidents and great men, others for descriptions of physical features. The sisters at Goodwin Mission also gave out names to students when they enrolled. Often they were given the first name of their father as a family name. In this way I once became Christine Joseph. Other families became known as Tom, Peter, Martin, and Alex. They did not have the opportunity to gain the name of someone famous.

II. SEASONAL ACTIVITIES

★

CHAPTER 8

The Fishery
at
Kettle Falls

I N CHOKECHERRY Moon (August), my parents moved their tipi to our prime fishing location at Kettle Falls on the upper Columbia. When we arrived, natives were already in the process of spearing king salmon, [then] making their annual run up the river. They were one of the five runs of salmon species that came this far up the Columbia and its tributaries during the summer.

The Indians gathered at the falls every year to spear salmon and dry it for the winter. All the surrounding tribes were welcome at this summer resort in the homeland of my Colvile people. It was a beautiful place to camp, with cliffs overhanging the falls on the west side and trails leading to the water between the high grayish-white rock formations that so often glistened in the sunlight. On the east side were flat rock slabs much closer to the whirling pools, where campers could most easily get water. The falls passed on either side of a large central rock that created a smooth backwater behind it. The area near the falls was filled with mist, ribboned with many colors creating a faint rainbow on a summer evening. A person with an artistic mind could easily draw a beautiful picture of this gift of nature.

Our camp was close to the Colvile on the west, beside our Okanagan distant relatives from Osoyoos. The west side was called La-chin (Woven Kettle or Bucket) because of the many depressions made by whirlpools there.[1] The east side was known as S-calm-achin (Dug Ground) because the ground was rough with boulders and looked as though nature had dug it out in places. Tribes generally camped in specific areas, and Colvile hospitality saw to it that no visitor ever left without a full load of dried salmon. The Colvile camped on both sides of the falls to oversee the fishing. The east side encampment included Kalispel, Spokan, Coeur d'Alene, and Flathead, while on the west side were the Okanogan, Sanpoil, Squant, and Wenatchi.[2] While wealthier families had more permanent homes in a central location, most people had tents made of tules, canvas, or, more rarely, smoke-blackened skins. In my time, flour-sack coverings were also much in evidence.

As soon as we arrived and my parents worked to set up camp, I ran down the side trail overlooking the falls. I could see the thirty-foot drop to the river, which was dotted with many Indian men with spears getting king or chinook salmon. Large log scaffolds extended over the foaming river where men stood to spear or net fish fighting to get up the falls. Some men had set up big baskets woven of red willow with serviceberry rims. These were placed just below the falls where salmon would occasionally fall back into them while they were trying to jump the wall of water to reach the spawning grounds upriver. The day was hot, but the men worked long and hard catching fish, while their women cut and cured it along the banks or in the camps.

The spearmen were using tools made in both the old and new ways. The iron spear made by a blacksmith had come into use by the younger generation, but the older men still preferred the native construction. It consisted of a sharpened deer horn or bone tied into a wooden frame and covered with pine pitch to hold it in place and make it watertight. A stout two-foot hemp line was tied through this head, and it was affixed to a long wooden handle. When a fish was struck, the head loosened during the struggling that followed. The fisherman let the prey tire itself out before he pulled in his line.

None of this fishing gear was ever touched or made by women, because they were classed as unclean mortals by the men.[3]

Periodically, the salmon that had been caught were gathered into a big heap under the shade of the cliffs. There a man called the divider or Salmon Tyee took charge of giving the fish to all the campers according the size of the family in each lodge. It was equally divided among all, both workers and visitors, regardless of how much labor they had put in, every day at noon and dusk.[4] Everyone got an equal share so that the fish would not think humans were being stingy or selfish and so refuse to return. The divider that I remember best was named See-pas.

Our lunch was usually boiled berries and steaming chunks of red salmon in a cloudy white soup. Father loved this, but Mother would never drink the broth of any fish. I always sat next to father so I could brace my back against him. I curled my feet underneath me. Mother said they were so big because they were an inheritance from my white [ancestor]. Father would joke, "Kee-ten will never make a good foot racer because her feet are in the way of the stumps." Mother also reproached me for going barefoot. I took off my moccasins as often as I could. This was unusual among native children. "Taking your moccasins off will make your feet grow big. She looked to Father for support, but he was quiet. She said, "You spoil that child. You should make her wear footgear." Father would look down at my dirty face and smile his sweetest, [most] understanding pal smile. But he never said anything, even while he gave me more salmon from either the kettle or the tule-mat tablecloth where chunks were set to drain.

The fate and well-being of the future depended on how people treated the fish.[5] In return, the fish indicated what kind of seasons we could expect. Before the bad winter of 1892–93, people knew to expect hardship because the salmon runs were plentiful and the fish had a thick skin. Nonetheless, we very much enjoyed boiling and eating these red, fat, juicy king salmon. The old people liked to drink the soup made from boiling the fish.

Fishing was not the only thing done by the campers, since time was also devoted to visiting, gambling, trading, and other types of labor.

One day Mother took me along when she visited the Kalispel tipis. As we entered, I could smell a terrible odor. I whispered to her, "What smells?" Mother pushed me as she waved her hand for silence. When we returned to the lodge after the visit, she told me the unbearable smell came from an herb used to prevent sickness or death caused by a shaman. Years later, I learned that the root is called *mus-aia* and is strong enough to keep evil away.[6]

While we were visiting, I learned that our Catholic prayers were in the Spokan language, which is also shared by the Kalispel and Flathead.[7]

In the evening, people made large bonfires in the open air and challenged other tribes to play stick games. Lively songs were sung by both sides, and each team tried to distract the other while it was trying to hide the two bones. The object of the game was for the other side to guess which hand had a particular bone. Each side had a long pole stretched across in front and pounded on it with short sticks, keeping time with the songs. Bets of robes, blankets, coins, and so forth were piled in the middle. Anyone could bet on a team, even women. Women also had their betting games, which could last for a few hours or several days. All bets had to be absolutely matched [equivalent]. Anyone who wanted to make a bet had to match it against one for the other side. After the game, a winner got back double on the bet.

Athletic contests were also held, native games of running, jumping, lifting, and shooting. A favorite one of old had pairs of men compete against each other. One player rolled a serviceberry ring along a trench while the other man tried to shoot an arrow through it. The ring was decorated with beads, dyed porcupine quills, or feathers. Sometimes a ten-inch ring had spokes laced to make a center hole two inches in diameter. The trenches were about fifty feet long. The players rolling the ring waited on a slight upgrade, and the shooters formed a line along the trench. The winner was the man whose arrow went through the hoop that matched his bow. If there were several "bull's-eyes," these men competed until the best shot got all the bets. It was an exciting game, accompanied by yells and laughter after each game. All gambling required good sportsmanship. It was shameful for poor losers to grieve. They would get no sympathy. Visitors left either walking because they had lost their ponies or gleefully driving a new herd.

Recently they also learned card games, such as Monte, a Spanish game. It is better known among my poeple as Wal-looks.

The granite around the falls had many uses. Women gathered the slabs on the east to make knives, scrapers, and other tools for turning deer hides into buckskin. This kind of rock (called quh-kam, tanning rocks) was well known and preferred, so it was traded widely. Since there was no flint in the area, this granite was the substitute, especially for tanning scrapers. These fan-shaped pieces of chipped rock were fitted into three-foot handles and tied with buckskin or hemp cords. The women made these scrapers by hitting the edges of a granite slab against a flat rock.[8] Slowly, one side became ready for use [to deflesh a hide]. When a hide was mostly clean, it was dressed out by stretching it tightly within a square frame made of two log supports with cross logs above and below. The scraper in the handle was used as a beamer to rub the stretched hide and to break up its fiber. A fire was built nearby, sometimes on both sides of the frame, to heat and help dry the hide.

The hide was considered to be "green" (unprocessed) as soon as it came off the animal. It was soaked in water, weighted down with rocks, for two or three days. When the hair was loose, the hide was placed on a smooth post about six feet long, six inches wide, and braced against a tree for support. A deer rib or later a dull butcher knife or slat of metal (often from a scythe) was used to scrape the hair off the hide while leaning against the end of the pole and pushing with both hands in a strong downward motion.

When all the hair was off, the hide was washed and hung up to dry thoroughly. Then it was given its first smoking over a smudge fire of rotten fir wood and soaked again in lukewarm water overnight. The next day it was drained well by placing a pole at one end, wrapping the other end around a sapling, and twisting it tightly. It was now ready to be stretched in the log frame and rubbed with the beamer until dry. It was again soaked overnight in warm water mixed with crushed brains and boiled in this whitish liquid. The next day it was again stretched, rubbed, and dried. This finished the process unless the hide was to be colored. Then it was smoked over a smudge of rotten fir if it was to be golden brown or over rotten cottonwood if yellow. The buckskin was now ready for use. The advantage of smoking was that it made the hide more water resistant and less stiff when dry.

At the fishery, my mother was well known for rising early. I often dropped back to sleep after she shook me the first time each day, and Father had to lift me under the arms to get me awake. I dreaded this early morning rising and was glad when fishing season was over. Mother got up so early because it was the custom to get water for the camp only in the early morning or in the evening, since women stayed well away from the fishermen during the day. It was believed that if women drew water, washed clothes, or bathed, the fish would react to the human smell and never return to that place. It was strictly against the rules during fishing season for anyone to take water from above the falls or otherwise pollute the area.[9] Water for human use could only be taken below the falls, reached by a stony, dangerous trail down the south side for perhaps two hundred feet through the Suicide Cliffs, so called because people who fell or jumped from them were lost in the swift, boiling waters below.

Many were the strict regulations governing my people during the fishing season. Women could never throw any salmon entrails in or near the river, where the odor might carry to the fish. The blood and entrails were usually buried safely away from dogs or from the footsteps of women who might be in their monthly periods of contamination. Women were not allowed to bathe or wash while men were fishing. They were to stay away from the water above the falls and only take camp water or do their washing below them.

Women had their sweat lodges about a half mile below the falls and used them only in the evening after the spearing had stopped. The men had theirs in a row above the falls, a short distance from the camps. This ground was particularly sacred and used exclusively by the male population, including boys old enough to accompany their fathers in the rites.

No fishing was done on Sunday, by orders of Chief Kinkanawah of the Colvile, who was camped on the east side across from our lodge.[10] He was a strict chief, so Indians usually made the best of this day by swimming, playing native games, and visiting. Women used the free time to search for new tanning rocks around the idle stream a mile below the falls. Sunday was known as Ska-ch-cist (Flag Hung up Day)[11] from an early frontier custom. Many Indians attended church at Goodwin Mission about ten miles southeast of the camps.

The first Sunday after we arrived at the falls, Mother took us children across the river in a canoe. We passed above the falls with some relatives who were also going to mass. Father and others took their ponies even farther upriver to swim across where the water was not so swift and dangerous. Their saddles were piled in the center of the canoe to keep them dry.

On the opposite bank, we walked up the steep trail that went back and forth to the top of the first bench where it met the main north-south trail. After walking a mile, we were in full view of abandoned St. Paul Chapel, northeast of the fishery. Mother stopped to rest and took this opportunity to tell me that she and Father had been married at that old church shortly before activities were moved to Goodwin Mission, where we were going that day.

The historical log church stood in ruins, overgrown by weeds and vines. It was on the spot that Father De Smet had blessed for a church in 1842. Later Jesuits built a little chapel there, which was eventually replaced by the church built of logs and shingle shakes by natives in 1856. The flooring was whipsawed and nailed down with wooden pegs. No iron was used in the construction, supposedly. The Jesuits may have used this site because it was also convenient to Fort Colville, approximately four miles north on Marcus Flat. Many of the French Canadians there, along with the half-Flathead wife of Angus McDonald, the chief factor, were Catholic.[12]

After we got across, we met father and mounted our horses. The large, modern church awaited us at Goodwin Mission. It was on a hill along a small bench, overlooking the rolling land of the Colville Valley, drained by a small river of the same name.

At church, Indians prayed and sang hymns in different languages. Their voices seemed to echo back and forth in that great building. After church, women went out the side door and men out the front. Everyone waited in front while our chief and other leaders spoke to the people from the steps, reinforcing the moral messages of the priest.

Mother held me at her side in the women's group. The aged chief Kinkanawah came out last, since he sat in the front pew. He used a worn willow cane to steady his footsteps. His eyes were beady and bright as he stopped on the platform above the wide row of stairs. He cleared his voice and spoke.

"My people, my children. We have again come to the house of Our Father, the Great Spirit of the Universe. We did not come here only to meet our friends and shake each other's hand in greeting, but to build a straight trail to lead us to home prepared for us above, in the skies with the Great White Spirit. Our lives are held [by] a small string, ready to break at any moment. Our moccasined feet may tread on this trail to home, to be judged by the Maker for our sins. It is well, my people, that we laid aside the sinful way of life and are prepared. Life is uncertain. Next year, we may be fewer at this time. I am an old man. My days are short. I grieve to leave you behind. My children, be faithful to this house of the Maker. I urge and command you to listen and obey its rules after I take the last trail."

Other speeches were made. At this time we learned who the divider was to be. He was called Kanatal, and I feared him. He was a tall man, with a wrinkled face, high forehead, even teeth, and square chin. He was the head councilman and adviser to the chief. He was also best friends with the chief factor. Early traders trusted him with their mail and valuables between Fort George (Astoria) and Fort Colville. He was famous for being honest and upright. If the priest was not there, he led services. He loved authority and despite his old age orated in a thundering voice.

One day we children were playing at bending willows into tiny horses, with split sticks to ride them. We were so busy with our toys that we failed to note the approach of the village whipper, the one-eyed Kanatal. He lifted me by the arms and started to whip me with one of the many willow switches he always carried in his wide buckskin belt. I screamed, and he went for another child, but all had fled by then. They went into the bushes and rough places where the old man had difficulty. He whipped me unmercifully until I kicked and broke away. I ran back to the tipi and my mother, but she smiled and said he whipped only the bad children. I had to obey my elder's words.

On Sunday afternoons, men went to the lodge of the chief to hold council, discussing camp problems, while the women and children went swimming below the falls or searching for tanning rocks.

Chief Kinkanawah and Kanatal were fanatical Christians. They were severe in their judgments both of the tribal laws and of those added by the traders and the missionaries.

When Kinkanawah became chief, he introduced a new punishment.[13] He had all offenders lashed with a twisted deerskin whip. For any crime, however small, he had a tule mat put down in his lodge. Offenses included not going to church on Sunday or feast days. The whipper was Kanatal, who is said to have enjoyed his position; many a man or woman fainted on the mat because of his stout arms. Yet cruel as it seems, it also took the place of killing a woman who had disgraced her family by committing adultery.

5. Tanning a hide laced onto a log frame. Courtesy of the
American Philosophical Society.

6. Roasting and drying a salmon. Courtesy of the
American Philosophical Society.

7. Fishing at a weir. Courtesy of the American
Philosophical Society.

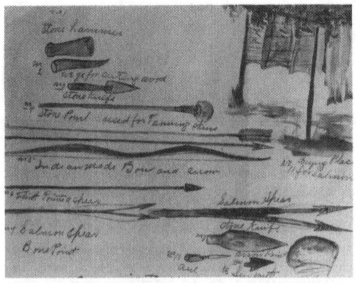

8. Sanpoil artifacts. Courtesy of the American
Philosophical Society.

9. Making a tule mat, with mat lodges in the background.
Courtesy of the American Philosophical Society.

In 1930 Mrs. Sam Pierre, then eighty-two and living at Kettle Falls, told me that she had seen several lashings by Kanatal. After the chief had specified the number, he sat in deep prayer. Arsell, an eighty-year-old Okanogan woman, confirmed this and said that the "cat of nine tails" had never been used before Kinkanawah became chief. Other chiefs, such as those of the Okanogan, took this punishment from him. When the chief died, the punishment stopped. Regrettably, it had a bad effect on native women. The younger generation had learned discipline in mission school, but the rest of white society led them astray. Without the dread of punishment, women got too free.

Kanatal began his service under Chief See-whehl-ken.[14] I heard a vivid story that suggests he actually began the practice of whipping, starting when this chief was old. When the men met in council, See-whehl-ken would take out his beautiful tobacco pouch and fill his long pipe with crumbled tobacco. With his head bowed in thought, he took several puffs and handed the pipe to Kanatal on his right, who took three draws and passed it on. It was empty by the time it had been silently passed to everyone in the circle. Only crying babies could be heard. Finally the chief lifted his head, and his deep voice vibrated through the crowd, saying "Kanatal will speak."

Kanatal pointed his finger at an accused man and woman. "This woman and this man (pointing at them) were seen embraced together by the path to the water. It is wrong for a woman who is not married to let a man hold her in his arms."

The chief asked the woman to defend herself. She replied, "I was going for water when he (pointing) forced me into his arms against my will."

Kanatal thundered, "That is a lie. You were not struggling to free yourself from his arms." The women who were there smiled at each other. Then the chief asked the man to speak. He said, "I held this woman in my arms because I love her. I will marry her if she will consent." The chief sat for a moment before giving judgment without [consulting] his council. "It is against the rules of our tribe and

*only the mama
my
whipped*

church for an unmarried woman to be found in the arms of a man. For this broken law, I sentence her to be a lesson for all women. Twenty lashes."

Kanatal took a worn buffalo robe and spread it out in the center, motioning the woman forward. The chief's wife handed him the whip, which was kept in their house.[15] He told the woman, "Take off all your skirts but one, so you will feel the lash."

This case was typical,[16] but there were many exceptions because some women learned refinement. I well remember one day at Goodwin when I saw a woman in the latest fashion. Kala'len (Caroline) Louie was smartly dressed in a long, sweeping dark skirt with a wasp waist and many ruffles down the back. She reminded me of the yellow jackets that infested the salmon drying on the fishery scaffolds. Many of the elders whispered criticisms about her, but I was very impressed. Later, whenever I would see her at traditional gatherings dressed in buckskin and basketry hat, I always made a comparison with her beauty that day. The only white women I ever saw were the sisters at the mission, and they were hardly women of fashion.

★

CHAPTER 9

Fall Hunting

WHEN THE chokecherry leaves were yellow and wilted, it was customary among all the Indians to go on an annual fall hunt arranged into groups of friends and families. That year Father made a decision that we should join the Colville on their old hunting ground in the mountain range northwest of our home at Pia.

We had been working hard until then. Many chokecherries still persistently hung half-dried on the bushes in the gullies and many small ravines on the big hillside near home. Pia was noted for its wild cherries, and that year the crop was unusually heavy. The old people said it meant another winter of deep snow. Mother contented herself with drying the abundant fruit and storing many hemp sacks of it. This was the industrious way of a good tipi housewife.

Father had made several stacks of bunchgrass hay, set in oblong shapes with long, sloping sides to prevent the rain from soaking it. He had stacked the grain in cones, with the bundles neatly placed inward toward the center. All his harvesting had been done by hand. He cut the oats and wheat with a cradle scythe and bound the grain with his hands without using any twine. He was an expert at tying the bundles with the plants themselves. He was so skillful that they never came apart during hauling. Mother helped him with the heavy work while I took care of the baby under the shade of the upright bundles.

We were short of pack saddles, and I watched as my mother made some extras out of dried forked thorn bushes heavy enough to hold together even under a big load. She whittled these down with a sharp knife to fit the sides before nailing them together securely. She covered them with wet rawhide and sewed it with buckskin thongs, making holes with a bone awl. In this tedious way, she made the new pack saddles. She made the girth from horsehair first twisted into small strands, then woven together in a wide strip to fit the large iron rings used as a cinch. She padded the cruppers to fit snugly under the horses' tails, to keep the load from slipping on a steep trail.

We had about ten packhorses all loaded with empty flat parfleches, extra ropes, and buckskin thongs. Father drove the long string of packhorses while mother and I followed behind. I rode my buckskin pony, having a lot of fun moving back and forth, chasing an old bay mare that had a habit of leaving the trail to snatch a few blades of grass.

We went down the steep trail from our cabin to Kettle River and the ford. The water was not too deep at that time of the year, reaching only to the flanks of our horses. I doubled up my legs to keep them dry because my pony was the shortest of the group.

Sulee had my former place behind Mother's saddle, and Keleta hung from her pommel in the single footer [braced cradleboard] used for all our babies. As usual, Sulee went to sleep from the rocking motion of the horse, but Mother frequently slapped her legs to keep her awake and prevent her from slipping off the rump. We were all happy.

My dogs went with us, and they now included a little yellow mongrel, perhaps with some fox terrier ancestry. He would not mind me, so Father tried to keep him behind his mount, but the dog would sneak ahead and chase everything it saw, just like when we went out into the woods together.

After we crossed the ford, the little dog saw some tardy ground-hogs that had not yet gone into hibernation. They were sunning themselves on a large flat rock close to the road. The mongrel jumped on the rock with his ears sticking straight up. The tiny animals ran quickly into deep crevices in the rock to get out of sight. The dog went on ahead, barking furiously and rooting out hiding creatures. Father rode up to the large boulders and shortly came back with a fat rodent my dog had killed by crawling into a crevice after it. This amused my parents so they were not particular about keeping the dog in the rear after that. Father tied the dead hog to his saddle and went on, saying, "We'll have a good supper tonight with this fat groundhog."

It was late in the afternoon when we crossed a big creek in a mountain gulch. The steep trail made a turn and came out at the top of a small clearing on benchland. We then came in full view of the Indian camp we were to join for the deer hunt. Some hunters had already been successful, since the drying scaffolds contained meat being smoked and dried over slow fires. The camp had about ten lodges, including some invited Spokan and Kalispel. These Indians spoke a different version of our language, but our older members had no difficulty conversing with them. We children found these conversations very amusing because some of their words sounded funny to us.

Among the Spokan were an old man and his wife who had no children. He was too old to hunt actively, so Father and Mother invited them to share our tipi and raw meat supply. They could cure it as they liked. My parents set up our camp, and Mother unpacked her kitchen. She took the body of the groundhog that my dog had killed, cleaned it, washed it in the creek, and laced up the belly with a sharp stick. She put the body over the fire to singe off the hair, scraped the hide with a knife, carved up the meat, and boiled it until the fat oozed into the water. When it was done, it made a great feast for all of us.

The next day, Mother rose before dawn and had everything ready for Father to start on his hunt. He was a good hunter and in the prime of his manhood, so we were not surprised when he returned that night with his pony loaded with deer meat. In her generous way, Mother gave some of the meat to the old Spokan woman to dry on the empty rack.

Mother continued to follow the old way. When my father was hunting, she never slept in his bed. His bedding was considered sacred then, and we were forbidden to play on or around it. She was very careful with the deer meat. The fresh kill had to be brought in through the rear of the tent and placed on a bed of boughs. It never came near the doorway where women walked. In this way she contributed to the continued hunting success of my father and the other men.[1]

Colville hunters always strung up deer heads on high limbs, with the nose pointing up so the deer could not smell the camp. They were never cooked or eaten until the hunt was finished. Only men and maybe a very old woman could do this. The same was true for the kidneys. Only adults, never children, could eat bone marrow. Were a child to eat marrow or fat, he or she would have weak legs and lungs. Only old people could eat unborn fawns, and they relished their tenderness. Children would be paralyzed (have dead bodies) in later life if they did so.

The old Spokan woman did not follow our beliefs. Once Mother was shocked to see the old woman skinning a deer head opposite our fireplace. She gouged out the eyes and threw them at the door, where the dogs eagerly gobbled them up. Such things were forbidden to women until after menopause. When our family had moved higher up into the mountains, the Spokan couple had been invited to share our tipi, so the breach of taboo made by the woman occurred inside our home. Mother did her best to make amends by cleaning up the area where the eyes fell and offering a prayer in apology.

Mother was very religious, believing in both our traditional ways and those of the Catholics. She saw no conflict between them, although others did. She always said grace in our language before every meal. The Spokan had been converted by Protestants like the Reverends Walker and Eells at Walker's Prairie.[2] The new neighbors thought this amusing, and some even said, "You Colville wear little medals around your necks like dogs. It is foolish to believe in the Black Gowns." Mother was a true Indian and so would always keep her reserve. Our canons of hospitality forbade her to insult our neighbors or guests. Whenever people like this were under our roof, she bit her lip tightly to prevent any angry words from coming out.

We were not the only ones in camp having trouble with the Spokan. The other Colville were becoming disgusted with a young Spokan girl who had become a bride that summer. When the women learned that she was to be a mother with her first child, they began to call her "the half-eye" because her husband had already had children with another woman.[3]

The new couple were supposed to follow many taboos very carefully. The Indian hunters were especially wary of having a husband with a young pregnant wife join their group. She was in a very contaminated state at this time. Everything she touched transmitted bad luck to others according to Colville beliefs, [which] the Spokan disregarded. It was a constant worry to the other women that the couple shared the same bed and would throw deer bones into the doorway for the dogs. The wife would also wander freely around the camp. When hunters did not do well, they blamed this couple for their bad luck. All of this was done in private because no one was brave enough to insult the Spokan deliberately by stating their dismay and disgust in the open.

We moved camp many times that fall as the hunters made their kills and scared the game farther and farther away. We moved to be closer to unhunted areas. It took perhaps two months to cross the mountain range across the big bend of the Kettle River, now part of the Boulder Creek District of the Colville National Forest. In actual mileage it was no more than thirty-five or forty miles along mountain roads, but the old Indian trail closely followed the creek, evading the steep canyons and rocky sides along the way. Where a log fell over the trail, the Indians made the trail go around it without further concern. It was only after we had packhorses that trails were straightened out and widened through dense areas. One of the reasons for this was that the packhorses were banging their loads against trees, rocks, and high stumps, bending our gear and cooking utensils all out of shape. By evening our pretty parfleches would be black from burnt trees. Such wear and tear slowed down our travel between camps, so it was easier to remake part of the trail.

As hunters from our camp filled all their packs, they would move home to winter camps. My parents moved west to reach the other side of the bend where the town of Curlew stands.

The snow was about two feet deep when we reached the summit overlooking the Curlew Valley. We did not stop. All our horses were heavily loaded with parfleches filled with dried meat. The old Spokan were satisfied with their own supplies because Father had divided every one of his deer with them. They continued to travel with us, as there was no polite way to send them off.

When we reached the steep decline in the trail, Mother was glad to see that some Spokan were camped on the land adjoining the little farm of her uncle Long Alex. She secretly told Father that they would now be relieved of the old couple. Her prophecy was correct, and our neighbors gladly joined their tribal members, saying goodbye with handshakes all around. We turned our long string of packhorses toward the cabin of my granduncle.

Old Long Alex was a character around Curlew, where he was born and lived out his life. He had cast aside his Indian ways to such an extent that he had invested in raising cattle and horses for a living. He was considered rich and industrious. He had built a flat scow for a ferry and charged people to take them across the Kettle River. On the river flats he raised vegetables and grain. He was not selfish with his wealth and had donated land for a cabin church built by Father De Rouge.

One of his daughters had been married to a white man named Gibbs and had two children, Marceline and Margaret. These children were both younger than myself and lived with their grandfather, as their mother was a widow. They went to the Goodwin

Mission school and were raised to be well-educated and accomplished women. I always admired their advantages and abilities.

Some people were not as poised and honest with their assets. Before we left Curlew, I saw a young man crossing the river on a beautiful black horse. He missed the ford and swam his mount through the deep water toward the home of Long Alex. He came up to my parents, looking very handsome as he dismounted, smiled, and extended a hand to them. He was the new husband of Antoinette, Chief Tonasket's young widow, who had reached our camp the day before. Tonasket had died the previous year at Marcus while returning from Spokane Falls, where he had had an infected eye removed. The infection spread and poisoned his system, killing him before he reached home.[4]

Antoinette had arrived riding sidesaddle and wearing a black skirt that reached almost to the ground. This was my first view of an Indian woman riding sidesaddle, as this mode had been scorned by our females. Later some did take to it, but it was still considered impractical. I recall that this young woman was both beautiful and well groomed.

After this young couple had moved on to their own camp, I heard the people talking about the young man, Johnny McDougal, who had married the widow because she was rich. Only one of his parents was an Indian, and he was considered reckless, spending his wife's money on liquor and gambling, both habits the venerable old Tonasket had strongly opposed in favor of schooling and work for his followers.

Tonasket came to wide attention when he made his "Paul Revere" ride from Vernon, British Columbia, to McLoughlin Canyon, just north of Riverside, Washington, to dissuade his father, an Okanogan chief, from fighting in 1858. His life was helpful and energetic. He was one of the men who signed the Moses Treaty in 1883 and used the occasion to ask for a school, along with a gristmill and sawmill. Shortly after the government built the school at Tonasket, Washington, for one hundred students, it burned down. The sawmill and gristmill fell into ruin when the chief began to ignore them in favor of the beautiful Antoinette Somday.

He left Tonasket to marry her and moved into the Curlew Valley to be near her home in Little Canyon (Inisiscachin). At Curlew, he bought two hundred head of sheep from Jack Ingram at Midway, British Columbia. My people called Ingram "the butcher" because he sold meat to the miners at the Rock Creek goldfields. He also sold to the relatives of his native wife. The sheep did well and increased. The next year the customs officials at Lake Osoyoos heard about the illegal transaction and asked Tonasket for Canadian duty on the herd.

We left Curlew and went home. We lived in comfort with plenty of food until about White Moon (February). It was nothing unusual for my parents to be out of food by this time of year. They were always generous to the poor and needy. Neighbors dropped by continually, and our fat parfleches were flattening out. There was still plenty of snow on the ground.

Mother began to ration our food, serving meals only when it became absolutely necessary. It pains me to recall that Mother would break off little pieces to fill our hungry mouths and save only a tiny morsel for herself. Then she would reconsider, and after some hesitation, break even her portion into smaller pieces for Sulee and me. She nursed little Keleta without eating anything herself. She was a mother who believed in sacrifice. Father too went without food, using as his excuse that he was not hungry after coming home from a fruitless hunt in the deep snow. He used snowshoes to keep from falling into the soft, melting slush.

Even now I am not sure how our neighbors, Ka-at-qhu and her husband, lived through.[5]

Late one evening, Sulee and I had gone to bed without food. I heard Father's footsteps approaching and jumped up to find out if he had any success. He called to Mother, "Open the back of the tipi," and I knew immediately there was meat. Mother had been nursing Keleta and put her down, although she yelled as she usually did. It seemed like ages before Mother cleaned away the old flooring of tules, bark, and dirt. Then Father rolled his pack under the cover and walked around to the front. He entered soaking wet from both thawing snow and sweat.

I shook Sulee awake, and of course we had a fight. Mother cooked the choicest venison, and we ate with relish. Before going to bed, Father took some food to Big Lip's tipi. The next day, Mother equally divided our meat with everyone else at our winter encampment. Father reported the deer were higher up in the mountains than usual because food in the lowlands was deep under snow. He had to travel to the place where timber moss grew to kill his deer.

Such hospitality by my parents taught me early to pick bones clean. Even today I enjoy bones and gristle because these were my foods. Whenever guests came, Father ate the best food with them. Mother waited to eat with us children, serving the meaty bones left by the honored, but toothless, diners. Also, bread crusts and other things difficult for the old to chew were luxuries to my hungry stomach. When company came, we were sent outdoors so we would not watch, saving embarrassment. Many times we went without food while watching my father and others devour a loaded table. I grew bitter toward elders and promised myself that both children and adults would share my meals. Thus children do not wait at my table; they eat with grownups to even the score from my own childhood.

★

CHAPTER 10

Winter Dancing

To be successful, a person had to have power from a spirit. This spirit came close to its human partner every winter, and their bond had to be expressed at a public gathering where individuals sang the songs that had been given to them at the first contact with the spirit. Although the song was given when a person was young, it was not "brought out" in public until he or she was old and respected. This added to the belief that every success was attributable to spirit power. Local whites sometimes call this a Chinook Dance, in the mistaken idea that the dancing calls Southwind to thaw the ground, but they are mistaken.

People gathered in a large home with a sacred pole set up in the middle.[1] An old man or woman would go up to it and start singing, while others sang and drummed along. A man might go up and sing softly and then pause to pray.

Sometimes he would begin again, telling everyone, "My children, follow my song," and everyone joined in with the old singer but using a lower tone so his voice could always be heard. In native theory this symbolized the whole tribe following a wise chief, shaman, or leader for the benefit of all.

A visionary might sing for an hour or less before abruptly changing to another song, slowly getting up while shaking the pole, and engaging in a few quick steps around the middle area. This was a sign that others could get up and dance in the same way, moving in place before resuming their seats. The shaman sometimes motioned with a wave of his hand, saying, "Come, follow my dance so your life may be spared long enough to see the sunshine of summer and the green grass under your feet again." The audience then came forward and closed in gradually around the singer, first dancing slowly with his voice easily heard, then growing more intense as they got the vibrating power of the spirit and the song as their bodies moved faster until they lost control in the joy of dancing. They began to imitate different animals as they danced. One would open fingers over the head and swing from side to side to indicate the alertness of the deer or the prowess of the elk. Another divided the two forefingers to imitate the running hooves of a deer or antelope.

Men largely imitated animals or prey important to successful hunters for help in the future. Women usually represented powers important for their own tasks as berry pickers, basket makers, or baby doctors. One woman sang, "I will find the largest patches of huckleberries when the summer comes again." Imagination had to be used as to what success they wanted from singing and dancing. Some appealed for health, gambling luck, a lifelong love, and so forth. After about an hour the leader stopped, and everyone else did the same. They went back to their seats to await the next singer. If there were many shamans, dancing continued all night. Occasionally the leader gave permission for intermissions when talking or smoking were allowed.

As each shaman left the pole, he or she said aloud, "I hope I am not lying. I hope your appeals are heard by the animal spirits. If I am a liar you will be unsuccessful in your appeals. May it not be so."

This pattern contined until midnight with each shaman taking a turn. At midnight a recess was given for people to smoke, eat, visit, or go home. Anyone who left without permission was vulnerable to attack by the spirits who were attracted to such gatherings and in readiness to kill or harm someone as a punishment or to get a companion in their loneliness.

The dancing continued for two or three nights before the sha-mans were ready to initiate a budding medicine man or woman. In large communities there could be several of these. When a man or woman had previously experienced the finding of a supernatural power to guide them, it usually left them alone in childhood. It came back when they were adults, appearing as a dream or vision to remind them of the contract, saying, "Sing my song and the world will shine for you."

While some persons might have been reluctant to take on the responsibility, or ashamed to sing in public, or too poor to give gifts at the initiation, they would die if they did not comply. Such per-sons were generally moody and deep in thought, lacking ambition to work or do anything else. They soon fell ill without knowing the cause, lingering a long time in a slow death until a shaman recog-nized the power and declared it time for a public initiation during a Winter Dance in the month of Spakt (February). The doctor could only delay death until the initiation by continuing to doctor and trying to find out the necessary song. If the warning was ignored, a person would suffer from the affliction and have it intensify during the winter until he either died or had an accident.

When the lives of visionaries were in danger, they received warn-ing from their guide in time so that they could sing the song to get over it by having the power come to their aid. If they were alone, the spirit might actually appear to them. This power was only for per-sonal use. You could never doctor someone else with your power unless you were initiated during a dance held at midwinter.

Most young people seldom tried to sing their songs in public until their hair turned gray with age. If they were anxious to show the power by singing, an older shaman was likely to get angry at such showing off and lack of respect, punishing them by taking the power and/or killing them. People said, "He is showing off and will die young. A big Indian doctor will bite his head off for showing such pride."[2]

When the time was right, novices collected robes, clothing, and ponies for a year before their Give-Away (Snee-wh-am, Drop-in) at the Winter Dance.[3] The gifts they gave away were called en-we-num. The dates of these dances were set by the leading shamans of the tribe at a joint meeting. Usually each area continued with the relative sequence and date used for past decades.

On initiation night, the lead shaman sang first in low tones to a silent audience. His voice grew louder as he walked to the medicine pole holding a strip of fur or other token of the power of the initiate. He attached it and continued to sing until his confident song vibrated through the people. Next he motioned for the initiate to come forward to the pole, saying, "take the cane [pole] and sing your song." Usually he or she forgot the song in the excitement of the moment. The lead shaman started the song so initiates could take it up and forget their surroundings as they got caught up in it. The spirit and song made them stronger.

When this happens, the sponsor says, "You sing to help your brother or sister." Everyone then joins in to help. Now the person is proclaimed in public to be a new shaman. This was very dangerous.

The novice was guarded and coached by a shaman during the entire winter season, taught mastery and ownership over the power during the nights of dancing. He was always seated beside experienced shamans and helped them while they worked on patients. They helped perfect the song and gave careful instruction as to the rules of the Medicine Dance. If the initiate survived the year following all this effort, he had the acknowledged ability to continue as a full-fledged shaman. If his power was weak, other shamans would take it from him while his hold was yet uncertain. He then would die.

The last two nights were set aside for a general curing of the afflicted. After the shaman grabbed the pole and sang, he asked those in need of his services to come forward into the middle of the lodge. He placed his hands in a basin of water and touched the patient on the top of the head, moving his hands slowly down the sides of the body to brush off any lingering illness. His fingertips quivered during this process, tracing the outline of the seated patient. His treatment covered the whole body all the way to the ground. If he missed anything, he dipped his hands in the water again and sang in a low tone while he repeated the brushing cure. When he was successful, the patient jumped up suddenly. Four to six chosen men came to the shaman's aid, holding his feet. Meanwhile the doctor fought for control over the illness, now held in his doubled-up fists braced in front of his body. If the sickness was caused by a very powerful shaman, the feet of the curer actually rose off the ground. The men held him until he could plunge his hands into the water basin and dissolve the disease object. For example, it could look like a worm covered with blood or a bloody feather. It had been shot into the body to make the person sick or die. If the disease was too powerful, other shamans or more experienced ones were called in to help. Sick people were always at liberty to try another curer if they were not cured or felt dissatisfied.

After midnight on the last night, after the recess, the host shamans chose members of the audience to distribute the presents brought by shamans and patients. The person in charge had the responsibility to see that everyone received a gift, depending on their standing in the community. A popular man or woman left with several large and expensive gifts, such as robes, blankets, silk handkerchiefs, clothing, bridles, saddles, ponies, and trade goods.

Although the Colville have embraced American clothing, food, customs, and religion, they still believe in the shaman. Missionaries preached against this at almost every service, but without effect. Even children fresh out of advanced education still believe. They may brag around whites and friends that [shamanism] is foolish, but their hearts hold fast to tradition.

In 1918 the daughter of a famous shaman [tempted fate]. Her father had cured many people and charged large sums. He was rich, respected, and sometimes feared. He sent his daughter to school and brought her beautiful clothes. At a dance given by her father, she went up to the medicine pole and broke out into song like a full-fledged doctor. Her father grieved at this but tried to initiate her at once. The old people just shook their heads and said, "She's proud, showing off her song. Soon she will die."

Her father was our greatest shaman, but even he could not protect her. She died the next summer. Whether this was malice or coincidence remains in doubt.

In 1930 I met a woman in the Yakima hop yards who was a Colville. I laughed at one of her jokes, but she hushed me up, saying, "Do not laugh out loud, because there are native doctors nearby." She was deathly afraid of them, despite many years of school.

The next spring I had a mild form of influenza during the epidemic, but she became more seriously ill. She died after a native doctor told her that a Nez Perce woman had witched [hexed] her over some disagreement about chickens getting into her yard. Her fear of shamans helped to kill her. People will try white doctors only when they cannot get native ones.

In 1932 a woman at Monse, Washington, became suddenly ill and sent for a white doctor. He told her she had appendicitis and needed an operation at once to prevent a fatal rupture. Instead she sent for a shaman with Bluejay power. He cured her, but it took six young men to hold him during the treatment. All six were educated, but as one of them said, "I never believed in Indian doctors, but seeing is believing. [The shaman] was a small man, but the six of us could not hold his feet to the ground. The object he took out of the woman was about four inches long, and it breathed in the basin of water as if it were alive. It was covered with blood and seemed to have eyes. A moment before, he had nothing in his hands."

While most whites were skeptical, I can testify that our shamans were very effective at curing illnesses that even physicians had given up on. Indians had a staunch belief that God made the world according to a divine plan that gave power from the animal world to our ancestors and now to us. Shamans understood this power better than anyone else, but they did not use it only for good things like nice weather and curing. Some were bad and used it to kill others so as to take the power that came to these weaker visionaries.[4] But the important thing was that the best power came when everyone was gathered together for a feast of First Foods during the summer or, most especially, for a Winter Dance when the powers and their representative spirit guides were strongest. Since everyone there was aware and watching, only good could come out of these gatherings.

★

CHAPTER II

The Seancing Rite

THE SNOW was deep enough to reach almost to the knees of my buckskin pony as we returned to our cabin at Pia (Kelly Hill). His unshod hooves sometimes slid on the narrow, icy trail. We were returning from church at Goodwin Mission in honor of Last Shoot Day. My people called Christmas "First Shoot Day" and New Year "Last Shoot Day" after these holidays were introduced by the Jesuits. These terms were invented because the celebration included shooting rifles off at midnight to mark the birth of Christ and the arrival of the "Baby Year." As a child I did not understand the significance of these terms until years later.

Shortly after we reached home, a man on horseback arrived to invite us to Northport the following week to attend a big Medicine Dance given there by shamans. Everybody in our community was invited, as it was customary for Indian doctors/shamans to wait until midwinter to have everyone congregate for our native way of worship.[1]

Although this practice had been forbidden by the church and Father De Rouge had the full cooperation of the stern chief Kinkanawah, both failed to erase this worship. After Kinkanawah died, De Rouge protested to the new chief Aropaghan, who only smiled in his kindly way and said, "Let my children enjoy their Medicine Dancing as their ancestors did for so many years. It is not harmful. We all go to your church first and only dance later for our own amusement." To our surprise, Father De Rouge agreed to this, and Winter Dancing was revived in our locality.

A few days after our invitation, we started for Northport on horseback to attend the big dance. Mother had packed everything we would need so we wouldn't intrude on others. Our trail was close to the west side of the Columbia most of the way. It took us one day to make this ride of twenty-five miles. As we came in view of the level stretch of land almost directly across the river from the tiny city of Northport, we could see many different families camping in an area freshly cleared of snow.

Mother put up our tipi immediately after we arrived, and Father took our horses to the field where haystacks had been provided by the shaman.

The Indians had already completed a long combination lodge with three fireplaces for heat and light along the center. In outline the structure looked like a long hay shed with a slanting roof. It was covered with canvas, tule mats, and fir boughs. It could accommodate a hundred Indians if all sat on their feet to save space inside. The lodge was unoccupied because people did not dance in the day, only at night after finishing the evening meal.

When that time came, I followed Mother with the other women into the long building, which was already filled with men, all seated in a group at one side. At the back sat the leaders and shamans, talking in low tones and smoking their medicine pipes. Some of these pipes were decorated with fur and feathers to indicate the special spiritual powers of the individual. In the very center was the sacred pole tied to the top of the lodge by buckskin thongs and covered with strips of fur, feathers, copper bells, beads, hooves, and claws. These represented the powers of the different shamans who were going to participate in the dancing. The pole was about eight feet long and had red face paint on places where the bark was peeled off. No one should touch this medicine pole except shamans who were going to sing and dance their powers.

A shaman always wanted a large crowd to attend a dance he sponsored, because this showed his power and popularity among the people. It was the only time and place where people acknowledged their powers in public. It was also the only way a new Indian doctor could be initiated into the rightful ownership of such status. It was a safe haven for these powers until a stronger shaman took away the powers of a lesser one, thus killing him or her. The sick and afflicted came to be cured by the assembled shamans, usually choosing one to start off, then asking others to help if the case proved difficult. If the patient was poor, a gift was promised for later delivery, or relatives came to the rescue with payments or gifts to "gladden the heart" of the curer toward a quick and safe recovery.

On this occasion the dance was hosted by three brothers, Conequah, Little Rock, and Coosta, who, as powerful figures in this district, had extended invitations to everyone.[2]

When the lodge was packed, one of the headmen came forward and sat down by the doorway to guard it until midnight. No one could leave the room while the singing and dancing were in progress. If someone had to leave, the head shaman had to give permission to the guard, causing public attention and embarrassment.

Conequah was the greatest shaman of the Sinschirst (Lakes) and the oldest of the brothers. He moved forward to reach the medicine pole and started the weird, haunting ceremonies of the native religion that few whites see or understand. As he moved the pole back and forth, it rattled with the animal hooves and tiny bells tarnished with age. While he moved the pole there was a deep silence in the room, except for the sound of the fire crackling. All my people were still, alert and waiting. Suddenly the song of the medicine man broke forth, in grunts and undertones until he gasped for air and his voice became stronger to carry the tune throughout the house.

Conequah walked to the middle and grasped the pole. He shook the pole with his hand several times, then started a new tune for another song. He sang many songs that night. His voice rang out clear for a few moments, but ended. Lifting his arm for a slow wave to the crowd, a gleam came into his eyes and he sang out, "Join . . . me. Sing. I . . . need . . . your . . . help to keep the spirits that have come here."

Men and women immediately joined in and sang louder and louder until the tipi rocked with the song. All of a sudden the shaman jumped up and simultaneously changed his tune to a more "jazzy" one. He danced alone for a few minutes, then he commanded the group, "Stand . . . up . . . and dance . . . I . . . need . . . your . . . help."

Everyone got up and danced except for the aged and children, first with slow movements till these became faster and faster in a frenzy. They made motions and sounds imitating animals of every known description. One would put hands in front of his head, palms out like deer antlers, another flap his arms like eagle wings, a third [undulate] like a swimming salmon. Dancing continued until the leader abruptly stopped and slid his hand from the top of the pole, just beneath the furs and feathers. He bowed to the pole and motioned to the ground, following his hand down the pole as he sat down, saying "oo . . . ooo . . . oo." All the other dancers did the same, sitting close to the eaves of the lodge to wait for another shaman to take the pole and sing his song.

The shamans continued in this way for ten nights. During the day they slept, while families visited and people entertained themselves with gambling.

On the tenth night, the anticipated highlight came. When the room was filled and the guard settled at the door, Conequah got up and walked directly in front of a double gray blanket hung along the back of the room. The doctors sat on either side of this curtain. The focus of all attention, Conequah sat down in front of the blankets and sang his song alone, with bowed head.

Then he stopped and said, "When I was a boy, I found my greatest power, the chief of all powers of the Lakes, in the middle of the big river that passes my doorway. This fish spirit is so powerful that it devours other fish. It is the spok-letch (Ling).[3] It has eyes that can see everything underwater. Tonight he is coming from the very headwaters of the Columbia. He is coming in person, his spiritual person. Anyone that wishes to be cured of sickness will be cured for free tonight. Yes, I have spoken."

The shaman started another new song; beginning as grunts, it became a tune. He motioned for his assistants, two men, to come forward. Each held some strong buckskin thongs. They used these to bind up the singing shaman. They tied his thumbs tightly together behind his back, then his toes. They doubled him up and tied his thumbs and toes together with his body bent backward. The doctor sang, "Yes, throw me behind the curtain."

The men lifted him and threw him roughly behind the curtain. Before it had stopped swinging, Conequah sang back, "Yes, lift the blanket." The men lifted the blanket, and he was sitting there singing, with all the loose thongs in his hands. He did this several times, with different men acting as assistants, to prove it was not a fraud.

He took some small red-painted feathers and blew on them. They disappeared, and he told people where to find them. Sometimes it was in someone's hair braids or at the tip of a tule mat in clear [view].

All three of the shaman brothers took turns exhibiting their skill and untying themselves. Then Conequah asked to be bound up again and thrown behind the curtain, because his power the Ling cannibal was almost due to arrive. Once behind the blanket, he remained there singing. In a short time, he said that animals were arriving to pave the way for the "Oldman." As each animal arrived, its voice was heard. The shaman imitated it and told which shaman it belonged to. Many animals came and told their stories through the tied-up shaman. They told how close Ling was in his canoe. At last he arrived, shaking the rear end of the lodge as he came over the tules. The audience could hear but not see this happening behind the curtain.

Ling yawned and grunted as though tired from a long journey.

Then he spoke through the medium of the shaman. "I have come a long way, my children. I am [too] old and feeble to travel. I heard your song and know the wishes of your hearts. I will cure all ills of anyone that follows my song." The doctor sang a short and weary song that everyone willingly followed in the [devoted] belief that they would be cured by the power accompanying the song. This finished, and the doctor acted as medium for the prophecies of the "Oldman."

"As my canoe was drifting along, a short way up the river, I saw a white body lying in the bottom of the river. I pushed the body to shore and it hooked on a limb." The voice continued, "Tomorrow at sunrise, a stranger is coming to your lodge. Before I leave, I will send you a deer for your breakfast. That is all. I have spoken."

Ling left through the back of the lodge. The assistants removed the curtain, and the shaman was still tied up behind it, bundled in a dead faint. Little Rock came forward with some sweet mountain herbs, lit them in the fire, and put the smoldering bundle under Conequah's nostrils and began singing his older brother's song. Slowly the lead shaman revived and joined in the singing. Little Rock untied him, led him to the medicine pole, and put his hand around it. This finished the dance.

The assistants brought forward heaps of blankets, robes, silk handkerchiefs, clothing, and cloth. These were distributed to the crowd, as a consequence of the spiritual gifts of the shamans.

The next day, the whites at Northport found the unidentified body of a drowned white man. About dawn, a Spokan shaman arrived on a white pony, and the dogs chased a deer into the village. It was killed and served at a feast celebrating the success of the dance.

These three brothers were the last of the ancient people to perform this secret rite. It is said that only the Colville "understood" the power of Oldman Ling.

★

CHAPTER 12

The Sweatlodge Deity

THE GREATEST of all deities among the tribes of North America was the sweat lodge. Its use was universal among the people of the forest, and many tribes still hold fast to its traditional sacredness. The Colville tribes were no exception, since they cherished a belief in this spirit of ancestral legends.[1]

During times of affliction or troubles in life, the Indian always turned to the sweat lodge to make a prayerful appeal. It was a place that made no distinctions. All could go there: rich or poor, weak or strong, simple-minded or great in knowledge, commoner or chief, uneducated or adept in shamanistic wisdom. All were equal to enter the lodge to pray and worship our Creator. There were no lines drawn between any of them: male or female, old or young. All had the same privileges to enter a church open to the public, regardless of race.[2]

In building the sweat lodge (Qsilatienge, the Warmer) a suitable level spot had to be located with water and wood available nearby or a short walk from the campsite. Campers always had in mind the need to have a sweat lodge close by and so selected a place along a stream, creek, river, or lake. Larger encampments would build more than one permanent lodge to accommodate worshipers. Although it was considered very improper for any individual to refuse another the use of his or her sweat house, it sometimes happened that someone would deliberately force himself to be invited to sweat with another group to have the advantage of knowing them. When this happened, the group did not rebuke him openly with words of insult. Rather, they looked at each other in mutual understanding of the intrusion and acted distant toward him. The sensitive nature of the Indian prevented open insult, no matter how angry they were at heart, but it also made offenders aware of how people felt from some not-so-subtle clues.

Men generally set up their sweat houses above the stream from the camp to save themselves from bathing in water contaminated by menstruating women. Water for the camp was also drawn from an area above the camp for the same reason.

Preparation for building a lodge included the choice of level ground at the edge of a water source with an intervening area for a fire to heat the stones. The ideal was to face the lodge downstream and toward the "trail of the sun." In practice this meant facing it east, west, or south but never to the north, because that was considered away from the sun. The sun and the sweat lodge were considered to be closely connected in native religion.

After the ground was leveled it was covered with long, straight green branches. The favorite was serviceberry limbs if they were available, because they bent easily without breaking. Other possibilities were maple, fir, and willow, which were somewhat more brittle. These substitutes were used mostly for temporary lodges built while away hunting or berry picking.

The framework was conical and usually had twelve poles stuck into the ground and bound together at the top in a smooth, rounded shape. The poles at the entrance were left oblong to allow people of any size to enter comfortably. The twelve supports of the lodge represented the twelve ribs of the Sweatlodge deity and of mankind generally. All permanent lodges had to have these twelve ribs, but one built in haste or in ignorance could have as few as eight. The back of the lodge was always arranged so that it was built against rocks or dense bushes to prevent a child or stranger from wandering in from that direction.

The covering was made of fir boughs, grass, bark, and dirt. In later periods tent canvas became the norm, because it was more durable and tidy than boughs. Dried twigs used to fall on bathers, and the grass, twigs, and fir boughs kept coming apart. A layer of grass or fir was placed directly on the framework and covered with bark before a layer of earth was put on. Only the door was left open, covered with a skin robe or, later, a blanket or canvas.

To the left, inside the entrance, a pit twelve inches deep and fifteen wide was dug and the rim covered with flat stones.[3] This was the [basin] to hold the rocks, after they had been heated in an outside fire buried between crisscrossed logs and left until they were white hot. The belief was that the hotter the rocks, the more successful would be the prayers, because the steam would go higher.

The heated stones were rolled into the sweat house by means of two forked sticks, usually of green wood to retard burning. Later the hay fork was used to perform this work.

The floor was covered with grass, dry pine needles, and fir boughs. Fir was known to be an effective spiritual cleanser after contact with death or a menstruating woman or almost any other unclean thing. These boughs were placed with the butt toward the walls and fire, the tip toward the middle. This flooring was like velvet and scented the air [to add to] the purification of the bath. The tips of green twigs were used to rub the body clean after dirt was sweated from the pores, because fir cleaned both body filth and spiritual contamination. Rosebush leaves did the same when they were crushed between the hands and the pulp rubbed over the steaming body to clean and purify it. Rosebushes were especially used after contact with a dead body or a funeral, augmenting a sweat or a cold bath.[4]

The stones used were usually gathered from dry land, as those from streambeds retained enough water to split or burst under heat. Preferred stones were smooth, round or oblong, and fine grained. Their size depended on personal preference, but easy handling with crude tools was always a consideration. Most were the size of a man's fist.

The mystic number of the sweat house was five, encompassing the fire for heating the stones, water for bathing, stone for sweating, wood for framework, and earth for covering. These five together accounted for the great strength of aboriginal belief in the ability to reach the Great Spirit of the Unknown by bringing them all together in this rite.

The use of fir and rose had symbolic connections with earth, moisture, and plants, but its origins in religious practice were unknown.

After being used in a sweat lodge, the stones were never discarded where anyone could walk over them. They were piled by the side of the lodge away from paths. The fir flooring was taken into the forest and placed between two trees or heaped around a stump. This kept it away from human activity and possible disrespect or pollution.

When preparing for a sweat bath, a person first built the outside fire and then cleaned the lodge. New fir boughs were placed inside, and refuse was removed. When the stones were hot, each was rolled into the basin to the left of the door. When all were in, the doorway was covered and the lodge left to heat up. Meanwhile, the person undressed and took a cold-water bath before entering the lodge with a pail of water that was placed at his right elbow when seated. This water was used to sprinkle the rocks to cause steam to rise and fill the space. The Indian sang his song of praise to the deity and prayed between verses. Often he or she would begin by praying for ten minutes in praise and thanksgiving. This was usually sufficient to heat the petitioner, who came out to cool off by jumping in the stream. Upon reentering, song and prayers were intensified to ask for health and to guard against death by accident. A man could enter

and leave the lodge as often as he wished. He could pray for benefi-
cial things but could never ask for luck in love, gambling, or increased property until the last visit.

Afterward he bathed in the cold water and dressed. Once the
lodge had been heated, the door was always kept closed, because
there was a belief that the longer the body of the lodge was kept
warm, the greater the likelihood that prayers would be answered.

Each tribe had its own songs appropriate for use in the lodge, and
some individuals had medicine songs they used. Some specialists
switched to a love potion song after the tribal one if they were doing
love magic. The greater the power someone had, the longer he was
expected to stay in the lodge. If a group sweated together, the person
nearest the door took the lead in deciding when to leave and plunge
into the cold water. There was no firm rule for this, however.

Clean boughs were used every time the lodge was heated, but
intact stones were used again and again, becoming more sacred with
each use. Similarly, anyone with power could purify and increase it
by using the sweat lodge repeatedly. A shaman fresh from a cure
used it to fight off the weakening of his strength and prepare himself
to fight off attacks from other shamans intent on taking away his
power during such a weakened condition. A person going to a celebration where there would be gambling never failed to use the lodge
for two to ten days to increase his ability to win over an opponent.
Warriors preparing for an expedition sweated for days in order to be
successful. Everything connected with an interest in life could be
improved by prayer and song in the sweat lodge. This ranged from
purifying the body to gathering together visiting relatives and
friends at this place of worship. Sometimes, if a desire were personal
or embarrassing, a petitioner would camouflage his or her intentions by praying before the group for health and common things,
keeping the private ones silent for the deity alone.

A man and woman never sweated together, and each sex was
expected to have its own lodge. Women either had one discarded by
the men or built one themselves below the camp near the water.

Children went in with a parent, but as soon as a boy was old enough he went with his father. It was desirable for old and young to sweat together, because then the adept could teach the inexperienced.

The early missionaries and teachers were often not aware how deeply important the sweat house is in native religion. Those who did often tried to stop its use, but while many other features of the old religion were abandoned, we remained devoted to the sweat lodge, and it continued to smolder at an even heat due to a firm belief in its benefits and its greatness as a guide during sorrow or need because this deity had long been so kind to all of us. Before the whites came, the lodge was all we needed to stay well. It helped everything from congestion to the stiff joints and rheumatism of elders. During the early epidemics of measles and smallpox, however, it helped to kill off many of our people because they continued to practice the old ways and did not know that these diseases from Europe required other treatments.

During these epidemics people made pathetic appeals to Sweatlodge and jumped into the cold water with their very high temperatures and fevers. It was the same as committing suicide, and many died. Tuberculosis also took a heavy toll after my people gave up the fresh air of the tipi and showed their civilized progress by adopting the cabin with its airtight windows and doors. The secret of fresh air was lost, and my people became weaklings, no longer strong and straight like arrows molded from cradleboards and healthy living.

Yet to some extent we have tried to live in both worlds. An Indian knew he could be faithful to his native creed and still pray every day to the God of the whites. When in actual need from the troubles of the world, however, he did not hesitate to turn to the sweat lodge, never understanding how this could conflict with the white God, since the missionaries always said that God had many ways of helping people in distress.

When I returned from school in 1912, people said I was another Indian going back to the blanket because I saw no conflict between the old and new [creeds].[5] I used the sweat lodge and one day remarked to another woman that I was pleased to see such a staunch church member in the lodge. She was horrified at my suggestion that the two did not belong together and flung angry words at me in defense of her own beliefs.

"The Great Spirit gave the Indian the sweat house out of sympathy because they were poor in the knowledge of how to pray and ask for what the body needs. There was no evil in that. If I was committing evil against the God of the white man, I would quit praying in the sweat lodge immediately. If the priest thinks it is all right for me to sweat and pray to the God of my forefathers, why should a common person like you try to stop me? You are not a priest to know about such things."

Thus she rebuked me with scorn in a manner most uncharacteristic of my people. It was useless for me to try to explain my intent with the remark that started it all. The roots of her belief were so strong and deep that there was no point in my carrying the discussion any further. My people have always believed that all roads and rituals lead to a common spiritual result, and they saw no conflict among these different approaches.[6]

III. OKANOGAN HISTORY

CHAPTER 13

★

Tribal Backgrounds

FOUR TRIBES made up what is known as the Okanogan group-
ing: the Colvile (Swhy-ayl-puh), the Sanpoil (Snpo-i-il), the
Lakes (Si-na-aich-kis-tu), and the Okanogan. [All of them belong to
the Interior Salish division of the Salishan language family] and
speak closely related tongues, with dialect variations chiefly in
pronunciation.[1]

The Okanogan had two main divisions, the Upper or Lake Okanagan of British Columbia and the Lower or River Okanogan, now
on the Colville Reservation of north-central Washington State,
where Colvile and Sanpoil still occupy ancestral lands. Most Lakes
have also moved to this reservation, although a handful remain in
British Columbia.

Before whites arrived, all four tribes had an estimated population
of ten thousand or more. Today their combined population does not
exceed three thousand, with perhaps half this number being of
mixed blood.[2] [Along with other tribes they compose the modern
Colvilles.]

The ancient territory of the Colvile proper embraced that part of
the Columbia Valley extending from the mouth of the Spokane
River to the Arrow Lakes of British Columbia. They were considered rich because they had the good fortune to have the prime
fishery at Kettle Falls. The friendly Kalispel occupied the Pend

d'Oreille Valley to the east. On the west were the Okanogan from the mouth [of the river named for them] to the Shuswap Lakes of British Columbia and [all the way] west to the summit of the Cascade range. The Sanpoil had villages on the Sanpoil and Nespelem rivers, with a few settled on the Okanogan and Columbia rivers. They hunted south of the Columbia in the area now known as the Big Bend country. The Lakes were on Arrow Lakes primarily, but their villages and camps could also be found on Kootenay and Slocan lakes in British Columbia and in northern Stevens County in Washington.

These tribes intermarried a good deal, some links extending to the Kalispel, Spokan, Peskwaws (Wenatchi), Columbia (Grand Coulee), and Kootenay. Many of the Lake Okanagan found spouses among the Thompson and Shuswap. These interior tribes were held together by bonds of marriage, trade, visiting, and common interests. Long before they had horses, the Colvilles would sometimes join the Flathead to hunt buffalo in Blackfoot territory east of the Rockies.[3] They went in large numbers because there were frequent clashes with the Blackfeet, who were relentless enemies of the Salishans. Once people had horses, these bison hunts were combined with raids on the Blackfoot pony herds. When fortunate enough to get some horses, the camp [broke up quickly and kept going without rest] until west of the Rockies.

Buffalo robes were greatly prized for their long wear, so hunting expeditions onto the Plains would sometimes last a full year because of the great distance they had to go and the amount of time spent dodging enemy Blackfeet. Buffalo was called kwas-peet-za (curly haired), the same term meaning both the animal and the robe. Women would scrape the hides until they were dry, white, and smooth. These hides were used for bags, tobacco pouches, war cases, knife cases, arrow sacks [quivers], parfleches, and medicine [bundles]. Most important, they were used for body armor vests and shields against arrows. Earth and herbal paints were used to decorate them with family-tree symbols or events from tribal history.

Many years before whites arrived, the Colville and others decided to consolidate [in common cause] against frequent raids from other enemy tribes, such as the Shoshoni, Nez Perce, Shuswap, and Kootenay, who frequently invaded their valuable land. Their friendly allies were Salishan tribes such as the Kalispel, Spokan, Coeur d'Alene, Wenatchi [Peskwaws], Moses-Columbian (Grand Coulee), and Flathead. The Colvile would join the Flathead to poach buffalo in Blackfoot territory.

Each tribe took its home identity from the site of the winter villages. The typical Okanogan and Colvile winter house had a [domed roof and] rounded ends. It was built on cleared, unexcavated ground. Three to eight pairs of long poles formed the frame, tied at the top with twisted willow shoots. This row of inverted Vs was formed by the pairs set about ten feet apart. Stringers were fastened across these, a foot or so below the apex, then lighter poles, eighteen to twenty inches apart, were leaned against the ridgepole from both sides and tied to the stringers. A stout pole was leaned against each end, in the half-tipi style. Then this frame was "shingled" with layers of tule mats, tied at intervals, but leaving the top ridge line open for light to enter and smoke to escape. If available, fir boughs were laid along the bottom, then two-foot strips of bark, and finally a layer of dirt. Mats covered the doorway. Lodges varied between twenty and sixty feet in length, occupied by as many as eight families. Two families used the space between each of the uprights, living on opposite sides of a fire. A corridor about four feet wide ran down the middle, with fires along the center. The floor, along the sides, was covered with tule mats, robes, blankets, and boughs. People slept with head to the wall and feet toward the fire. The rounded ends were used for storing food.

These were the ancient winter dwellings, not pithouses, as some have said. The old people told me that the Okanogan did not use pithouses until the Nicola introduced them.[4] The Colvile had no pithouses because none of the Nicola took up residence there.

Just when the Nicola entered Okanogan country cannot be determined. Reliable people have told me it was not so very long before the first whites came, probably toward the close of the eighteenth century. All agree the Nicola came from the south, and [they may have been] a "lost" band of Wasco-Wishram, Chinookan living around the Dalles neighborhood of the Columbia River.

Modesta, an aged Okanogan woman, told me the legend of the Nicola. "They were a people from the south who left their homeland on account of a quarrel that started when two men argued over what caused the soft, whistling, whisperlike sound made by a flock of geese in flight. One man said the noise came from their wings flapping, the other that it came from their bills. People took sides. Finally the issue was submitted to the chief, who decided the noise was made through the bill. This angered the man who thought it was caused by the wings. A council was called to consider the question, and it decided for the bill. The man still believed in the wing. His relatives and friends got angry with the chief and council too, so they packed up and left the tribe. They [went up] the Columbia, traveling slowly, stopping for a year at one place after another. None was satisfactory. At the mouth of the Okanogan River, they turned upstream and turned again into the Similkameen Valley under the grandeur of Mount Chopaka. There Okanogan people treated them well, better than any other tribe they met. So the Strange People (En-koh-tu-me-whoh) stayed, intermarried, and learned the language. Their women were fair and pretty. In return, they taught the use of pithouses (qua-zee'ah).

These were eight feet deep and fifteen to twenty feet in diameter, accommodating two or three families. Tops were conical in shape, made with pole rafters covered by matting, grass, bark, and six inches of packed soil. A roof hole [hatch] served as doorway and smokehole. A tree trunk with branch stubs protruded through the opening and served as the ladder. As it was inconvenient [and immodest] for women to go in and out, they stayed home and sent children for necessities like wood and water. Water was carried in tightly woven baskets, lowered into the house with ropes. Women did not drink much, so they would not have to leave the house often. A tiny fire kept the underground house warm and comfortable.

After some time, the Nicola finally wanted a home of their own and found it at Douglas Lake. Today they only use a few words of their original language.

In 1932 I met John Poke, a Wasco about sixty years old. He confirmed the Nicola migration story. "When I was a boy, my grandmother used to tell me we had relatives who left after an argument about how geese made a noise while flying. My ancestors knew they went north, but where they settled we do not know." When I related the Nicola legend about the Spider, told by my father sprinkled with Nicola words, Poke understood perfectly. Both he and his wife said that Spider story was one of their own tribal tales.

When Lewis and Clark made their famous exploration, they did not reach Okanogan territory, but my people heard many stories of white-skinned strangers who wintered at the mouth of the Columbia.[5] The stories came from the south—from Yakima who told Wenatchi [Peskwaws], who told Okanogan. Living between the two tribes who spoke such different languages, the Wenatchi were usually able to speak both the Sahaptian Yakima and other languages more closely related to their own Salish tongue.

The first white explorer to enter our country was David Thompson of the Northwest Company of Montreal, a rival in the fur trade with the great Hudson's Bay Company.[6] Thompson came down the Columbia River in the late spring of 1811 and arrived at the falls while people were busy with the chinook/king salmon run. He saw fish traps lining both sides of the river. My great-grandfather, Chief See-whehl-ken, welcomed this small party of travelers, including several half-breeds, which my people had never seen before. As a good host, he gave them the finest salmon. Thompson called my ancestor by the name Big Heart, apparently because he had trouble pronouncing his real native name.[7] He named our fishery Ilthkoyope Falls, staying there long enough to construct another boat to take him the rest of the way down the river.

The same summer, representatives from the Pacific Fur Company of John Jacob Astor established a trading post at Fort Okanogan, at that river mouth.[8] This was about one hundred miles from Kettle Falls. My people began to hunt and trap fur-bearing animals and trade them for guns, cloth, blankets, and trinkets. Eventually they began to think of these as necessities.

During the War of 1812, the Northwest Company acquired the American Fur Company and all its trading posts.[9] In 1821 the Northwest Company merged with Hudson's Bay, which began a post at Kettle Falls in 1825 named for Andrew Colvile, London governor of the company.[10] The name of the fort was transferred to my tribe by usage over time. Before then, visitors knew us by several names. Early French-Canadian trappers called us les Chaudieres (the Kettles) and the Americans knew us as the Kettle, Bucket, Cauldron, and Pot Indians. Always we were linked with the falls, probably because the foaming and boiling of the water in the potholes below the falls reminded people of huge kettles cooking. We called these depressions klek-chin because they looked like our cooking baskets.[11]

Our ancient name for the big falls was Swah-netk-qhu, which I wish had been retained. It was rendered by early whites as Sionetkwu, Schwankoo, or Schwan-ate-koo.

When Fort Colville was established, the traders assured my people they were not after land but only exchanging furs for goods. When some of the company began to farm some of the fertile bottomland, the Indians did not object. There was much trust in the hearts of my people. If anyone had become suspicious of losing their country, I am sure there would have been a massacre.

Chief See-whehl-ken exerted a strong influence on maintaining cordial relations, encouraging his men to hunt and trap for the post so whites would gain confidence in his people. When he died about 1840, both races mourned him deeply, and the memory of his generosity, kindness, and good deeds lived on for many years. He left no sons to take his place as head of the tribe, and his three daughters had male children who were still too young. The tribal council therefore elected his nephew, Kinkanawah, to take office as the closest eligible male relative.

In 1842 the famous Jesuit Pierre Jean De Smet came to the fort to buy seed for his new mission of St. Mary's on the Bitterroot River among the Flathead.[12] After he finished his business at the post, he visited the fishery and was surprised to hear the Indians saying prayers in Flathead (Salish) and trying to sing Latin hymns. This mystery was explained to him when people told him about Ignace Saxa, one of Thompson's boatmen locally known as En-yas. He was a half-Iroquois from eastern Canada who married a Flathead woman. He recalled the prayers and rituals he had been taught by Jesuits as a child and in turn taught them to his own and other children. Thus he converted many to Catholicism long before there were any actual missionaries in the Northwest.[13]

Chief Kinkanawah welcomed Father De Smet, later known as Kwy-lux (Black Robe-Gown), who stayed at the fishery for several days before going downriver to Fort Vancouver to successfully convert many of the coastal people. Before he left, Kinkanawah was converted and christened Pierre Jerome. Also converted was the chief of the Arrow Lakes, Martin Ilemux-solux (Chief of All). When he left, De Smet promised to urge his superiors to send priests to the Colvile, and three years later, in the summer of 1845, Father Anthony Ravalli arrived to build, with Indian help, the chapel of St. Paul a short distance northeast of the falls.[14] Some say it was a log cabin, but in 1930, shortly before she died at the age of 105, Old Lady Marchand said the first chapel was made entirely of cedar bark. Soon after the chapel was done, Father Ravalli left.

In 1847 Father Peter De Vos arrived, and people helped him build the mission of St. Francis Regis with log walls, a shake roof, and a floor of lumber whipsawed at the fort.[15] The fasteners were wooden pegs instead of iron nails. This church was a mile southwest of the town of Ward. There my parents were christened as infants and married as adults. It was our place of worship for a quarter of a century, abandoned only when a frame church was built in 1872. Later the old church burned down, but the ruins can still be seen.

Old Indians remember that the frame church was put up soon after the great 1872 earthquake. While many Indians had joined the church before this, most still held to their native beliefs and were derelict in the observance of Catholic teachings. My father was eight then, and he said the earth began to tremble and rock violently, sounding like big trees cracking. Boulders rolled down hillsides, fissures opened in the ground, and some tipis collapsed. People were panic stricken, fearing the end of the world was at hand. Inveterate gamblers threw away their gaming [pieces] and tried [desperately] to say what few prayers they remembered. People confessed to one another in public without shame. The tremors recurred with diminishing intensity and violence for three days. During that time my people stayed close to the priests. The Black Robes had no difficulty making lifelong Colvile and Okanogan converts at that time.[16]

The Colville remained at peace with the whites due to the influence of the Hudson's Bay Company and the Jesuits. One of the most influential men to hold the position of chief trader at Fort Colville was Angus McDonald, known as Whoop-chen (Hair on the Chin) because of his heavy red beard.[17] He was considerate and kind. His wife was a Flathead woman named Catherine. Some of our women helped care for their children and household because they had such a large family. In return, she taught us to eat clabbered milk sweetened with sugar, a dish regarded as a great luxury.

Kinkanawah always went to McDonald for advice on matters of tribal policy, which included staying out of the 1855 Yakima War and the 1858 Spokan War. Our first official contact with America came in December of 1855 when Isaac Ingalls Stevens, first governor of Washington Territory and acting superintendent of Indian affairs, met with several tribal leaders on the Little Spokane River.[18] He had already visited Fort Colville in October 1853 on his way from the East to the territorial capital at Olympia. When he arrived, Mrs.

McDonald made a nice supper of steaks cooked in buffalo fat for him and for Brevet Captain George McClellan, who was exploring in the vicinity and would also return a few years later.[19]

Stevens found the Indians "well disposed and religious." There were twenty-eight miles of settlements in the Colville Valley, most inhabited by former Hudson's Bay Company retainers who wished to be naturalized and gain legal title to their improvements.

When Stevens held his famous treaty council at Walla Walla from 29 May to 11 June 1855, Chief Kinkanawah was there as a spectator. Six thousand Nez Perce, Cayuse, Walla Walla, Umatilla, Yakima, Klickitat, and others were assembled. Three treaties were made, and three reservations were set aside in return for more than sixty thousand square miles of ceded territory.

Afterward, Stevens went to the Bitterroot Valley to treat with the Flathead, Kootenay, and Upper Pend d'Oreille. Then he went to the mouth of the Judith River in Montana to treat with the Blackfeet and worked out a truce between them and the Flathead and Nez Perce.

On the way back he received word that Yakima, Cayuse, Walla Walla, Umatilla, Klickitat, Palus, and some coast tribes had gone to war against the whites. His party then paused at the Little Spokane for three days to meet with the Spokan, Colville, and Coeur d'Alene to keep them from joining in the war. Trader McDonald and the Jesuits were also invited to the conference. Stevens met with Chief Jerome Kinkanawah and his tribe during a council at the falls. They could not reach an agreement for a treaty. The Indians were reluctant to sign because so many were away for spring root digging that the council was not representative. Stevens promised many things, saying, "This is your land. No white man shall take it away from you without your consent." This impressed everyone, and the treaty was postponed for a later time. But this never happened because shortly after this meeting Stevens went to war against other Indian tribes. He was killed fighting other Americans in the Civil War.

The Yakima asked for help, and Chief Jerome consulted with the

Jesuits, who advised him to stay out of the war and remain peaceful. He asked McDonald, who told him the same. The Interior Salish stayed neutral, keeping out of the way and hidden until the fighting was over. Only later did the Spokan become angry with the military sent into their country, and they defeated a group of soldiers in 1858.

Before Stevens could return, he was called east by the 1860 Civil War, and he died with great honor for his country at the Battle of Chantilly. The Indians did not get this news for many years, so the old people continued to wait for him. By then they had learned to eat white food, since corn and potatoes were issued to them when winters were severe and food was short.

In 1846 a treaty was signed between America and Canada, but their common border was not surveyed until 1857, when a large group of officials and Canadian soldiers arrived at Fort Colville. They selected a spot north of the fort and built log huts of thick jack pines. These headquarters were on the south bank of the Columbia four miles from the fishery. Unfortunately, these Canadians were thirty miles too far south according to the 1859 American Boundary Commission with George McClellan. These soldiers cut a swath through the thick virgin forest without asking the Colville, leaving an open space sixty feet wide, running east to west through the center of our lands. Wherever a trail crossed this space, piles of rock were left to mark the line.

Perhaps if Chief Kinkanawah had known that the postponement and the lack of angry response to trespass was going to cost our people their land, he would have been more firm and demanding of the whites. It was characteristic of Indians to have many talks and conferences before deciding on any business and putting the decision into effect. A chief usually liked to have all members present and satisfied. He was still waiting for consensus when the government declared the rich land of the Chewelah and Colville valleys open for settlement.

Our tribes lacked land of their own until 1872 when President

Grant proclaimed boundaries for the six tribes, using the Columbia River as the border on the east and south. The Okanogan River set the western one, and the International Boundary with Canada was the one for the north.[20] The Colvile had to move west across the Columbia, leaving their beautiful lands for rough and rocky ones more suitable for deer hunting than for farming. The Okanogan had to move east to the benches covered with sagebrush where bitterroot grew abundantly.

My people did not farm and had no use for crops until the fish runs began to disappear from the streams and rivers. White activities causing pollution, and commercial fishing projects were the cause of this. Every year the Colville found fewer salmon to take, not enough to live on, and so began to turn to farming to stay alive. Finally, dams were built on the Columbia and the salmon were stopped altogether from coming above the Grand Coulee. The salmon were gone, and high-powered rifles are doing about the same to our game animals.[21] By the time we saw the need to farm, the younger generation realized that their ancestors had let the whites have the richest and most fertile of our bottomland, and it was too late to get it back.

For many years the old people waited for the return of Stevens to set the record straight. They still believed in the traditional law that held everyone responsible to honor their word once it was given. Indians were used to leaders who served for life and did not know that the Great White Father in Washington changed every four years and that laws were constantly being rewritten by Congress.

My people were waiting in a humane and patient fashion for promises to be honored and justice done; waiting until the sun had set on the natives of this great nation.

When the Colville Indian Association was organized in February 1931, Chief C. B. Suzen Timentwa strongly opposed it and tried to have his Okanogan people reject the new form of government intended to replace the chiefs of old.[22] His efforts were in vain; the young, educated, and mixed-blood generation brought it about. The older people stayed staunchly with him, and a generational split developed on the reservation.

This chief was selected by the Okanogan in 1915 to fill the vacancy left by the death of the venerable Chief Swimptkin, whose son had died shortly before him and whose two grandsons were too young. Timentwa was not descended from chiefs, but his family gained prominence when his great-aunt Sara married Alexander Ross, the trader at Fort Okanogan. During the fourteen years they lived there, they had four children. In May 1825 Ross [sent] his oldest son Alex along with Spokan Garry and Kootenay Pelly to the Red River settlement to be educated. Later that year Sara and the other children moved [there] too, and the Okanogan never saw her again.[23] The Timentwa family remains suspicious of white husbands ever since, fearing they would desert the children or take the wife away.[24]

CHAPTER 14

★

The Big Snow
and Flood Rampage
of 1892-1893

W E WERE settling in our winter home when the men decided to take the ponies far into the heart of the reservation so they could graze on the lush grass there and get fat before the snow came.[1] Most of Father's horses were of the cayuse type, much smaller than regular horses but with greater endurance, able to work long and hard on meager food. They were almost as vigorous as the deer of the forest and could live on the same foods.

In previous years, Father took his ponies thirty-five miles up the Kettle River in Canada. The Canadians did not think it was worth the effort to set up a customs office along the Indian trail, though there had been one at Lake Osoyoos since 1860. Hence we could come and go as we pleased. The pasture was located at the first big bend of the river in an open valley with rocky cliffs and small boulders. It got less snow than other areas, or perhaps the numerous rocks helped to melt the snow faster and keep the bunchgrass clear for feeding animals.

The men gathered their fat, sleek horses into a log corral. The ponies snorted and frisked, with quivering nostrils and wild eyes. Father smiled with satisfaction when his herd left the corral, kicking and playing. The hair of my pinto shone in the late fall sunshine glistening off the crusted snow. On the day set, the men moved the horses to the winter pasture and returned on foot three days later, resigned to stay around camp for the long days of winter. Cooking utensils and saddles were cached at the pasture in preparation for spring roundup. After their return, the men had a holiday, their hard work done for the year. Some of the old men made holes in the ice at the edge of the river and fished, while others helped the women gather firewood. The men seldom carried water, as that was considered a chore for women and children.

Before the snow, Sulee and I played with the other children, making tipis out of the thick green moss that carpeted rocks beside the creek. When the snow deepened, we amused ourselves by climbing young saplings and swinging back and forth. We used to see who could climb highest and spy the fishery that most of us called home.

The long and tedious winter evenings were devoted to visiting and feasting, and it was the proper time to tell stories, legends, and sagas. The old people told their families about past tribal customs, laws, habits, and wars. In the quiet of winter, much of our important traditional knowledge was passed on to a willing audience. Our tipi was a favorite gathering place because my parents were generous hosts. As a child I found the stories monotonous, but I always stayed awake beside my father.

We children played in our section of the tipi until visitors came; then we were hushed and told to sit quietly and listen while our elders conversed. We were not allowed to ask questions or interrupt the conversation.

The snow came down slowly at first, but by midwinter it filled the sky and ground with a vengeance. It was as high as my father's knees. Blinding white sheets came down faster every day until it was waist deep by the time of the church holidays at St. Regis Mission. We were anxious to celebrate Christmas (First Shoot) Day. The day before, some Indians crossed the river in canoes and walked on foot with backpacks of blankets and food to spend the night at the mission. My mother went with them, but Sulee and I stayed home with Father. The holiday continued until Last Shoot Day or New Year, when guns were also fired at midnight.

A few days after, father grew worried about his horses, laced on snowshoes early one morning, and put on his pack to trek to the pasture. He was gone for more than a week, returning sad and disheartened. After walking for two days, he had made a desperate attempt to save the ponies in the deep snow, but to no avail. The horses were pawing up the snow, but it was too deep and crusted for them to reach the grass. They were starving when he reached them. For a week he used a slab of wood to try to expose enough feed for all of them, but he could not. He was especially concerned about my pinto, but by then my pony was too thin to save. Father lost his fine herd of horses.[2]

We were not the only ones hard hit that winter. Everyone lost their herds, whites and Indians alike. The deer came down low and tried desperately to survive the long, cold winter.[3] Many of them starved beside the Columbia. They were at the mercy of Indians on snowshoes. The small hoofs of the deer sank into the crusted snow, burying them to the belly, where they were easily taken by hunters. From this and other small favors, Indians were able to keep somewhat happy and indifferent to fate for the rest of the winter. People became restless only at the first signs of spring when the snow began to thaw.

Just before spring, hundreds of deer died, unable to exist on tree moss, pine needles, or bush tops. Game was very scarce for the next several years. In the Buttercup Moon (March), Father dressed me warmly and sent me outdoors to play until he said I could come home. He said my mother was ill. It was a very windy day that shook the tipis in the slushy snow, but the sun was shining. I went out and joined a group of children riding down a nearby hillside using mats with bark runners as sleds. We had great fun, but our moccasins got wet. While some used the sleds, the rest of us scrambled over the ice sheet to bare patches to pick the buttercups just coming into bloom. Spring was in the air, and we were happy.

Some of the children wandered farther into the deep ravines to jump into the snowdrifts there. They worked hard to extract themselves until they reached safety at the edges, laughing the whole time. Our parents seemed indifferent to our health, since they let us stay in our wet moccasins. Every spring was the same as we came home soaking wet, covered with snow and mud, and gathered around the central fire to get dry. Yet their indifference seemed justified, because we never caught cold. We were very happy and free. We did not go to school and set our own schedules, playing and eating when we wanted. We had pure, clean air both outside and inside the tipi. We lived among friends and relations, free to enter every home and eat there.

Late that evening, Father called me from one of these homes. As we entered the doorway of the tipi, I heard a funny noise that sounded like a baby crying. Then I saw a wee babe in my mother's arms and appreciated that we had a new member of the family and I had another sister.[4] She was tiny, with a wrinkled face that I liked to watch as her mouth opened in search of food. It reminded me of the little birds my friends had found the summer before. Sulee cried from the grief she suffered at the tragedy of being replaced as the youngest in the family.

Father always wanted a son, so his disappointment was great when this third daughter arrived. She was given Keleta as a pet name. This was the last in a series of disappointments Father had that spring. He had lost his horses, his food rack was disappearing, and his family increased. He lost his jovial spirit and looked sad, [brooding around the tipi]. He did not laugh or talk as much as before.

The snow slowly melted away, but the nights would freeze the water into ice to thaw in the sun of the next day. The ground was bare in spots.

Early one morning I overheard my parents talking. They decided the family should stay in the winter camp while Father went across the river to the white towns to seek work. This was necessary because we had no horses or ponies to carry all of us to another place. The rest of the day, he prepared for his departure. The next morning he put on clean clothing and gave what few coins he had to Mother. He had no blankets or food, nor did he have a destination. He was desperate and in need of food for his family.

After he left, Mother held Keleta to her breast and cried in silence. Sulee and I did not understand any of this and so played around the dying embers of our fire. She had always been generous to the poor and needy with our food. All winter long she had given away some of the food Father had saved the previous summer. Father said nothing because he also believed in helping the needy. That was the reason we were short of food before the spring plants were ready.

It was only when I was much older that I realized the sacrifices made by my gentle mother. She would cook a very small piece of venison and divide it equally into three pieces. Sulee and I would swallow ours almost whole. Mother would then divide the third piece again and go without any food for herself. I did not stop to wonder why she fed the baby after each meal with tears in her eyes. It was because she was hungry. Our childish selfishness did not understand that our mother was going without to keep us alive while she yet had to nurse a third. My heart aches with remorse as I write this. She died long before I realized any of this, and now I cannot ask her to forgive me for being so selfish. When we cried for food, she could only turn her back to the fire, away from us, and weep quietly. While neighbor women were complaining and [broadcasting their troubles], Mother remained silent. She never complained of her ailments or misfortunes and never aired her troubles in public.

Mother was a reserved woman, almost to the point of coldness, and many people misunderstood her aloofness and the hidden warmth of her character. She had a heart of gold that showed only to the poor and unfortunate. I knew her to give away our own food to the needy so that we went without for a time. It was the way she and Father were raised, and they had watched their own parents do the same.

When all our food was gone, Mother did the next best thing. She dressed us each morning and bathed the baby before lacing her into the cradleboard. She took her digging stick and led us to the hillsides to dig up the tender shoots of the balsam sunflower and feed them to us. We did this for two weeks until the shoots were high enough to develop a thin skin that had to be peeled off. These shoots were called "famine food" because they were the first fresh food available each spring.[5] It tasted like celery and was considered an aid to digestion. It was best mixed with other food and meat because a steady diet of it was not healthy.

One day Mother led us up the Kettle River to gather mussels from the shoals to eat with the shoots. Back home she buried the shells under the fire to bake in the sandy loam. Even so, they were tough and we had to work very hard to chew them. Still, we enjoyed this change of food.

Mother trapped ground squirrels when they first emerged from their burrows after winter hibernation. Groundhogs were fatter but had a stronger scent than the squirrels. They were a luxury we all enjoyed. As always, Mother divided our catch with the old people in camp. We also ate tree squirrels and all kinds of birds Mother snared with a hemp string.

That spring of 1893 everyone was starving. Those who were able-bodied had moved on in seach of food, work, or money. We were stranded in camp with the old and feeble because of our lack of horses.

Early one morning I awakened to hear the singing of meadow-larks. I had had no supper, and my stomach ached for food. I could not abide the happy sound of the "tattler" of legend and began to cry quietly to myself. By now I had learned to be patient and not complain, for it was useless to share my grief with Mother. She remained true to her education and was stoic with everyone. Mother did this even with her own children, never cuddling us or saying soft words. I was [a bit] afraid of her and in consequence held her words in great respect.

Yet that day my mother was very kind and understanding. She interrupted my tears by saying, "What is the matter Kee-ten?" using my pet name. It was too much to bear, and I told her I was hungry and lonesome for Father. I heard her sigh as she got up to start the fire. I got up quickly, dried my eyes, and warmed myself at the fire. We said nothing else, but we had shared our sorrow.

Mother dressed Sulee and the baby in clean but worn clothes, better than we wore for every day. I wondered why we were wearing them but was afraid to ask. My questions or inquisitiveness were always rebuked because it was not the Indian way to learn anything.[6]

Instead, I waited to see what would happen. When we were dressed and ready, Mother placed the cradleboard with Keleta on her back, and we went directly across the river in a fragile canoe lent to us for the trip to Marcus. Mother placed her daughters on the bottom and paddled from the stern. With each dip of the oar, the boat leaped forward. Mother was expert with a canoe, and we went in speedy safety.

At the little city of Marcus, we followed Mother from one house to another as she knocked on the back door to ask for food for her family. At each door she was refused admittance and would silently leave while Sulee begged and cried for food in our language. Perhaps this prevented whites from learning the true nature of our distress. By afternoon the sun beat on my bare head and I felt weak [from hunger]. Mother stopped in the shade of some jack pines near three lone houses set in this shade. She rested there for some time before she determined to go to the door of a house where we could hear men and woman laughing hilariously.

A woman came to the door wearing a long dress with many ruffles along the bottom and her hair curled and piled high in a roll behind her head. Her smile was sweet and dimpled. She was beautiful, with pink skin, red lips, eyes as blue as the sky. Mother talked to her and she nodded. She came outside and shut the door, giving each of us children a pat on the head. Then she went back inside and returned with some fluffy, lacy clothing for my mother to wash and mend. She also brought out some bread and food that Sulee and I ate in haste under the jack pines.

Out of respect for the dead and their kind deeds, I will not use the real name of this woman but will supply a substitute. The city of Marcus was filled with nice churchgoers who did not believe in associating with a prostitute like Nellie. She made her money from providing the nightlife in the sleepy little burg of Marcus, a character of the Gay Nineties with a kind heart who was shunned by the decent society of this pioneer town. Yet she alone was willing to help and provide our salvation until Father returned. Every week Mother went to get washing and mending from Nellie and returned with food and spare clothing. Mother had no idea where or how Father was. She could only wait for him patiently and continue to support the family by digging roots, trapping animals, and doing laundry. She never stopped dividing our food with those less fortunate, even though the worst was yet to come.

As the days passed and the spring sun melted the snow, the Columbia rose with increasing speed until it became a roaring and ferocious monster. One morning Mother shook me awake because the water was at our doorway. I helped her gather up our most necessary possessions, and we escaped to higher ground. Mother went back and forth all day to move everything to safety. She also helped the old people move away from the flood. She did not rest until everyone was safe on higher benchland.

Within a few days the river rose to threaten us again, and we had to move up farther to be safe. It was a sight I will never forget. We children stood in a group while driftwood and other debris passed by our tipi. It was so dense that nothing could get across. It included whole trees, houses, barns, chicken coops, fence rails, intact haystacks, and ferryboats. Some of the homes were complete even to the floors. Once a chicken coop went by with a rooster and some hens sitting on the roof. As it passed close to the bank, the rooster

10. Situated along the Columbia River below Grand
Coulee Dam, this forty-foot tree with wood debris lodged
midway along its trunk testifies to the kind of flooding
described in this chapter. Photo taken about 1978–79,
editor's collection.

crowed. All these things were destined to be smashed to splinters at
the falls just below.

The flood went on for some time before the water receded. The
high water left grayish rings around the pine trees as high as fifteen
feet above the ground. These marks were evident for years, bearing
witness to the force of the destruction.

The Creator had been kind to provide the famine food that got us
through the early spring as it had our ancestors for eons before. But
nature had whims of its own, playing havoc with the property of
Indians and whites who lived along the Columbia. The big snow
destroyed all the ponies, preventing us from seaching for food, and
the melting snow caused the rampage that wiped out everything
else. We had to start over and became stronger than before as a

result. Anyone who had food or a warm place shared it with others so that all might survive.

Father returned to plant a garden, but when harvest time came he had to borrow tools to bring it in. When he began to build up his herds again, he needed hay and had to borrow a scythe and wooden rake to collect bunchgrass. He could not find a wagon to borrow to haul it, so he devised a pole sled to haul it to storage. His only remaining personal tool was an ax, and he used it to start a new log cabin. This was too slow, and my parents decided that my father would go back to working at Fort Steele in British Columbia until he could save enough money to start over.

All of this was hard work, but the important lesson for us all during that time of hardship was that we could best survive by working together. We learned the important thing about being Indians was the willingness to share whatever we had and the determination to survive with renewed intent and wisdom after any calamity.[7]

CHAPTER 15

★

Early Farming

AFTER the bad winter and flood, ponies and game were gone and families were confused. That spring, some people began to attempt to farm in earnest for the first time. My people loved the free life and were reluctant to stay in one place.

Only a few had started farms on a crude scale. Most had gardens full of potatoes and weeds. Some had fields of wheat and oats surrounded by split-rail fences. This grain was used to feed horses, and the women threshed the wheat by hand or by driving horses over it. Then it was [winnowed] from dishpans. The kernels were boiled until soft, with tallow flavoring and a little flour thickening. This dish was as common as beans are today.

The rails had been carried on human or pony backs. These fences were made of nine rails piled on top of each other like a log cabin, with two posts in an X shape [at the junctures]. No nails or staples were used; some used twisted willows to tie the fences together.

It was more convenient for people to plant little plots of grain and potatoes secured from the ponies by fences, tie the cabin door with a buckskin string, and leave to follow everyone living on the chase.

After the hard winter we moved to Pia, about ten miles north of the fishery. It had a wide sidehill and many little stretches of bench-land heavily covered with bunchgrass. Pia means "bald eagle," and many of them nested on the cliffs north of the treeless sidehill.[1]

We made camp close to a spring in a ravine, surrounded with birch, alder, willow, and aspen. The water was hard and full of alkali. Soap did not lather up there, but the soil was a rich loam and the bunchgrass was taller than my head as a child. There were no trees for fence posts around the hill, and springs oozed everywhere. The climate was wet, and flowers, weeds, and grass grew abundantly. Our ponies could not eat it all.

Some native families had homesteaded on a bench three-quarters of a mile below us. They had built three or four little huts near a small church founded by the Jesuits, who held services there occasionally. People had set out little gardens and fences, as the priests had encouraged. They had learned to relish vegetables at St. Regis school.[2] They worked with shovels, and one or two had wagons with wooden wheels made from tree cross sections with a hole bored through the middle to hold the axle. The huts had no stoves; heating and cooking were done by means of fireplaces with clay chimneys [chinked] with bunchgrass and stones.

Gardens were planted with a shovel. Very few people had the money to buy secondhand plows from the settlers across the Columbia. Most of our people did not raise chickens, swine, or cattle. The many ponies ran wild and unbranded like deer. Stock raising hindered people from roaming after the wild harvest and attending festivals. Favorite horses had ears cropped or manes roached or tails clipped for identification.

Horse thieves were unknown. Anyone suspected was openly criticized and laughed at with scorn.[3] His family was disgraced and constantly reminded of the deed. Only recently has stealing become a problem, as the young have learned the flaws of the whites. At school they learned about constitutional rights and the need to prove evidence and call witnesses. It is no wonder that some elders kept their children from school, having seen that a good education sometimes forgot honesty and morality.

It was not unusual for people to store their food and extra clothing in their cabins and tie the door with a buckskin string. A lock was needless. Neighbors knew their property and respected it. If the fence broke while they were away, someone would repair it. If someone needed food, he took it, either mentioning or offering compensation for it when the family returned. If the crop was threatened by wind or weather, neighbors harvested it. Colville lived in friendship and harmony.

[Father set about making his farm.] He managed to borrow a hand scythe and a large wooden rake to harvest his bunchgrass for hay. As he mowed it down in gullies and meadows, Mother came behind him to rake it [into heaps] for hauling. Father had to take off his shirt, it got so sweaty from bending over to make back-and-forth hand strokes at a slow pace. When they were done, they were dismayed to learn they could not borrow a wagon. Eventually Father made a "stone boat" or "go devil." He cut two curved wooden poles for runners and made a platform of poles tied across these with heated and twisted red willows.[4] He had no wire or nails. My parents used it to make two haystacks.

From the ravine with the spring, he cut posts to make a fence around each stack. He hauled each post with a long rawhide rope tied to the saddle pommel, and the cayuse pulled it uphill. This was tedious, but Father was never easily discouraged. He did not fear work, and he was strong and healthy then.

The site he selected for our log cabin was two miles north of the haystacks. He had only an ax to cut the logs, and he worked for many days cutting and hewing them. When they were ready, he rode around the neighborhood to borrow a wagon to haul them to the site. His borrowing expedition was a failure. There was no wagon or harness strong enough to get the logs out of the brushy woods and up the steep hillside.

Instead of getting disheartened, my parents talked it over and decided that Father should search for work that winter. Because he had previously cut cordwood there, he went to Fort Steele, British Columbia.

The leaves were all gone off the trees and the late fall was cold when we moved camp again. Mother stored extra food and clothing on a high scaffold near the haystacks, which were settling lower from all the fall rain.

My parents said good-bye to our new neighbors, and we started on another traveling adventure. My parents had made many trips to the Kootenay country, where my grandmother lived, so we took the shortest route to Fort Steele. At the little town of Bossburg, an Indian named Adolph took us across the Columbia in an unusually long dugout canoe, made in the Arrow Lake pattern.[5] Adolph belonged to that tribe and was well qualified as a canoe maker. It was roomy enough to take all our things across in one load. Then the men came back to take the horses across. Sulee and I had a lot of fun watching the old bay and her six-month-old colt swim the river. The dugout followed behind its little head. We were glad when mare and colt arrived safely.

After the pack animals were loaded, father took the lead, as usual, holding the rope on the oldest mare. The other horses naturally followed the old mother and colt. The family caravan came next, and I had a lot of fun riding back and forth between Mother at the end and Father at the front. Some of the boys wanted to go to British Columbia with us, but Father would not encourage them, fearing they would get homesick before spring.

We followed the mountainous trail till it branched toward the Kalispel country. We saw many deer and other animals along the way. Father wanted to stop and hunt, but Mother thought it was too late in the season to cure meat. So he killed blue grouse and pheasants as we needed fresh food. Eventually we reached Kalispel living by the Pend d'Oreille River at their winter encampment across the river from Cusick, Washington.[6] The following day some of them joined our caravan as far as Bonner's Ferry, Idaho, the home of most Lower Kootenay. Instead of going to the Indian camp, we stayed the night with the Frye family.

Dick Frye was a white married to a Colvile woman, Suesteel, my grandmother's first cousin, who was pleased to see my mother. She was fluent in Colvile and Kootenay but awkward in English. She was godmother at my christening, but this was my first meeting with her. [As a token of our bond,] she gave me the cutest gold earrings shaped like women's old-fashioned high-button shoes. She pierced my ears with a thornberry needle and left the earrings there so my ears could heal around the openings. A rather small woman, she must have been beautiful in her youth when Richard married her. She raised many children; the girls were beautiful with fair skin, dark hair, and jet-gleamed eyes. They all learned to speak our language, although they never lived close to the tribe. Frye was a pioneer in Idaho, highly regarded in regional history.

They became my godparents after I was born en route to their tree-shaded home, overlooking the Kootenay River. Their land was fine, and they were well-to-do.

The next day, we crossed the river below their house and headed due north through Moya and what is now Cranbrook.[7] Finally we crossed the river to Fort Steele, and Father found a job cutting wood for his former employer, Major Steele, who was in charge of the barracks of Canadian soldiers.[8] We moved into the virgin timber and joined other families cutting wood on contract, but Father was considered the best of them.

The mining town of Fort Steele was still booming because, although placer gold was extinct, quartz claims were paying well.[9]

I heard a story I could never confirm about this area. Some Kootenay were on a fall hunting trip, far back in the mountains. Around the camp they found some black, shining rocks. While supper was cooking, a man kicked one of these rocks into the fire to level out the ground for his bed. Instantly, the rock began to burn. The curious Indians took samples back to the mining town. One man offered a Kootenay a new plaid shirt and blanket if he would point out the place the rock came from. For this meager pay, the miner found the very rich coalfield at Fernie, British Columbia.

[Father worked hard that winter but was paid well. In the spring, we went back to the homestead. From Fort Steele, we took a] direct trail leading to Spokane. There my parents bought many things, but the most important were a shiny red wagon, a set of stout harnesses, and two stoves. The cookstove had two oven doors much beflowered with cast-iron ornaments. Each flower had a round yellow center. The heater stove was an old-fashioned box affair. Mother got a hoe, rack, and cooking utensils for the new stove. The storekeeper induced her to buy them.

Our ponies had hardly been in harness, so some white men helped Father hitch up some cayuses to the wagon, which was loaded with our purchases, the parfleches off the bay mare, and the pack saddle. When Father took the reins, the horses ran like wildfire across the Spokane Bridge. Mother and I followed on horseback, driving the rest of the pack animals. I vividly remember that Mother paid with a gold piece at the toll bridge. My mind could not understand that she got more money back than she had given. She tried to explain that gold was more valuable than silver, but my mind did not comprehend the difference. When we camped that evening north of Spokane, Father was amused by this.

The road was rough and rocky, [barely] a trail to Marcus. The Colville Reservation had no roads at all. Mother and I had a hard time staying with Father in the wagon, or even keeping him in sight. Father could not coax Mother to ride in the wagon. She had never ridden in one before and was afraid. Nor would she let any of her children ride in it. Three days out from Spokane, we arrived in Marcus.

Instead of taking the usual canoe across, we rode the flat-bottomed ferry operated by Bob Baily. The ferry was rowed by two to four men with long paddles at the front. The big boat was pulled upsteam by a saddlehorse until it caught the current across. When the wagon was put aboard, the cayuses were as frightened as we were. They tried to jump off, and Father was obliged to unhitch them to quiet them down. It was strenuous work to cross a customer, and the price was high. Before this ferry started, old, crippled

Broken Nose Abraham was a wizard with a frail canoe. Using only one paddle, he could skip across in no time.[10] Nor did he charge much. Yet the ferry could carry much more.

Once across, we had trouble finding a road wide enough to wheel the new wagon through. Trails had to be widened here and there in some places. At the homestead, Father drove directly to the ravine where the logs were. He unhitched the wagon and used the front part to haul the logs out, after he was obliged to cut four feet off the end so the cayuses could pull the wet wood two miles uphill to the cabin site.

After all the logs were hauled, Father hired another Indian man to help. He knew something about fitting corners together. They made one room, eighteen by twenty feet, and chinked the cracks with clay and bunchgrass. We did not need a fireplace because of the two stoves. Later a lumber kitchen was added to the house.

That summer, Father cut fence posts in the ravine to go all around our new land. During that period, natives were at liberty to take land anywhere on the reservation without permission from the agent or the chief. The best agricultural land eventually was taken by whites, some already on the land illegally and others who came later with the Homestead Act. There was still a lot of level land around, but being an inexperienced farmer, Father fancied the big, rocky hill, admiring the abundant bunchgrass growing there to feed his ponies.

Before the snow fell that [winter], Father had fenced the bench-land on the sidehill overlooking the valley of the Kettle River. [He used] many hundred posts around that three-quarter section. Mother sometimes protested that he was taking on too much, saying he should be satisfied with a garden plot. He told her, "When I was a gambler, I wanted to be the best, and when I cut cordwood, I wanted to cut more than the others. Now I want the largest ranch here."

Once the cabin was finished, we used it only occasionally. Usually we lived in a tipi in the backyard, where Mother cooked over a campfire on warm, sunny days. We enjoyed this life-style much more.

Cookstoves were rare among the natives. One day a family came to visit us from the fishery. Their little three-year-old girl ran directly into the red-hot stove and put her whole palm against it. Her flesh sizzled as it cooked, and she screamed in agony. Her parents rushed to comfort her, saying she had never seen a stove before. Yet only a few years later, this same family lived in a comfortable dwelling south of Kettle Falls. Their farm prospered and the daughter grew to womanhood, educated at the Goodwin Convent.

My parents were not alone in the sudden progress of their farming. After the 1893 winter famine, people saw the need to farm for food, first on a small scale, then on a larger one. Necessity is the best teacher, and the terrible destruction of the cayuses and deer urged people to take their livelihood from the soil.

Although we now had a farm, my parents still [indulged] the traveling fever. Occasionally we would leave the ranch, after the crop was planted, to gather native foods, which were always relished more than potatoes and vegetables. We never missed the annual fall hunt until it was forbidden by the state game department, supposedly to protect the diminishing herds.

During another bad spell, Father decided to try his gambling luck among the Kootenay. Before he left, he killed many deer to keep us fed. He planned to be gone only a few weeks if he were successful at winning Kootenay ponies. Father and his teammates took sweat baths to prepare for the competition. The Kootenay are great gamblers, eager to take on a party of Okanogan or Colvile. Wagers included ponies, robes, and money. After Fort Steele sprang up, the Kootenay were considered rich and proved it by gambling for lavish [stakes].[11]

Father went alone because there were too many of us and Teequalt was too old to ride horseback. All summer, Mother took care of the patch of potatoes and watermelon. When the chokecherries ripened in August, there was still no word from Father. Mother was silent, but she looked worried. Our meat was gone, much of it given away to the needy or rationed, and we were getting hungry. Father could not write, and Mother would not think to look for mail. When the fishery started up, Mother could not move us there because there was only one pony. She did ride over occasionally and bring back fresh salmon.

As people prepared for the fall hunt, which Father never missed, he was still not home. One day Uncle Andrew returned and said Father was broke and on foot, vowing not to come back until he had made [money]. After Uncle left, Mother's eyes filled with tears and her lips trembled, but she never complained. [Eventually Father did return.]

Hardships like these instilled a spirit of progress everywhere. It became feverish as more and more white customs were adopted.[12] People liked the luxury of sugar and coffee, bannock bread, pots and pans, cotton clothing, and cowboy duds. Buckskin items went out of daily use, but they were made to sell to whites. Fancy and work gloves, moccasins, shirts, beaded vests, and fringed clothing were designed to appeal to the eye of a white buyer.

A few elders still used deer-antler saddles, but most people bought leather ones from the store, along with bridles. These were decorated with bright nickel-plated rings or celluloid ones in red, white, and blue; expensive ones were made of silver. A pretty bridle was worth a horse.

Women mixed [styles of clothing]. Those who worked for whites doing laundry wore much beruffled or pleated dresses, later replaced by bustles. More traditional women wore long, sweeping cotton or silk skirts, whose tight-fitting waists had large pearl or porcelain buttons in front. Wide plaids and bright colors were used for shawls with long fringes. Silk handkerchiefs were tied around the head. Only young ladies wore coats, machine-made capes, or feathery hats. Old women braided their hair, but young ones had their hair done in the latest style.

Men dressed like cowboys, wearing jeans and straight-brimmed gray hats. Older men wore buckskin clothes only for council meetings. By this time most men cut their hair, although the old men wore theirs long.

★

CHAPTER 16

The Invasions of
Miners
and Settlers

THE NEW Year of 1896 was a notable event for the Colville
Reservation. The Indians called it the Mineral Law, but it
actually involved the opening of the reservation for whites to take
mining claims. The law was to become effective on 21 February
1896, but long before that date arrived whites were swarming over
the reservation trying to set mineral claims despite the deep snow
covering the region. When the day came, whites came in hordes,
startling the peaceful isolation of my people.

It seemed that every projecting rock that showed any promise of
a mining lode was claimed by these fanatical men. Indian protests
were disregarded, and the agent told the Indian police to keep their
own people out of the way because all this confusion was The Law.
By this time Indians had learned that these laws, regardless of how
bad or unfair they were, must be obeyed. Our leaders were discouraged by the activity and the realization that outsiders could
take any land with mining potential. Within a few days, however,
the grand rush seemed to have receded, and only a few men strug-
gled through the deep snow in search of claims. We thought this was
the end, but it was only a temporary respite.

When spring came, miners returned and continued the search in
the hills and mountains where deep snow had prevented travel
before. A rumor began that a rich mine was found at Kel-yel-pas

(Tree in the Center of the Land) on the ranch of Batise Tonasket, the eldest son of the great chief. They called it Camp Eureka [later Republic], and whites began vigorously to congregate there in large numbers. Many Italians were hired to widen the trail with picks, shovels, horses, and plows. They were expanding almost the identical route to Curlew that my father helped Chief Tonasket and Joe Seymour build. This route was intended for the first wagons brought from Spokane to the new store Tonasket had just built at his homestead in the Curlew district.

Later Edwin Morrison used it for his stagecoach line. I vividly remember the stage as it passed below our house, rocking from side to side over the rough new road, pulled by four to eight horses. The stage ran at full speed to cover the eighty-five miles from East Marcus to Republic. Way stations grew up like mushrooms along the route. The closest one was located six miles due north of our cabin at the ranch of Pete Pierre, a half-breed Iroquois, and his wife, a quarter-Flathead. Pete had charge of the Morrison stage horses, and he was very conscientious. He had the new team ready in harness and hooked together when the coach arrived so the horses could be exchanged quickly, while the passengers took time to eat lunch at the halfway house run by his wife Maggie, a notable cook who attracted the best people as her customers. While their farming had been unsuccessful, the couple made a lot of money from this boom of several years. Six years later the railroad came to Republic, and all this came to an end.[1]

Once Morrison urged my father to build another stage stop, so he would have a place to leave horses ten miles farther than the Pierres. Whites were not allowed to establish businesses on the reservation unless it was a mining claim or townsite. Father moved us to the location in his wagon, and Mother set up the tipi. He employed men to help him cut and skid logs for two large buildings, a barn and a boardinghouse. He had them almost done when a woman who lived about four miles south arrived one morning and gave my parents a real tongue-lashing. She said her husband was thinking of building a stage station on their garden plot, which extended to the site of Father's buildings. Father, ever the sensitive Nicola, when told he was an intruder on the Colville Reservation, decided to vacate. Before we left he started a large fire at the corners of the buildings. The green logs were not all consumed. For many years, these lopsided buildings remained as a mockery to my parents for trying to make money during the boom of 1896. The woman and her husband never did anything with the land. Such petty jealousy has stopped the progress of other business ventures, retarding Indian success.

When the road was finished and level, wagons became very common because the freight charges averaged about eighty dollars a ton between Marcus and Republic. Marcus enjoyed the boom, and new buildings crowded away the old log shanties of pioneers and the early log store of Marcus Openheimer, founded in 1860. Log shanties were replaced by fine homes, hotels, and restaurants. Both Marcus and Republic ended up with dozens of square-front saloons. The church bells on the Sabbath were drowned out by the laughter of men in bars, dives, and brothels. Such were the contributions to our locale made by greed and lust.

This clash of cultures is illustrated by a humorous story. Three men from Colville went to a restaurant in Spokane when it was a pioneer town. They learned that people could go in these and buy food to eat. The two most adventurous men went in and paid for their first dinner. To play a joke on the old man with them, they went back to the camp and invited him to eat with them. They went to a restaurant and he was served all kinds of food, greatly enjoying himself. He thanked the owner for his generosity and walked out full. He was surprised to be pulled back inside and asked to pay money. He was startled and said, "You should be ashamed to ask for money when you feed a guest." Of course the owner did not understand the Salish words. After much merriment, the two younger men paid for his dinner, while the elder walked out muttering angry words. He could not understand how anyone could charge for food under his own roof.

The reservation was violated again at noon on 10 October 1900 when it was opened for homesteading. The law to enable this was the result of a bill passed and approved by Congress through the efforts of the Indian Department and the secretary of the interior. The Colville tribes had no voice in the matter and only heard about it at the last moment. People were frantic and desperate, being content to always live separately from whites. Like their fore-fathers, they wanted only to be free and left alone. Gradually whites moved in, but they were there as traders, missionaries, and agents working for the benefit of the people. Then others arrived and began to take instead of give. Favorite lands were claimed by whites. Sections of the reservation to the east and north were lost forever. The older generation recalls this mistreatment vividly. Now they viewed this new law as the climax of the plan to take all the land. The rich and fertile valleys of the Colville and Chewelah had al-ready been lost, and now the rest was to be taken.

Our chiefs and community leaders gathered to stop the takeover. After many council meetings by groups in various localities, every-one decided to meet with the superintendent at Fort Spokane to make a formal protest against the invasion. They wanted the na-tives, the original landowners, to be asked for their consent. When the meeting was held, Major Anderson, the agent, tried to explain his predicament and obligation to follow the orders of his supe-riors.[2] The elders, however, recalled the 1855 meeting with Gover-nor Stevens when he said, "Your land is your own. No one shall take it away from you without your consent." Anderson explained that there never was a treaty or any ratified agreement, so words were worthless. The Indians could not comprehend why a great man like Stevens should have broken his word to them. They continued to insist it was their right to protest for protection from the govern-ment. Later Anderson was obliged to rebuke the appeals Indians made through his office. He also made some insincere promises that a man of his education should have known could never be fulfilled. Perhaps his fear of opposing orders from the greatest office in the land, combined with a concern for a (possible) uprising among his charges, forced him to make rash promises. He could not go against the Homestead Act.

Before the Indians left Fort Spokane, they held a meeting among themselves and decided they would not let the surveyors tape [off] blocks of their land for allotments. They would also boycott any orders or directives from the Indian Office. They therefore left in better spirits than they had arrived.

Fort Spokane was on the river of the same name, an eastern tributary of the Columbia River. It was placed on level benchland bordered by rough, wooded hills. The central area, known as the campus, was surrounded by large frame buildings previously used by the army garrison stationed there in the event of an Indian uprising after the 1855 Yakima [Treaty] War. After the fort was abandoned, some of the smaller buildings were used by Indian agency personnel and their families. Major Anderson lived there with a few clerks to care for the legal business of the Spokane and Colville reservations. The garrison jail was maintained to hold unruly Indians guilty of small offenses. Serious crimes such as murder and grand larceny were taken before the federal court in Spokane. All the Indian communities were starting to have their own police to enforce federal laws relating to Indians. Such policemen were paid twenty dollars a month and given a service revolver and billy club by the agency. Their families received a small amount of rations, but they had to furnish their own ponies. The police took turns making the long trip to Fort Spokane every so often to serve a week watching the inmates in the jail. They did not get travel expenses for this, however. It was part of their duties.[3]

The police chief of our district was James Bernard, who was nicknamed Captain Bernard by Major Anderson. Bernard also served as adviser to Chief Andrew Aropaghan of the Colville because he had some education and could read and write.[4] I presume he may have gone as far as the fifth grade, which was the high average for so many of the Colville of that time. The captain had an energetic nature and

[keen] intelligence, earning him the goodwill of the confederated tribes. His position and literacy made the older Indians believe that Bernard was qualified to do legal business between the tribes and the government. People did not know how to hire a lawyer or get another opinion. Even if they had done so, the 1887 federal laws prohibited them from employing a lawyer on their own or for their own defense without the consent of the agent. Everyone was at the mercy and whim of the Bureau of Indian Affairs because the courts had decided we were "wards" of the government. This injustice has been a great handicap to our advancement and self-respect.

Such a retarded education was not the fault of the Catholic mission schools, for Indian children were given excellent teachers and a set of firm lessons to aid them in their endeavors. They were able then to go on for advanced courses at colleges and universities in Spokane and Seattle. The only drawback was the need for the children to leave home to go away to school, causing sorrow and sadness to the rest of the family. Indian people do not like to be away from relatives and loved ones for very long.

Another detriment to our education was the early age at which our girls married, giving them husbands and families before they could finish school. Parents pampered the couple until they could support themselves, often raising the children for them.[5]

The surveyors arrived in the early spring of 1900 under the leadership of Clair Hunt.[6] They came across from the town of Marcus, and the Indians were there to meet them. This confused the crew, and they halted their plans until they had word from Major Anderson. When he heard, the major gave orders to the police to round up the leaders and place them under arrest. The police and Captain Bernard had already decided they could not do this, and so they resigned. Chief Aropaghan remained in the background during all of this, unwilling to commit himself to either side, Indian or white.

Finally, Bernard urged the chief to go to Marcus and forbid the surveyors to ever enter the reservation. The chief then rode his pony five miles into town. On the other side of the river, he was immediately met by some half-breeds, who invited him to the hotel for a big dinner. Then they took him to a store and bought him new clothing and underwear. In this way they won over the chief to allow the Hunt crew to come onto the reservation. He also promised the half-breeds they could have allotments like full-bloods if they would buy him food and clothes for as long as he lived.

The chief went to the crew to give his permission, and they had him place his thumbprint on a document giving his consent. Hunt immediately moved the crew onto the reservation, wasting no time. This caught Bernard and the others by surprise and prevented them from rallying against the crew. The first allotment they surveyed was that of William Miller, an uneducated half-breed. Peter Alex, brother of Chief Aropaghan and barely able to speak English, was hired onto the survey crew. We watched helplessly as the crew advanced steadily toward Pia each day. The crew employed other tribal members to ease their way. Charley Brown, a half-breed cousin of Bill Miller, acted as interpreter, and his white wife was camp cook. The half-breeds sold their birthright for a job, and people said the chief sold their reservation for a pair of underwear.

Many of the older Indians refused to take their allotments and lost their rights as a consequence. Clair Hunt tried to be fair and so assigned land to such people if he heard about their refusal so they would have something for the future. For all of his bad actions, he had a sympathetic nature and fine character, and he loved the Indians. He said he was only following the law. In later years the elders came to love him in return and appreciate his foresight.

Mother held with the older Indians and would not take what was allotted to her. Father took the opposite position and was firm in his resolve to take allotments for himself and all of us children. Jimmy Ryan and Clair Hunt, together with Major Anderson, encouraged him in this. He tried to arrange allotments for my grandmother and her husband, but Mother opposed this. Father respected her wishes, and thus we never came to own any inherited land like some families who took advantage of allotting all their relatives. Some were even able to arrange land for relatives born and raised in Canada, who had no legal right to our land.

Early in May, the crew came to Pia during the time my sister Maria was born, and Father immediately took an allotment for her without telling Mother. This amused Hunt, who remarked, "Joe, you're lucky to get eighty acres for a baby so new." Everyone was entitled to the same eighty acres as long as they were tribal members living on the North Half after the reservation was declared open.

While the crew was camped below us, I rode down the hill to play with the two Brown girls. Their mother included me in meals with the crew, and I got to know Mr. Hunt well.

When objections were raised to half-breeds like the Browns getting land without the consent of the tribal council, the chief would say, "They are the descendants of Indians and are landless. We have a lot of land, so it is better that we give it to them than to whites who are strangers to us." Such was the kindheartedness of our chief. His character gave mixed-bloods a place on our reservation, and his gentleness made Marcus the entry point for the October opening of the North Half to white homesteading.[7] Youngsters appreciated the chance to mingle with these strangers, but the old people developed an aversion to the class they called "breeds" and predicted they would cause all the rest of the land to be lost in the future.

Long before the 10 October date for the opening, whites [roamed over] the North Half looking for the best homestead locations. On the date set, the grand rush began at noon, with people coming in all kinds of conveyances, from horses and old buggies to worn boots and knapsacks. Homesteaders were none too careful; some claimed allotted lands and would not get off until Major Anderson ordered them away under escort by Indian police. This was both amusing and pathetic, because the whites were so desperate. A poor family with many children took land that was part of our allotment. Father raised no objection because he had allotments for seven children.

When that family learned the truth from the Indian police, they left quickly without causing any trouble.

This influx of whites gave me new experiences. I saw a cow milked by a white woman. I had never known that cow milk was used until then. The woman gave the milk to her children, and that startled Sulee and me even more.[8] When we went home and asked mother, she laughed at our ignorance, explaining that whites had many uses for milk. I only learned to drink it years later on doctor's orders.

One day we went to the Pierre's Halfway House. When the passengers arrived for a quick lunch, a jet-black man was among them. I was really afraid of him. His eyes looked much lighter around his dark pupils. Maggie Pierre and Mother were amused at me. He so impressed my mind that I had nightmare fits that night because they teased me so about my fear.

Until the invasion, we traveled on horseback, rarely in a wagon. With improved roads, people started buying buckboards and hacks. The father of a family living below us, who came to be called Alex Hayes when the sisters at the mission gave his daughter Emily the last name of President Hayes, bought a beautiful surrey with a flat top, double-seated rig, and fringed canopy for his wife and educated daughter to ride to church. I looked longingly as the bay team carried them into the distance. Emily dressed in the latest fashions, with large "mutton chop" sleeves and dresses of pale blue China silk. Her hats were covered with artificial flowers. She was a pampered only daughter. I watched her clothing during Sunday mass, wishing to dress like her when I grew up. She became my ideal of womanhood, although I knew I would never be her equal in singing. She led hymns when her Aunt Collet was absent from church.

My father hired on with freighters. Starting as a helper, he earned his own wagon and a team of cayuses for hauling freight from Marcus to Republic. The roads were in terrible condition and dangerous. One day the teamsters met a wagon above Rockcut where there was no turnout despite a long, rocky grade. The [oncoming] wagon was empty, so the men hung it off the cliff by ropes tied to pine trees until the loaded wagon got past.

Father came back from one of these trips with an orphan white lad, about thirteen, named Jimmy Ryan. He had previously lived with his uncle in Butte, Montana. He ran away from home because he did not like his uncle's wife. He drifted among strangers until he heard of the Eureka strike and joined the horde. He did not talk much, could be gloomy, and seldom laughed out loud. If amused, he grinned without comment. He never showed ill temper and was a willing worker around the ranch, doing his chores silently. He fed the stock, chopped wood, and carried most of the water. Mother and I appreciated his releasing us from that [wet chore].

When Jimmy first came to live with us, Sulee and I were amused by his strange speech. We used to mimic him until Mother scolded us for being impolite to our guest. It is peculiar that Jimmy learned to understand every word of our language, but he never tried to speak it. He always replied in English. Soon Sulee and I began to learn English from our adopted white brother. He was never legally adopted, but he lived with us at intervals for many years. He was part of the family. My parents always called him their son.

Jimmy was a great reader of yellowback novels. It was from one of his books that I learned the alphabet. I could spell the word Kentucky before I ever had a primer because it occurred frequently in the novel Jimmy taught me from. One day Mother papered our cabin with Jimmy's novels. When he got home, he made no protest, but he got busy and continued to read from the wall, with me helping to find the next page. Mother used to secretly scold me for being so interested in books. She wished me to spend all my time in the backyard tipi with Teequalt learning our traditions. Long Woman [Long Theresa] declined the invitation to live in the cabin during winter, when we needed the warmer housing for the new baby, Louis Eneas. Teequalt said the house lacked clean air and light, but my parents suspected that she did not like Jimmy's company. He was unconcerned about this, so we all lived in happy harmony, regardless, and all of my siblings learned to read English from Jimmy.

The Kelly family took an allotment on the hillside near our farm. Mrs. Kelly claimed a strain of Indian blood, but it was never made clear which tribe. She looked white because of her gray eyes and very light skin. All her children were fair, and she was married to a white man. She arranged allotments for herself and her children in very fertile land suitable for growing wheat. Once they were settled, people began to call our place of old by a new name, Kelly Hill. The Kelly family lived there for many years but seldom mingled with Indians. All their sympathies were with the local whites. All this change was due to the tricking of Chief Aropaghan, who never received anything else from the mixed-bloods after they promised to take care of him for life. He died poor and rejected as people turned more and more to Captain Bernard for advice and wise leadership. True to his traditional training, however, Bernard always tried to seek out and respect the opinions of the old chief before any decision was reached. We always gave our elders the fullest regard and respect by virtue of their age and experience, regardless of any mistakes or bad judgments they had made. While the younger generations turned away from the chief for creating the modern mess, the pedigree of his ancestry, store of traditional knowledge, and continued dignity protected his chiefship. While he had proved that he could be influenced and bribed, his kindness and love of the people dominated his life and career. This could not be ignored by our elders and leaders. He was poor and miserable in his last years, but he was buried as a chief.

Appendix

Since this autobiography is not, in final form, a fair example of Mourning Dove's own literary efforts, a draft of an article that, according to her own letters, pleased her is included: "The Red Cross and the Okanogans." This is reprinted as written by Mourning Dove except for the editor's clarification of spellings in brackets.

THE RED CROSS AND THE OKANOGANS

The Red Cross today has a far more significant meaning to the Indians of the Northwest than ever before. It is no longer a mere "money making scheme of the white man", but in reality an institution of charity. The soldier of the trenches and prisoners of war have long known its worth, the Belgians, young and old have blessed it, but not until now, since the coming of the white man among us with his new ideals, have we from our hearts felt gratitude for his coming. The charitable efforts of the Red Cross has put us in touch with the unselfish side, with the true nature of the foreign brother who lives in our midst. It is an historic fact that the Indian in general entertains no love for the "higher civilization", and that he is ready to grasp at the most forlorn hope held out for the recovery of his halcyon tribal days. Perhaps this Government will never know the full extent of the German propaganda that was spread among the different tribes, how the old and ignorant were excited by the promises made them by mercenaries of the "Baby Killers", how their vast hunting domains would be returned to them if only the arms of the Kaiser prevailed. To this end the Red man should join cause with his overseas friend. Many disputes arose among the tribes. The old and uneducated sympathized with the Hun, while the younger and more enlightened counseled peace and continued allegiance to our own country. It is to these half-educated tribesmen that the nation owes a debt of gratitude for fidelity mentained [maintained]. The splendid patriotism of the thousands of our best young men who joined in the world fight for democracy, attests the true steel of the Red race, hampered though it is by undue

Governmental restrictions. And now the Red Cross has effected a change of heart among many of our fathers and mothers, and we younger Indians feel a joy in the closer union of the two races, the brotherly love which "peace on earth" should bring to all peoples.

Marcus, a little town on the Columbia River, was the first to come to the rescue of its Indian population suffering with the dreaded Flu. Assisted by the Deputy Sheriff, John Lane, the Red Cross reopened the old hospital which was proffered free by its owner, a physician residing at Newport. Liberal donations poured in and commodious quarters were provided for the stricken Indians, who were wholy unable to cope with the strange malady. Mr. Lane found several homes with corpses lying in the same room where the remaining living members were too weak and emaciated to bury their dead or care for themselves. Using pursuasive methods, with that generosity of heart for which he is noted, he carried these poor invalids in his own car to the "Sick House" of the white man. In some cases the aged and superstitious could not be induced to leave their squallid homes, but remained to fight fate with that stoic indiffernce to death for which our race is renowned. To these, such aid and comport was rendered as possible under the conditions.

The Indian population of Kelly Hill and adjacent valley would no doubt have been wiped out by the epidemic had it not been for the Red Cross. The lady members of this humane body devoted themselves to the dusky patients who filled the wards of the hospital. Day and night they relaxed not their vigils, but cared for the sick with all the tender patience of the true mother and sister. The simple minded recipients at length understood and appreciated this care and attention. Dr. Parker donated his services and his wife and others kept close watch over the afflicted. One boy in particular, an only lad, the sole comfort and aid of his aged parents, came down to death's door, but was saved by the experienced nursing of the Mother Superior of Ward Mission, who came daily until the danger point was passed. Father Schyler of the same Mission visited the hospital whenever called, sometimes on foot and untiring. The Catholic Indians wanted to be right with the white man's God before leaving for the Happy Hunting Grounds, with its visions of wild freedom which finds place in the mind of every tribesman, however Christianized.

Dr. Lane, in company with Dr. Parker, went down to the South half of the Colville Reservation, visiting all the sick and arrousing the Red Cross spirit of Enchelium. Aided by the Indian Agend [Agent], they partitioned the dance hall into wards, where many lives were saved to the tribes. The Indians were cared for, either by the Red Cross or the Indian Agency, as far North as the international boundary line; and we feel that we are fortunate in having a place in this great republic. In the upper part of the reserve, about Oroville, there were no deaths from the Flu; but just across the boundary, where lies Smilkameen, Penticton and Inakmeep [Inkameep] reserves, the grim reaper harvested unstaid [unstayed]. Canada, renowned for her generosity and wisdom in her management of Indian affairs, rendered no aid. War-worn and exhausted, with her thousands of maimed and health-ruined soldier boys to care for, the Government seemed powerless or inert to the condition of the tribesmen, and the suffering and mortality was/has been appalling. Many pathetis [pathetic] incidents could be narrated. Chief Antoin Nachumchin lay ill in the same room where his younger brother was dying from the dreaded scourge, tuburculosis. It devolved on a young sister to care for the two brothers, in addition to the necessary work both inside and outdoors. One day the girl spoke of feeling unwell and Antoine warned her not to leave the warmth of the house. But fuel must be had. She went out, gathered wood and began chopping it. Soon the sound of the axe ceased. Antoine arose from his fevered couch and went out to find her lying unconscious by the little armfull of wood which she had succeeded in cutting. The brother carried her into the house, and a half hour later, her spirit fled. Her teeth had burst in the aweful agony of death. Despite such suffering, this devoted sister had not to the last atom of her strength desisted from ministering to the wants and comfort of her sticken brothers. The patience of the Indian woman endures without murmur or complaint even unto death. Can greater love and fidelity be found in any race?

An old blind Indian lost his four children on whome he leaned for support. His aged wife was nearly as helpless as he. He rallied from the Flu, went out willingly to try doing the work which would never again be done by his children, took relaps and/and sank rapidly. While dying, he said: "God has surely forgiven me my sins, for the blindness and afflictions which I have suffered. The sunshine I have missed in this life, will be all the more resplendent in the next world. With sight restored, I will there see my children again. I am willing to go."

In Penticton, were many deaths. The custom of indiscriminate visiting of the sick among the Indians is prolific of fatalities. The Indian police forbade this, and by enforcing the edict, many lives were saved. At Inkameep, notwithstanding no medical aid could be had, there were no deaths. The Indians began sweat-housing as a "sure cure" for the Flu. I warned them of the danger of such course and they desisted. It was soon learned that keeping warm was a better system of dealing with the scourge. We also found that mentholated Okanogan sage brush was an infalable remedy for the Flu. Made into a strong tea and drinking it hot, effects a cure within three or four days with no after attack of neumonia [pneumonia]. It is a vile smelling, nauseating liquid.

The Flu put fear into the Indians as much as did the dreaded smallpox which swept them off by the hundreds in past years. So long as the Indian can understand what he is combating, he has but little or no fear, but it is the subtel [subtle], incomprehensible which mystifies and terrorizes him. When the scourge first struck the Okanogan country, many of the Indians said: "It is the white mans' sorethroat disease which is killing him off. The white man dies too easily. It will never hurt us." It is different now. Many of our people have died. Some resisted it from the first with good results, while others made light of it until too late.

The casting aside of the tepee and adoption of modern houses has had an evil effect on our race beyond calculation. Fresh air is lacking. Owing to his former mode of life—in the open and well ventilated tepee—the Indian does not understand how the air can become poluted and deadly, does not understand the value of clean air. In his ignorant and primitive state the Government and misguided reformists thrust upon him a condition unfitted to his needs and bodily comfort. Windows are for the admission of light, the tepee had none. Oftimes a large family will occupy a single room, day and night with the windows hermetically sealed. Diet is also neglected. Many die from overeating. They believe that food is strength and why resist an inclination to take it when wanted?

But while we are proud of America's part in the Red Cross, thankful for what it has done for the Okanogans, there is something lacking in its true efficiency, in all that it is supposed to stand for. No aid had been offered the stricken Indians across the Canadian border. Relief is sent to foreign lands, not even denighed [denied] the baby murdering, women mutilating Hun, but none has been forthcoming for the dying, simple minded natives at our very door on the North. Perhaps this is because of the lack of publicity. Whole families have been, and are afflicted, in many cases not one is left to provide firewood for warming the fevered sufferers. Oftimes corpses have rotted in the room where the sick lay moaning in delerium—dying with the piteous cry for water scarce articulated by baked and parched lips. I would that there were more white men and white women like those of Marcus, the little hamlet on the banks of deep rolling Swanetka.

Notes

INTRODUCTION

1. A more detailed account of Mourning Dove's life appears in Miller (1989).
2. Department of the Interior, Office of Indian Affairs, file 16326-1921-312, letter dated 3/16/21 from O. C. Upchurch.
3. Markowitz 1987:132.
4. Lucille Trosper Otter (pers. comm., 1988).
5. Theresa Broderick, *The Brand: A Tale of the Flathead Reservation* (1909).
6. Ryker 1962.
7. Fisher 1979:130.
8. *Ibid.*, 139.
9. The Peskwaws are the subject of a work assembled by high-school students from Wenatchee (Scheuerman 1982), which is amateurish at best. It even denies the tribe its own name in favor of that of the modern town, which derives from the Yakima Sahaptian name for the tribe.
10. Ross (1968), Brunton (1968), and Schultz (1971) deal with the 1960s on the Colville Reservation, building on the earlier work by Boas (1917, 1918), Teit (1917, 1930), and Ray (1932, 1933, 1936a, 1939).
11. Schultz 1971:14. Ray (1939:24) reported that the Southern Okanogans and Lakes had women chiefs, while Fraser River Salishans allowed women to be chiefs only to perpetuate a hereditary office in the absence of male heirs. The greatest of the Lakes chiefs was a woman. As Ray writes, "It is quite clear that female chieftainship is here a simple outgrowth of the principle of political and sexual equality."
12. Ross 1968:46.
13. Schultz 1971:12.
14. The Nez Perces loyal to Chief Joseph remain on the Colville Reservation near the grave of their beloved leader. Their saga is long and complicated. A disputed 1863 treaty deprived Old Joseph and his people of their

Wallowa Valley home in present northeastern Oregon. Whites moved in, and conditions deteriorated until hostilities erupted on 14 May 1877. After a valiant defense Young Joseph, the famous leader and son of Old Joseph, surrendered on 5 October 1877 with an understood promise that the Indians could return home. Instead, 431 survivors were shipped to Fort Lincoln, Dakota Territory, then to Fort Leavenworth, Kansas, and then to Indian Territory (present Oklahoma) in 1879. Many died of the cold or later because of the heat, desolation, and poor sanitation. After a national outcry they were allowed to return to the Northwest, arriving at Spokane Falls (modern Spokane) on 27 May 1885. Colville elders say that Young Joseph and Chief Moses, Columbian and Colville leaders, were briefly educated together by the Presbyterians at Lapwai, Idaho. They remained friends, and Moses invited the Wallowa Nez Perces to the Colville Reservation when the Idaho Nez Perce majority preferred to have Joseph's band settle elsewhere. By December 1885 they had taken prime land along the Nespelem River. More detailed information can be found in Ruby and Brown (1965), Gidley (1981), and especially Josephy (1979).

15. The McLaughlin Agreement was named after James McLaughlin (Pfaller 1978), a Special Inspector for the Bureau of Indian Affairs and a controversial figure in reservation history, particularly among the Sioux. The Colvilles knew him because in June 1900 he toured the Wallowa Valley with Chief Joseph, trying to find land there on which to relocate these Nez Perces. The relocation did not take place and Joseph's people remain among the Colvilles.

16. Ross 1968:67–84; Schultz 1971:54–93.

17. Brunton 1968:17.

18. The most available portrayals of Colville life today are two photographic books by Mick Gidley (1979, 1981). My 1983 review of *Kopet*, on the passing of Chief Joseph, and Gidley's reaction, requires some explanation. I had met Gidley during his year in Seattle and aided his work. At the time I wrote the review, however, I was a tribal employee and decided to collect some local reaction to his more recent book. People were still upset with *With One Sky above Us*, focused on photographs by the agency physician, Dr. Edward H. Latham. There are many different tribes on the Colville Reservation, and the book offended many by misidentifying individuals by name and by tribe. Over the past few years, however, people have come to appreciate the book for its photographs, although

they now supply their own captions. As a foreigner and a stranger on Colville, Gidley was in the position of the author Mourning Dove described in her novel.

19. For this falling out see Ault (1959:5). The quotation from *The Brand* about a tipi is in Broderick (1909:13).

20. These sources for native autobiography are discussed by Wong (1987), Brumble (1988), and Ruoff (1986).

21. Bataille and Sands 1984:1–25.

22. Showalter 1977:15, 25.

23. Baym 1978:17.

24. Bone 1958:25; Baym 1978:31.

25. Rafert 1982:70–104.

CHAPTER 1: MY LIFE

1. Although Mourning Dove refers to many people in this text by native names, all Colvilles had Christian names by this time, the result of their new faith and daily contact with whites. Many of these early names were French in origin but were so changed by Salish pronunciation as to be almost unrecognizable as European. Most were given to people during the annual Holy Week encampment before Easter. Father De Rouge (see note 28 below) delighted in meeting the new church members, adults or infants, and giving each a name and a gift. After some time, when everyone had both first and last names, he began to give out middle names to keep the practice going.

2. Elsewhere we learn that her father was born at Penticton, British Columbia, a large town in the vicinity of Arrow Scraper, identified as village 6, immediately north of Penticton in the list of Okanagan settlements by Hill-Tout (1911:130). Kelowna itself is farther north and derives its name from the Okanagan word for grizzly bear. The Nicola tribe, since absorbed by the Okanagans and Thompsons, were a small cluster of Athapaskan speakers. Such widely scattered pockets of Athapaskans were not uncommon throughout the West, most of them small, isolated communities between the Athapaskan homeland to the north and the populous Navaho-Apache migrants into the Southwest.

3. The Oblate mission of St. Joseph among the Yakimas was founded in 1879, a month after the Whitman massacre, by Fathers Charles M. Pandosy (son of a French admiral), Eugene Chirouse, and Pascal Richard,

priests who had came along the Oregon Trail with Augustine Blanchet, bishop of Walla Walla (Bischoff 1945:182). While at Yakima, Pandosy grew close to Owhi and his family. He also prepared a famous grammar of the Yakima language. St. Joseph's had three locations before it was burned by the American army on 14 November 1855 during the Treaty War. During these hostilities, Pandosy wrote down the letter dictated by Kamiakin to Major Gabriel Rains (Brown 1961:144). The Oblates spent the winter of 1856–57 at Fort Simcoe before they scattered. Afterward Chirouse founded an important mission at the Tulalip reservation north of Seattle, and Pandosy worked with the Jesuits until he established the Immaculate Conception Mission midway along Lake Okanagan, which became the nucleus for the town of Corona (Splawn 1917:355). He died there in 1891 (Buckland 1966:19).

4. Other members of Mourning Dove's family deny that their father's father was a Scot or Celt. They say he was a native, but Mourning Dove chose to ignore this with a fiction that would appeal to white readers. As an orphan, Mourning Dove's father had an uncertain position in society, especially since he was raised, at least in part, by non-Indian families. Mourning Dove may have learned to question her traditional knowledge as a result of her father's reluctance. In any event, the experience was too significant to overlook, especially as it relates to his oldest child.

5. See note 2 in chapter 16 for a sketch of "Major" Albert Anderson.

6. Trout Lake, east of Upper Arrow Lake, drains into the Kootenay River. It is a fascinating exception to the generalization that each drainage shared a common language and culture throughout native North America. An even greater exception to this rule was the Klamath River of northern California, where at least three tribes from as many different language stocks shared a similar culture and sphere of interaction.

7. Sulee is a Salishan version of the name Julia.

8. This is the term used by a daughter for her mother. Males used another word for parents of the opposite sex. For other details see Elmendorf (1961).

9. Tobacco Plains was more than the main Kootenay camp. It was the center of their territory, and its chief was the nominal high chief or leader of the tribe. According to Turney-High (1941:23, 150–51), "When there was a movement over the mountains to the Plains, other Kootenai who joined the party were considered under the leadership of the chief of

Tobacco Plains, even though they were chiefs at home. This was likewise true for joint war parties. This is partially substantiated by the feeling that the chief of Tobacco Plains was warden of the bison." Accordingly, Maria and her family had a much higher status than Mourning Dove chose to indicate. To have been a rich Kootenay was one thing, but to have also been from Tobacco Plains was a great honor.

10. Julia, Mourning Dove's sister, is listed in the Colville census as married to a Shuttleworth. A man named Galbraith started the ferry at Fort Steele. See chapter 15, note 8.

11. Kettle Falls has long had a strong Catholic presence. St. Paul's Church was an early mission station, later eclipsed by the second of the St. Francis Regis missions, although it was long used for brief services during the fishing season. Nearby was the soldier settlement, called Harney's Depot before 1860 and Pinkley City afterward, in honor of Major Pinkley Lugenbeel, commander at Fort Colville. At least half of the soldiers there were born in Ireland and attended the local church. The major center for missionary activity, however, was St. Francis, founded at a settlement of mixed-blood Cree métis now called Chewelah, Washington. Father De Smet visited there on 4 August 1845 (Schoenberg 1962:19, no. 126). The second mission of St. Francis was built halfway between Pinkley City and St. Paul's in 1869. St. Paul's had been closed in 1858 as a full-time mission, but it was reopened in 1863 for occasional use.

In 1872 the Colville Reservation was both created and shifted to the west side of the Columbia. St. Francis was accordingly moved to the other side of the river in 1873, onto land given by Chief Kinkanawah with the stipulation that the church also include a school. This became the Goodwin Mission at Ward, Washington, administered by the Sisters of Providence (Charity). Although they ran a school for boys that closed 1 September 1908, their best-known activities centered on the Goodwin Mission school for Indians and the Sacred Heart Academy for white girls, which closed 30 July 1921. St. Francis had many setbacks during its time. Gristmills and sawmills were added from 1875 to 1880. A larger church was built between 1877 and 1881 and used until it burned on Christmas morning of 1888, the year Mourning Dove says she was born. Another building was started but not finished until 1911; it burned in June 1938. By then St. Mary's Mission near Omak, on the western side of the reservation, had long replaced St. Francis Regis as the religious center. Raufer (1966:89–119) devotes chapter 5 to St. Francis Regis Mission in the Colville Valley.

12. Although many Colvilles know and use a few names for the months in their language, two elderly women supplied me with a full year. Each month name indicates the appropriate activity for that season. The names are listed below with their equivalents in the Julian calendar, along with timely activities. Horatio Hale published similar calendars for the Flatheads and Wenatchis in Wilkes (1845, 6:410–11).

January	sk'ʷsus	"Taken or burned fast" (food and wood were used up quickly at this time, and eyes were blackened with red cedar soot when hunting)
February	spaqt	"Pinch" (hands stick to frozen surfaces)
March	s-kn'ir-mn'	Buttercups
April	skpəckɬtn	Budding out
May	s-kʷən'-kʷín'əm	Roots: wild potatoes, balsamroot, camas, bitterroot
June	k-məktútn	Wild carrots, balsam seeds (also called xwmina, "steelhead")
July	k-síyaʔ-tn	Serviceberries, up to eight varieties
August	ɬəxʷ-ɬəxʷ-tán	"Holes, holes": chokecherries, huckleberries (some root digging)
September	snk'əlkwis	"salmon spawn": cedar bark roots for basketry, salmon run in Okanogan River
October	sʌqmis	Salmon run in Columbia, traps set up at Brewster
November	sqʷl'it	"Gather tree moss, fall hunting (sKaym)
December	sk'ʔay	Winter

13. None of the Plateau tribes abandoned the aged or infirm, so something else must have been involved with Teequalt. Most likely it was her own grief and despair following the death of a dearly loved spouse. Since it was her own decision to wander away, I presume her neighbors would have respected it and not intervened. Still, her encounter with the Quintasket family was sufficient to give her a new lease on life.

14. In her collection of *Coyote Stories*, Mourning Dove (1933:11) credits Teequalt (Long Theresa) as the source for "How Coyote Broke the Salmon Dam" and "Coyote and Buffalo." See also Mourning Dove (1976:8).

15. Although the Jesuits did preach against killing, Ross (1968:43) has pointed out that it was the Hudson's Bay traders who most effectively imposed an end to Plains-Plateau hostilities, so that full time could be devoted to acquiring pelts for the fur trade.

16. For Ka-at-qhu see chapter 7 and chapter 9, note 5.

17. Although Mourning Dove describes only a single dwelling, homes were rarely isolated. Rather, people lived in small communities or neighborhoods during good weather, then gathered in communal winter villages. In general plan, a village or encampment was arranged along a watercourse, with the large winter villages usually at the confluence of the Columbia and a major tributary. The chief, leader, or headman lived at the center in a bigger home, suitable for holding general council meetings of adult men and women. Every settlement had a speaker to broadcast news and a series of scouts or lookouts watching the movements of game, people, and sky for expected and unusual occurrences. There were several types of housing, ranging from individual mat lodges to long multifamily dwellings with a fire trough down the middle. Locations within a lodge were generally assigned by age. Old people, usually a grandmother, slept nearest the door (other tribes say this was because they were "on the way out"), older children farther inside, and the married couple toward the back.

   Dried or cooked food was always available for snacks, but usually a family took one or two daily meals together. During the day, women worked together gathering and processing food or craft materials, while men worked separately. Women cooked, wove, and sewed inside, but they did their tanning outside and away from the camp because of the odors involved. Children had specially designated playgrounds, usually on a beach, sandbar, or cleared area along the riverbank. Sweat lodges and menstrual or birthing huts were set away from the camp for seclusion and privacy. Graves were placed in the nearest talus slopes, marking the continuity of living and dead with the land.

18. These paints were produced from various natural substances mixed with grease or some other binder. Color ingredients mentioned by Isabel Arcasa, a Colville elder, were red (red ocher), black (soot mixed with grease), blue (clay or copper ore), green (grass stain), yellow or orange

(birch bark or mountain ash berries), brown (inner tree bark or skin), purple (mature sage flower buds), and white (kaolin or other clay). Other details of parfleche design and manufacture are provided in Spier (1925).

19. Bitterroot is still an important if limited part of the Colville diet, served at all meals with a religious purpose, whether Catholic or traditional, especially modern versions of the First Food rites. In addition to traditional baking, it is now also prepared in orange-flavored gelatin.

20. Such cross-cultural encounters are examples of culture shock. Different viewpoints lead to different interpretations. When Harriet Shelton Dover, a Coastal Salish lady, described a football game from her own perspective, the game and cheerleaders seemed shocking.

21. The story of Camas Woman or the Hee-Hee Stone is told by Mourning Dove in her *Coyote Stories* number 23 (1933:191–96). The family's route was northwest into Canada, then west to the lake.

22. As used here, "bench" is the local term for a terrace or bluff along a river, made during its geological development. These formations are points of reference when in tiers, so landmarks can be described as being on the first or second bench above the river.

23. These references to warfare are a fiction, presumably inserted to accommodate a white audience. As Ray (1932:25) pointed out, the dominant Plateau values were pacifism and equality. Militarism was not highly regarded, except for Plateau tribes near the Plains. Present-day Sanpoils still preach against revenge, even for murder, because it cannot bring back the dead.

24. Father Peter John (Pierre Jean) De Smet organized the first Catholic missions in the Inland Empire of Washington, Idaho, Oregon, and Montana. Born 30 January 1801, he was assigned to this work in 1840 and 1841–46 as the result of three separate expeditions (1831, 1835, 1837) of Flatheads and Nez Perces under Iroquois guidance who had come to St. Louis to ask for Catholic missionaries to bring them the Great Prayer (Mass). These Iroquois had been converted by French Jesuits before moving westward in the fur trade and had been living among the Salish since 1816. After 10 December 1846, De Smet was procurator of the Rocky Mountain missions, with a residence at St. Louis (Schoenberg 1962:nos. 15, 21, 31, 143). Raufer (1966:60–88) devotes chapter 4 to De Smet. A charming and informative image of these early missions appears in the crayon drawings of Father Nicholas Point (1967), who came into the

missions with De Smet. See also note 7 of chapter 8 and note 13 of chapter 13.

25. The records of Goodwin Mission are scattered. The school chronicle, kept in French until 1900, is in the archives of the Sisters of Providence in West Seattle. School records after 1906 are in the archives of the Bureau of Catholic Indian Missions, Marquette University, Milwaukee.

26. Although she calls him Carnia, Mourning Dove alludes to Father Joseph (Giuseppe) Caruana. The memoirs of Father Parodi include the observation that "Kutene'-us was the name of Father Caruana, because he is a big fat man" (Raufer 1966:168). This is another version of the name Mourning Dove spelled T-quit-na-wiss, Big Belly. He was born 24 August 1836 on Malta of noble family, entered the missions in 1862, and died at De Smet, Idaho, on 29 October 1913 (Carriker et al. 1976:10). Among the papers he left is an interesting day-by-day account of his 1883 trip from St. Francis Regis to St. Joseph's Mission at Yakima.

27. St. Mary's Mission remains an important Colville center, where the school is now operated by the confederated tribes as the Pascal Sherman Indian School. Pascal Sherman, first named John Wapato, was a member of a prominent Chelan family. His name was changed by a priest during Holy Week (see note 1).

28. Like Mourning Dove, many Colvilles have much their own version of the saintly life of Father Stephen (Etienne) De Rouge, a tribute to his dedication and their love of him. A more historical account of his life and of Colville Catholicism was provided by Sister Maria Ilma Raufer (1966: 173–364), cited in the notes to the section on early reservation history. De Rouge was born 28 January 1860 and died 9 May 1916; he was a younger son of a French count with strong ties to the old nobility, but the family was not wealthy.

29. A cayuse is a small, sturdy horse, especially bred for life on the Plateau. It was named for the Sahaptian tribe shattered by the 1847 Cayuse War, after Marcus and Narcissa Whitman and others were killed at the Waiilatpu Mission near Walla Walla.

30. Father Celestine Caldi was actively involved in building many of the churches of eastern Washington. When he was stationed at St. Francis Regis around 1900, he held mass at Pia on the first Friday of every second month. As Raufer wrote, "Here was a large church for Indians and half-breeds who had good homes and were very religious. About 80 to 90

people attended the services, often coming great distances" (1966:115). Caldi followed De Rouge at St. Mary's, but his unstable mental state did much to undo the good work of the founder before Caldi was hospitalized; he died 3 February 1938 (Raufer 1966:387–412).

Father Edward (Edoardo) Griva was born near Turin, Italy, on 20 September 1864 and died 21 October 1948 (Carriker et al. 1976:12). A hardworking missionary, responsible for building sixteen churches, Griva was most proud of his title as premier Jesuit linguist. He studied Assiniboin (1894–95, 1904–7), Crow (1895–98), Yakima (1898–1902), Colvile (1902–3), Kalispel (1907–12), and Nespelem (1913–48) in addition to Nez Perce, Kootenay, Gros Ventre (Atsina), and Chelan. He assembled dictionaries of Columbian, Colvile, Crow, and Kalispel. Father Griva served at St. Francis Regis after Father Caldi in 1902–3. As Hanzeli (1969:45) has noted, "Missionaries were persuaded that their language learning was not inspired by a thirst for knowledge, but rather was a means of co-operating in the divine plan of salvation."

31. It was long a concerted policy in federal and church-sponsored schools to forbid students to use native languages. The policy was often enforced by punishments ranging from whipping to taking away meals and privileges. By forcing children to learn English, the intent was to turn natives into whites, at least in dress and speech. This was effective enough to suppress the public use of native languages and encourage the development of Red English as a substitute. Nevertheless, the native identity was not extinguished. Particularly encouraging for the present generation has been the 1972 passage of the Native American Religious Freedom Act, guaranteeing Indians the same right to practice their indigenous religions as those of European and Asian faiths have always had.

32. Throughout her life Mourning Dove was driven, anxious, and highstrung. She had repeated bouts of illness, the likely result of overwork and poor diet. Interestingly, her cures, like her life, combined native and Western allopathic treatments. When physicians were ineffective, the family turned to traditional healers, who usually were successful. Her invoking of both native and Catholic faiths is a reflection of native ecumenical attitudes. According to her family, Mourning Dove devoted considerable energy to looking for a "true religion." To that end she dabbled with the Jehovah's Witnesses and the Seventh-Day Adventists near the end of her life. Even so, she continued to attend Catholic services.

33. Fred Galler was Mourning Dove's second husband, whom she married in 1919. He was descended from both prominent Indian and pioneer white families, particularly John "Dutch" Galler, who moved to the reservation and died there in 1918 at the age of 105 (Hull 1929:190).

34. This image of a reflective woman meditating in a tree or on a rock was transposed into her novel, with the addition of a bison skull. She felt strongly enough about this image that a letter asks McWhorter about a copy of the picture of herself with a bison skull.

CHAPTER 2: SPIRITUAL TRAINING

1. A general survey of this time in the female life cycle, particularly with respect to puberty practices among Plateau tribes, appears in Verne Ray (1939:52–61).

2. An even more effective technique, used for one elder as a child, was to be sent out on a mile's journey to return to the river some crayfish placed in a dry pail. Their constant scraping against the metal sides created eerie sounds that helped both to induce fear and to bring on a supernatural encounter.

3. The spirits conferring power on an individual are now often called "pardners" in Colville English. Indeed, they do work with humans as though bound into something like a joint merger. Ray (1939:76–77) reported that a person refers to "my own partner(s) or power(s)." He called their bond "a highly specific relationship with a powerful ally available for personal action in any contingency" (p. 75). Regrettably, he quotes himself as saying that the beings of the Myth Age, from whom modern deities and species have differentiated, "appeared in the superficial guise of men" (p. 114). As I have been told repeatedly, they were and still are essentially human (humanoid), donning the covering of their species when interacting with *Homo sapiens* outside their abode or holy home.

4. The practice of inheriting power rather than questing for it is now the norm in Colville native religion.

5. As a general statement, "the more spirits one has, the greater power and invulnerability" needs to be modified in terms of the types and associations of each spirit. Quantity alone was not as significant as quality and intensity, although the famous case of Syolm indicates that it was possible to have it all on rare occasions. This greatest of the Methow shamans went into a trance for ten days while his essence met with immortals

gathered inside the highest peak in the valley. Pattern is also important, since shamans rely on the tribal sacred number for defining the range of spirits. The Methows had a 5 x 5 table of spirit types much like the 4 x 4 system for shamanic powers among the Lakota Sioux (and 7 x 7 for the Kootenays). These were the pattern or sacred numbers of each multiplied by themselves to define the types and classes of spirits.

6. Personality traits were also taken into consideration, since elders closely watched all youngsters to select those few with the best memory, discretion, and attention span. Such a child was called a lone arrow and carefully instructed in the traditions, laws, and commandments applicable to the kindred, community, and landscape.

7. During the menstrual seclusion, a girl took care of her body wastes in a deep hole dug along the inside edge of the shelter. She covered every elimination with some dirt until the hole was filled and the hut had to be moved.

8. See chapter 3, note 1, for a discussion of this virgin's cape.

9. Mourning Dove's first menstruation occurred about 1900, when she was twelve years old (see chap. 16, n. 6).

10. Throughout native America, just as in the Plateau, rock art identifies locales of sacred significance. Often it serves to verify the ancestral location of a mythological event or a communal ritual. Lightning-struck trees are loci of concentrated power. Even now Colvilles are well aware of these sites as zones for power acquisition, although very few use the decreasing number of locales still available. White settlement, constructions such as Grand Coulee Dam, extensive flooding, and desecration have taken their toll.

CHAPTER 3: COURTSHIP AND MARRIAGE

1. This cape for virgins has never been mentioned in print, but it is plausible on the basis of the available ethnography. Capes were worn, and people often chose the skin of their spirit partner for articles of clothing (Hill-Tout 1907:68). Sources are clear, however, that most social distinctions were indicated by headgear. At puberty, Lakes boys wore a hat with an animal tail at the back (like a coonskin cap) so their trainers could tell by the angle of the tail how fast they were running along the ridgeline of the hill behind the town of Kettle Falls. Hill-Tout (1907:69) also confirms

the wearing of tight-fitting, legless trousers of thick buckskin by girls between puberty and marriage.

2. During a recent visit to some archaeological sites, Sanpoil elders explained a few tipi mounds set off from the rest of the encampment as the likely abodes of girls under chaperonage. Just before marriage, girls were sent off by themselves to ponder the seriousness of their new responsibilities.

3. This parallels the Mediterranean notion that the honor of the family resides with its women, who must be modest and protected for the well-being of all. Billy Curlew, the late Columbian (Sinkiuse) leader, always said, "My wife is my wealth," meaning that she had to be well dressed and have expensive horses so that she would properly reflect his (and her) status in the tribe.

4. These gifts were not a payment or bribe. Rather, they expressed the sentiment of sharing so important in the evaluation of any individual in native America. A son-in-law who shared from the beginning would establish himself as a good provider.

5. None of the Interior Salish had clans in a strict sense, so Mourning Dove is using colloquial English here. There were totemic groups associated with certain locales (Miller, n.d.d), but these lapsed in past generations. There were social classes, however, of old families who formed intermarrying aristocracies like that of Mourning Dove's own family, and of good families without the ancient pedigrees but still notable as hardworking providers. The poor families did not have disciplined habits, good luck provided by immortals, or prestige. They were given or begged produce from the other families.

6. The advice given by a chief at a marriage was mostly to remind the couple that they were to act like adults and to be fully aware of the important step they were taking. There was no instruction in the physiology or practice of sex. Nor did people make comparisons to animal behavior, because animals, after all, were not human and had rules of their own to follow, as specified in the mythology.

7. This glimpse of the skin of a new wife was in keeping with the extreme modesty required of proper females. In the old days, to see a woman partly uncovered meant death or forced marriage, depending on the relative rank and marital status of those involved. During the Prophet Dance of a century ago, mass marriages were held in which males merely touched females in public to institute the bond.

8. The stated preference was for the couple to live near the husband's family, especially if an office was to be inherited, but in practice residence was a choice among several options. Bride service was not required, only a continuing exchange between the in-law families. Nor was anything allowed that was as formal as the northern native Californian half-marriage, where the groom joined the family of the bride. Flexibility was the major rule, especially since families would relocate if they became angry or displeased with someone or something in a community. This kept hostilities to a minimum among the Okanogan Salishans, who valued pacifism.

9. In native America, suicide was definitely a form of revenge against a loved one. Women were the most frequent suicides, then children angry with their parents. Women in the past threw themselves on their digging sticks (dibbles), the tool most associated with the role of a woman. Father Ravalli began to make converts after he worked long and hard to revive a woman who tried to hang herself in 1857 at St. Paul's Mission (Raufer 1966:77). She had just quarreled with her husband. Such tragedies continue, although suicide messages from some modern teenagers give despair and hopelessness as reasons.

10. Polygyny (multiple wives) was a privilege of the wealthy. As long as a man could support several wives, these marriages were favored by the families involved. Intermarriage has long been a particularly Salishan strategy on the Plateau, while the Sahaptians prefer to use large social gatherings to forge alliances. Chief Moses of the Columbian tribe used this strategy of "royal marriage" to good advantage among the Columbian Confederacy, which became the kernel of the modern Colville polity (Ray 1960).

11. The marriage of widows and widowers to surviving same-sex siblings of the deceased spouse (sororate if sister, levirate if brother) was recognized in practice and in the kinship terminology. Such marriages perpetuate the alliance between the two families and protect the children of the previous marriage from trauma. Family members safeguard each other, so a sibling is a proper replacement for a deceased spouse.

CHAPTER 4: THE DUTIFUL WIFE

1. Ray (1932:49) gives other examples of decorated dress indicative of status and abilities. He notes that the combination of quills and feathers, dyed

red, distinguished a shaman of great prestige. Red bands were a particular hallmark of shamans, placed around the sleeves and body. A powerful woman shaman wore a dress with a wide, red-painted hem, showing her ability to treat menstruation troubles and signifying that she was "standing in her own blood that deep."

2. Basketry has by and large fared better among Canadian tribes along the Fraser River. Its technicalities are described by Haeberlin, Teit, and Roberts (1928). Most recently, Colville elders have begun to revive their traditional twined flat bags and coiled baskets, now using rug yarn instead of natural fibers.

3. Balsamroot was more than just a "famine food." It was the most versatile staple, used in at least seven ways during stages of its maturation (Turner, Bouchard, and Kennedy 1980). These foods include the first sprouts, prebloom (peeled) stalks, threshed and dried seeds, roasted seeds, a ground seed flour, a gruel like peanut butter, and baked roots. Another famine food was rose hips (cf. Eidlitz 1969).

4. Bitterroot gathered when the flower is still in the bud peels easily and quickly. If it is gathered before or after then, peeling is a laborious process, damaging to fingernails, knives, and patience.

5. The use of herbs and plants throughout the coastal and interior Northwest is the special concern of Nancy Turner (1978; Turner, Bouchard, and Kennedy 1980).

6. This is an accurate reflection of disease in North America before European contact. Diseases were limited to the stomach, senses, and skin. The cold barrier between Asia and America, scattered population, and lack of domesticated herds to act as intermediate disease hosts prohibited large epidemics until Europeans, acting as biological reservoirs, introduced devastating pandemics.

7. When she married, every woman was supposed to start a calendar, consisting of knots in a string. A large sample of such string calendars is illustrated by Leechman and Harrington (1921). Most are from the Nicola and Yakima valleys, but they were not collected from the women who made them, so much important information was lost. A Methow woman told me that each calendar was begun by a bride to record important events in the life of her family, their pets, and their fortunes. Mnemonics included the size and type of knot, its color, and whether or not a string, ribbon, or figure was tied into it. The sequencing was very important, so that every day had a knot, bigger ones marked Sundays and

weekends, and those for a month or year were larger still. When the woman died, her calendar was either buried with her, burned, or hidden away.

Regardless of the events, the exact chronology and interpretations were known only to the recorder. In the old days, of course, the overlap between calendars of adjoining generations created a sense of continuity. Now that calendars are no longer made, elders complain that their memories are not "long enough." For mnemonic calendars from other regions, like the Papago carved-cactus sticks and the Plains bison-robe winter count, see Underhill (1938).

CHAPTER 5: BABY CARE

1. Men and women engaged in mutually dependent but separate activities. Young women were watched, advised, and warned by other women, not by the general community or its officers. The female sphere was often unto itself, as was the male sphere. In this separation, native people see cooperation and complementarity rather than antagonism.

2. Such extreme modesty was the rule during birth. Among the Wishrams along the Columbia farther south, "The patient remained covered with the buckskins both for warmth and modesty. The midwife never saw the mother uncovered; she did not see the baby come. She knew how far the baby was by feeling the woman's abdomen, and as soon as it was born reached under the coverings and got it" (Sample and Mohr 1980:430–31).

3. A woman was expected to reflect the values of her upbringing at all times, but most especially during birth and menstrual seclusion, when her actions had direct bearing on the whole community. Her pain and discomfort were a sacrifice, a part of her overall contribution to the community. She acted with resolve because of her obligations to everyone else.

4. Reports of massaging to mold the baby are all too few. This adds a Plateau example to what was once probably a general Native American practice. It is best reported for the Southwest, where I have seen it performed at the Pueblo of Zuni in New Mexico.

5. There is a strong belief among modern elders that mothers should provide milk for their own infants. Otherwise some moral or physical

problem is suspected. Among the Cheyennes, the use of cow's milk to feed modern babies is believed to make children stubborn, like bovines (Straus 1976). Note also Mourning Dove's first encounter with the milking of a cow (chap. 16).

6. See the discussion of rose branches in chapter 12, note 4.

7. Waste from a baby's diaper had to be ritually deposited in a specific hole, in a hidden location, to protect the child from sorcery or ill-will. Ray (1933:128) also reported that "a baby's excrement was always deposited in the same place, a hole in the ground. If this were not done, the child would become mischievious and later refuse to obey."

8. Although there is a general folk belief that nursing is a check on large families, lactation does not rule out pregnancy.

9. This reference to baby language reflects a wider context of beliefs about human existence, which begins in babyland, blends with biology during this world, and continues as essence and memory in the afterworld. Unfortunately, we know little about the belief in babyland. The most detailed discussion occurs in the unpublished Tillamook ethnography by Elizabeth Jacobs.

10. This ingenious swing was widely distributed. I first heard about it from the Lenapes (Delawares), who in ancient times lived on the East Coast, and most recently it was described to me among the Suquamish across Puget Sound from Seattle.

11. An often overlooked aspect of the relations between culture and biology involves what was done with the milk or baby teeth when they fell out. No elder could remember when I asked. This information was saved for posterity, however, in the Okanogan notes of Norman Lerman (1952:file 1, 155): "The first tooth lost was wrapped in a piece of meat and thrown over the shoulder to a dog to eat. This gave the child strong adult teeth like those of a dog."

12. Parents usually refrained from physically disciplining children for a wide range of reasons well summarized by Pettitt (1946). Instead, the Interior Salish relied on an unrelated man who served as the whipper for each community. Among the Columbians a child was threatened, but if this did not bring reform, the whipper would come, place the child face down, and use a red willow switch on his or her back. Then the man danced with the whip held in his mouth, rejoicing at the child's change of heart. The mother usually gave the whipper a gift, often a blanket, as he left.

CHAPTER 6: CHARMING AFFECTIONS

1. Mount Baldy was well known among Colvilles because it was the nearest place inhabited by grizzly bears.

2. This arrangement of the chief in the center duplicates that of any idealized encampment in native America. The chief was centrally located because he (rarely she) was the nexus of the community. By extension, this metaphor can be applied to all communities of plants, animals, and crystals.

3. According to the cultural definition of gender among the Interior Salish, plants that bloom are the males, literally "men plants." Since their flowers grow on stalks, this phallic aspect of the plant probably led to the classification as male. Also, Plateau men wear fancier clothing than the women do.

4. Turner, Bouchard, and Kennedy (1980:117) report that red columbine is still used as a good luck charm.

5. Funerals and other sad occasions have an adverse affect on spirits and the transmission of power because these are telepathic. Spirits are keenly sensitive to sorrow and distress. This is turned to human advantage during vision quests, when petitioners suffer various hardships or pain while fasting.

6. The first meeting between McWhorter and Mourning Dove probably occurred at the Walla Walla Indian Days of 1915. Walla Walla was also the home of her mother's brother, Louie Stui-kin.

CHAPTER 7: WIDOWHOOD

1. This chapter was found after the manuscript had been largely assembled. Its disjointed beginning suggests that it was intended for the chapter on early farming.

2. Funerals, more than any other event, bring Colvilles together and remind them of the bonds with each other and the land. The procedures described here have been modified by the requirements of law and mortuary practice, but family and friends still sit with the body all day and night. It is dressed in good clothes, and traditional families make sure moccasins are put on the feet or in the coffin. Old ladies tell wonderful stories all night to keep everyone alert and less sad. Catholic prayers and

hymns occur at intervals, along with the Rosary. A few years ago the Salish translations of these were revived.

Many elders say whites are cruel because they desert their loved ones at night during the wake. Natives show they care by staying close by for as long as possible.

On the day of the funeral, labor is divided among the gravediggers, cooks, and other mourners. The grave is not dug until it is to be occupied; leaving an open grave for too long would encourage more deaths. Here as elsewhere, the native view is that everything is interrelated. Similarly, cemeteries are cleaned only once a year, the weekend before Memorial Day, because clean cemeteries with rows of graves allow more deaths. Whites rarely understand this link with the land and thus unfairly criticize unkempt cemeteries.

The reservation has many small cemeteries. Where the body is buried indicates a last important link with a tribal past. People are buried by family and tribe, unless weather or personal wishes intervene. Mourning Dove bought a plot for herself in the local white cemetery near her home in Omak; otherwise she should have been buried with her family at the Pia Mission.

People moved constantly, although everyone had a place that was home. This was also the site of their cemetery. Sometimes mother and father are buried in different locations, usually because they have children buried in each and so can "look out for the kids" after death.

A Colville tribal fund provides money for the burial for each enrolled member. Relatives, friends, and neighbors rally to help with food and hospitality during the wake. Elders are now transported to wake and funeral in a tribal van. After a funeral service, usually a mass, the body is taken to the cemetery of choice. The service continues, and elders make speeches at the graveside. The coffin rests above the open grave during all of this. When all have said good-bye, it is lowered into the grave while everyone waits or sings a Salish funeral hymn. A man stands at the foot of the grave holding a shovelful of dirt. First men, then women, file past and throw a handful of dirt into the grave. Meanwhile, male family and friends are filling in the grave with shovels. Such human labor by relations and friends is a last gesture of love for the deceased. Most Colvilles still object to the use of backhoes or other heavy equipment either to dig the grave or to fill it in.

As the grave is filled, people wander through the cemetery visiting the graves of their kinspeople. On very hot or cold days, elders stay in the van until the body is lowered into the grave, then they come out and stand nearby as a gesture of respect.

A feast or dinner is held for everyone after they leave the cemetery. Traditional families still empty their closets of household goods and other possessions of the deceased. A year after the death, often during the July Fourth celebration at Nespelem, families hold a memorial giveaway and reassign the native name to a living relative.

Colvilles are justly proud of the care shown to their dead, their heightened sense of community, and their strong ties with the land. In some cases, as with the cemetery at Manson on Lake Chelan, these links continue with ancestral land that is not part of the main reservation.

CHAPTER 8: THE FISHERY AT KETTLE FALLS

1. By supplying these terms for areas around Kettle Falls, Mourning Dove made a significant contribution to our knowledge of this area.
2. Squant (skwant) is a term generally meaning waterfall but also serving as a place-name. Scraps of paper indicate that Mourning Dove used this term specifically for the Omaks, Omak Lake, and St. Mary's Mission, noting the bitterroot grounds in this area. Others use it for Nespelem Falls. The Nespelems, closely related to the Sanpoils and Okanogans, are not treated as a separate tribe in the manuscript. I feel sure that this is more a reflection of missing pages than of any oversight.
3. Women stayed far away from fish and other game, in part because their odor during menstruation had a decided effect on animals, attracting carnivores and repelling grazers. Only the possession of power could change this condition, as in the case of a woman who used her Kingfisher power to draw salmon to a weir at Malott and then swam downstream of it. "Though women should not come within half a mile of a salmon weir, those who had [S]almon power, or who were attended by a man who had such power, could do so with impunity" (Cline in Spier 1938:160).
4. Such a division, twice a day, had to be absolutely equitable among everyone there at the time, even brief visitors. Failure to share this bounty could offend the Salmon Spirit, who would end the run.
5. No mention is made here of the series of rituals held throughout the summer to express thanksgiving for each of the foods as they become

available. These First Food feasts continue as a special part of Colvilles' relations to the land. The rites are held in turn for first crops of roots, plants, berries, and fruits important in the aboriginal diet. Central to all of these was the First Salmon rite (Gunther 1928).

For the Sanpoil First Salmon, women prepared a ramada or shade and covered the ground below it with sunflower leaves. Then they camped away from the river for five days. During that time, the men went naked ("with nothing between themselves and the Creator," I have been told) and feasted on fresh salmon. The first four days they ate flank sections, boiled the first two days and roasted the next two. The fifth day they ate a soup made from the dried odds and ends of all the previous salmon, mixed with roots and berries. After this, women and children rejoined the fishing camp and work began in earnest to dry salmon for the winter.

Different species were honored in different areas. According to notes left by Norman Lerman (1954:file 2, 179), Riverside held a ceremony for suckers in April, Tonasket for rainbow trout in May, and Oroville for Sockeye in July.

In an article in the *Nespelem Tribune* (vol. 2, 4:1, 4) of 10 July 1935, Mourning Dove reported First Foods for bitterroot at Omak in April, for salmon at Keller in May, for serviceberry at Osoyoos Lake in late June, for chinook salmon at Kettle Falls in July, and for dog salmon at Oroville when they were available there.

6. Colvilles use this plant, valerian or stinkroot, as a food and as a rat-tlesnake repellent (Turner, Bouchard, and Kennedy 1980:142).

7. Throughout the American Plateau, hymns and prayers composed by early Jesuits are in the Spokan-Kalispel-Flathead dialect. De Smet estab-lished his first mission among the Flatheads after they and the Nez Perces had sent three delegations to St. Louis to ask specifically for priests. Ignace, a Catholic Iroquois married to a Flathead woman, con-vinced the leaders to specify Roman Catholic missionaries because only they had the Great Prayer (Mass). The native-language hymns and pray-ers have all but lapsed with the death of the older generation. At least one Jesuit still conducts services in Spokan. At present, however, Jesuits are actively trying to revive their use at Colville funerals and feast days. Hymn texts printed in Spokan have helped with this revival. Curiously, the prayers composed by Father De Rouge in Okanogan are almost unknown. See also note 28 to chapter 1 and note 13 to chapter 13.

8. The inspiration for this account of chipped rock scrapers was the visit to

Kettle Falls that Mourning Dove made as a chaperon for a group of seventeen schoolchildren on 30 May 1930. In her letter to McWhorter, she mentions that she collected the raw material and practiced the manufacturing technique so she could give scrapers to elders who would appreciate them as tokens of their past.

9. See chapter 13, note 6, for David Thompson's experience of the salmon fleeing from Kettle Falls when one of his crew threw a horse bone into the river.

10. The strict observance of Sunday was adopted from whites of past generations, with the fervor of new converts. Now some Colvilles speak of Christianity as their Sunday religion, regarding their traditional beliefs as their daily one. Hence such strictness once a week, after they had learned to distinguish a week, was not very difficult.

11. The days of the week were introduced by whites, since the Salishans needed no such units. Sunday is the point of reference, so it might be best to say that missionaries were the direct stimulus.

An interesting aspect of these names relates to the use of the flagpole. The traditional religion placed great emphasis on a world axis that united all parts of the universe. Presumably, the flagpole was considered to do the same for whites. This also helps to explain why the various historic prophet cults on the Plateau had their own flags flying from poles set up in the sacred precincts. Anthony Mattina explains the term for "flag" as meaning "tied," making reference to the knots in the string records kept by married women.

Sunday	s-kʕac=íw's	Flag Day
Monday	s-k-yxʷ=iw's	First Day
Tuesday	s-ʔasl=ásqʼət	Second Day
Wednesday	s-kaʔɫ=ásqʼt	Third Day
Thursday	s-más=(s)qʼət	Fourth Day
Friday	cil=kst=ásqʼt	Fifth Day
Saturday	s-k-ɫaʔ=ásqʼt	Last Day

Chance (1973:78) mentions the adoption of flags and their close association with Sunday. For some elders, flagpoles still are linked with the pole used by the Creator on Naming Day to hold the rings representing the names given to the prototype of each species. When Coyote, whose name ring was at the base of the pole, became the first creature to think for himself, the Creator upended the pole and made Coyote first among his creations.

12. Angus McDonald's wife was Nez Perce. He is discussed in chapter 13, note 17.

13. According to Garth (1965), this whipping complex came to the Plateau from the Southwest, perhaps via captured slaves returning home. He associates it with the adoption of horses and with the long journeys onto the Plains to hunt bison. As such, it helped tighten the control of the leaders during these dangerous trips, and over time it became applied in their home communities. I would add, moreover, that the whipping of children seems to have been an old practice among these Salishans and may have had something to do with the later adoption of a Spanish punishment. Malouf and Malouf (1945) indicate other effects of Spanish slavery.

14. The chiefly succession at Kettle Falls from ethnohistorical sources largely agrees with Mourning Dove (Chance 1973).

15. Note that modesty was observed even during the most severe punishments. Further, by having the wife of the chief retrieve the whip from their home, the tacit approval of senior women is also indicated. As the chief allowed the punishment of the man, so, it seems, his wife approved that of the woman. Among many tribes, the wife of the chief served as the de facto leader of the women in their community.

16. A stray page or two indicates that Maria, Mourning Dove's mother's mother, left Kettle Falls with her husband, son, and daughter because she was outraged by the use of whipping as a punishment. The family settled at Windemere among the Kootenays and eastern Shuswaps. Interestingly, McNickle (1978:206) treats whipping as a purification in a novel about his own Flathead community. Charles Quintasket insists that whipping was introduced by the "church police," tribesmen appointed by early Jesuits to maintain strict adherence to Catholic doctrine and Victorian morals.

CHAPTER 9: FALL HUNTING

1. During the sacred period of the fall hunt, all camps were under special ritual restrictions like those described by Mourning Dove. Only after the game had been welcomed and cut up on a layer of fresh fir boughs could

the meat then be taken out the front to be dried and processed. See also Hill-Tout (1907:167).

2. The families of Rev. Elkanah Walker and Rev. Cushing Eells conducted a Protestant mission among the Spokans at Tshimakain, also called Walker's Prairie, from 1838 to 1849. The mission was abandoned in the aftermath of the massacre of Rev. Marcus and Narcissa Whitman and eight others at the Waiilatpu Mission (near Walla Walla) on 29 November 1847. (See Drury 1940, 1976.)

3. Elsewhere in this text, other Spokans violate Colville hunting taboos. Earlier in this chapter, an old Spokan couple fail to show proper respect to the head of a deer. Despite their close linguistic, cultural, and spatial proximity, there are some profound differences in the practices and historical backgrounds of Colvilles and Spokans.

4. Chief Joseph Tonasket is fondly remembered on the reservation because he was all that a chief was supposed to be: kind, generous, wise, and always looking out for the welfare of others. While Chief Moses is sometimes called greedy and self-laudatory, Tonasket is not. He asked for a school, church, and gristmill instead of a salary for himself. He donated land for cemeteries. When whites began settling along the Okanogan River, he moved his family and herds to Curlew near Kettle Falls. He sold that land in 1884 and moved back to the vicinity of the town now named for him. In 1890 he supported the system of allotting the North Half, for which he is still criticized. He died in 1891 returning from unsuccessful eye operations. According to his gravestone, he was not born to the chiefship but earned it through ability.

5. Ka-at-qhu (Big Lip) is mentioned in *Coyote Stories* (1933:11) as a noted storyteller, the source for "Coyote Kills Owl Woman." Her death is described in chapter 7.

CHAPTER 10: WINTER DANCING

1. This sacred pole put up for each Winter Dance has ramifications throughout Interior Salish religion and culture. It relates to the tree or pole set up by the Creator at the beginning of the world to serve as its axis. It is also represented by the posts or poles marking graves and sacred places. As mentioned before, it is one of the reasons the prophet cults of the last century included flagpoles as part of their ritual equipment. Sunday is called Flag Day because of this overlap in sacred associations.

Ray (1939:120, 126, 129) makes other references to the use and importance of center posts.

2. Powers should never be made explicit because it was usually fatal. Only the most powerful of shamans would presume to do more than hint vaguely about the exact nature of their partners. The better idea that people had about them, the more likely they could be lured away, leaving the person defenseless. Instead, visionaries took the expedient of evoking or simulating some aspect of a power only in the most obscure way. Every power conveyed a token to the person, but usually this token was not as direct an emblem as it might appear at first. Certain animals were considered "friends" of others, so the token might be that of a friend of the partner, rather than itself. The evocation [sncuʔcuw'istm] and emblem-token [siyaRwt] remain vital parts of the traditional religion.

3. The Give-Away has long been a vital feature of Interior Salish culture and society. Its value rests on the general view that sharing is the most important of all the expressions characteristic of humanity. There is a rich and complex vocabulary for sharing in the Colville languages, specifying whether it was done in the context of Winter Dances, marriages, funerals, or other seasonal and life events.

4. Thefts or duels between shamans were conducted on planes other than that of ordinary reality. All some people ever know is that a person died, not how or why. For example, shaman X decided to kill shaman S by plucking a dead eagle at a Winter Dance and passing out the feathers among the audience. Since S had Eagle power and died shortly after, X is considered to have been the cause of the death among those in the know. Later X himself died in a contest with a shaman from the coast because he thought he was fighting a battle with Spider power. It actually was Octopus power, and this misjudgment killed him. Some shamans died defending their families from hostile shamans. Aboriginally, every family kindred was supposed to include at least one shaman among its members for this reason. Most relatives could be trusted, but not other people.

CHAPTER II: THE SEANCING RITE

1. This is the most sensitive chapter in Mourning Dove's work. This ceremony, usually called Conjuring rite, is still closely guarded among the Lower Kootenays (McLeod 1971; Schaeffer 1969, n.d.). Only they and the Colviles proper practiced it on the Plateau (Ray 1941). Earlier, Ray (1939:

116–19) described the Kootenay rite, compared it with the Ojibwa Shaking Tent (Djisakid), and noted that the Colviles included it within their Winter Dance, while the Kootenays held it separately. It is more important among tribes to the east, such as the Ojibwas and other tribes of the Great Lakes and Plains (Hallowell 1942; *Primitive Man* 1944; Densmore 1932). Of special note is that its distribution is circumpolar, common to native peoples of the Northern Hemisphere. Native people who are upset to see Mourning Dove's description here should be aware that theirs is but a version within a much greater pattern among humanity.

2. The three Indian shaman doctors at Northport have not been identified further. Colville elders suggest they may have been some of the five Jerome brothers who were religious leaders in that region.

3. The significance of ling fish is not well understood. Among the Lakes, special regard is shown it not only in the Seancing rite, but also in the name of their southernmost village, "Having Ling Fish" (see Bouchard and Kennedy 1979:293). The common name for this big-headed, slim-bodied fish is burbot (*Lota lota*).

CHAPTER 12: THE SWEATLODGE DEITY

1. This is a great overgeneralization. Although the sweat lodge was used throughout native North America, it did not always have attributes of divinity. It has a definite religious purpose, to be sure, but more as a means to an end. In other regions, such as the Southwest (Oasis) and California, the sweat lodge also served as a men's club.

2. Mourning Dove wrote that Sweatlodge was the wife of the Creator Chief, but all available information indicates that Sweatlodge was a "man." Ray (1932:177) reported information for the past generation identical to my own, received from the lips of the renowned Chief Jim James. The most likely explanation for the discrepancy is that the men's lodge, being the more general one, descended from the Chief, but the one for the women came from his wife, unless data are being deliberately disguised. There is also the possibility that Mourning Dove is reporting Flathead rather than Okanogan belief. A half-page of the manuscript has Sweatlodge addressed as E-ya-ya-ya Taa-to-pa (Great Grandparent). This is Flathead usage. According to Merriam, "Flathead assert that sweating and a being called *'topie* are closely connected" (1967:63). The term *'topie* refers to great-grandmother or grandparents in general.

Anthony Mattina, who had researched extensively in the Inchelium area on the eastern side of the Colville Reservation, has recently told me that he collected a story in which Sweatlodge is a woman. Thus it may be a regional feature of the eastern plateau Salish that comes as far west as the Colviles and Lakes.

3. The Okanogans have different styles of sweat lodges for men and women. Those for women have a higher roof, and the basin for the rocks is inside the door on the left. In the men's sweat house, the rocks and basin are on the right. By placing the basin on the left, Mourning Dove again shows her use of a female example as the general one.

Each of the twelve (or fewer) supports is named for a specific intention in a prayer said while the frame was built. Often it was a request for the well-being of a particular group, place, or race. The supports were said to equal the number of ribs of the Creator Chief. Other tribes had different symbolism for the lodge. For example, the Palus believe the supports derive from the legs of the Spider who turned into the first sweat house.

4. The use of fir and rose, together with other prickly plants like juniper, Oregon grape, and stinging nettle (Turner, Bouchard, and Kennedy 1980:152) accords with the concept called Sharp-Against in the folklore of European peasants. The notion is that these sharp or pointed items set up a barrier between worlds or existences to keep each in its own place. This is the reason rose branches are still used to sweep out fresh graves before burial. See photo in Turner, Bouchard, and Kennedy (1980:130).

5. The expression "going back to the blanket" is a slur directed against traditional Native Americans. In the same category are the terms "blanket Indian" and "huckleberry Indian," indicating the kind of racism Mourning Dove had to deal with constantly. The literary use of such pejoratives is discussed in Bone (1958).

6. In a fascinating article, Lopatin (1960) indicates the close parallels between the sweat lodge of eastern native America and the sauna of Scandinavia.

CHAPTER 13: TRIBAL BACKGROUNDS

1. According to current usage, Interior Salish along the Columbia River are divided into two dialect chains. The Colvile-Okanogan chain begins in the north with the Lakes and moves south through the Colviles, Sanpoils, Nespelems (virtually gone), and Okanogans. The Columbian chain moves farther south to include the Chelans, Entiats, Peskwaws (Wenat-

chis), and Moses-Columbias. Intermediary between these chains were the Methows, historically in the process of giving up their distinctive dialect, probably under the influence of the Columbian Confederacy.

When a story is told in any of these groups, the audience is supposed to respond with "yes" to show sustained interest. In each case, the word uses the characteristic vowel of its chain. Hence, Sanpoils respond with "aa," Methows with "ii," and Chelans with "ay."

2. Population figures are uncertain for the past. As of 1980, there were 6,134 registered members of the Colville Confederated Tribes. In 1978 the reservation itself included 2,850 members, 1,360 nonenrolled natives, and 2,450 non-Indians, for a total of 6,660 (Colville Confederated Tribes 1981:2–3).

Recent research indicates that the population of the New World was considerably larger than suggested by previous estimates, a woeful commentary on the initial devastation caused by European-derived epidemics. After steady contact, moreover, additional epidemics added to the already heavy toll. Population estimates for the southern plateau in 1805, 1835, 1845, and 1853 appear in Anastasio (1972:202), along with the dates of various epidemics.

3. These Inter-Salishan bison hunts onto the Plains in Blackfoot territory took place after the horse reached the Plateau and made long-distance travel practical. The original Split-Sun (mistranslated as Half-Sun), father of Chief Moses, organized such equestrian bison hunts and so formed the Columbian Confederacy among the Columbian, Peskwaws, and Chelan tribes, with some support among the Entiats, Methows, Okanogans, and tribes farther east (Ray 1960; Ruby and Brown 1965).

4. The Nicolas were a small Athapaskan-speaking group, since absorbed by the Okanagans and Thompsons.

5. Lewis and Clark, of course, went along the south side of the Columbia through modern Oregon. They were far from Kettle Falls and the middle Columbia Salishans (Thwaites 1904; Josephy 1979), yet their movements were widely known.

6. According to David Thompson, when he and his crew arrived at Kettle Falls (which he indeed called Ilthkoyope; see below), the chief gave the crew a roasted salmon and some roots, but this supply was too little for nine hungry men. So, after trying unsuccessfully to barter for more provisions, they killed a horse. This does not accord with Mourning Dove's account of the generosity of her ancestors.

Thompson arrived five days too late for the First Salmon rite. While there, he commented on the large village of plank sheds, which he described as clean and comfortable. The boards had been split from driftwood cedars. Everyone took the greatest care to keep the Columbia clean during the run, when a lone man speared salmon for the community. If a fish escaped, he stopped spearing for that day. The third day of the visit, the spearman came too close to a bleached dog skull, and he had to purify his spear and himself with the steam and cooled liquid of redthorn bark. By noon he was able to fish at the falls.

One morning about 10:00 A.M., one of the crew threw a horse bone into the river, and the salmon fled. They did not return until the afternoon, long after an Indian had retrieved the bone. By the end of that day, eleven salmon weighing fifteen to thirty pounds had been speared. These were "not fat but well tasted."

Thompson marveled that these salmon came 740 miles upstream from the Pacific Ocean to a falls three hundred yards wide. He never understood why only one spearman took fish when thirty could have been accommodated. As Chance (1973:18) has explained, it was a requirement of the salmon priest that the run not be abused or exploited. There was enough for all to share, while many salmon were able to spawn.

Thompson characterized the Colviles as arbitrators. Their village was a general rendezvous for news, trading, and compromises. The area above the falls had been depopulated by the pressure of Piegan raids, but the village itself was filled with intertribal visitors. The surroundings were rocky, with few trees and animals. He said that locals were poorly clothed, but they may have been careful to underdress during the grimy work of preparing the salmon.

Thompson intended to build a canoe to take his party down the river, but no single tree was suitable. Instead, a canoe was pieced together from several trees. It was finished on 2 July. The next day the horses were left in the care of the village chief, and the crew (five Canadians, two Iroquois, two Sanpoil interpreters, and Thompson) left. During the next few days they camped with Sanpoils, Nespelems, Methows, and Peskwaws (Wenatchi).

Thompson returned to the falls on 28 August, finishing another piecemeal canoe by 2 September. On 30 October he found the village at the falls deserted while everyone was off hunting for meat and hides. His last visit to the falls was on 22 April 1812, when four canoes were made, two of cedar boards and two of birch "rind" (Glover 1962:xcviii, 335–58, 379, 385, 395).

7. I have been unable to establish that Thompson called this chief Big Heart.

8. David Stuart selected the site at the river mouth for Fort Okanogan on 1 September 1811. The trading post was maintained that winter by Alexander Ross for the Pacific Fur Company of John Jacob Astor. The fort was sold to the Northwest Company after the War of 1812, enlarged by Ross Cox in 1816, and finally eclipsed by Fort Colville after 1825, since there was no competition after the Northwest Company and Hudson's Bay Company merged in 1821. An entertaining novel based on this period in the fur trade history is Sperlin, *The Heart of the Skyloo* (1934), which lists Mourning Dove in the acknowledgments. The best recent treatment of this period is Chance (1973).

9. Ross Cox took over Fort Okanogan on 30 April 1816, finding it a "horribly dull place." Tea and tobacco were his only luxuries, along with homemade beer from the essence of spruce. Standard fare was lean venison and dried salmon. His men were mixed Canadian and Hawaiian. He had them rebuild the fort, despite scorching heat, mosquitoes, and rattlesnakes. During August and September sturgeon were taken, some eleven feet long and three hundred to four hundred pounds when cleaned.

He found the natives honest and quiet, though shrewd traders. Regional dangers included wolves and ferocious bears. More personally, Cox admitted to fears of sharks, hawks, and rattlers. His Irish background led him to invoke Saint Patrick for the last.

Among the incidents he recalls was rushing tobacco, an essential trade item, to a needy colleague. Traders from rival companies had both run out of tobacco just before meeting a group of natives with furs. Cox received the urgent message and got a supply there first to save the day for his firm.

Sometimes relations with local natives became highly charged. The Sanpoils once stole ten horses because they were desperate. They were already starving when wolves killed all but five of their horses. The Okanogan chief, Red Fox, urged Cox to confiscate these, but instead Cox issued a warning that the next offense would be treated more severely. He also shot a horse for them to eat. Cox observed that the Sanpoils were envious of the trade goods that came to the Okanogans and Spokans because these were so near to trading posts.

Medical care was provided by shamans, one of whom performed a bizzare treatment. The paralyzed native wife of a proprietor at Fort George had her feet thrust daily into the fresh carcass of a dog. In all, thirty-two dogs were killed for this treatment, which proved effective. A similar cure was performed on a man from Fort George who had "overindulged" with local women so as to "fatigue" his health. He was placed into the bodies of a series of slain horses.

Of his isolation during the winter, Cox (1832:218) wrote, "Bad French and worse Indian began to usurp the place of English, and I found my conversation gradually becoming a barbarous compound of various dialects."

He described his September visit to Kettle Falls as unpleasant because the village was full of what he termed "piscatory offal." He was received as a friend and given an abundance of boiled and roasted salmon. Between the falls and Spokan House, there were lots of waterfowl. A small tribe of fifteen families there was led by a transvestite ("of epicene gender") chief with a rough beard and a deep voice, who interrogated him about English customs.

Cox (1832:225) noted the linguistic similarities throughout the area but characterized these dialects as "decidedly the most unpronounceable combination of gutturals ever formed for the communication of human thoughts, or the expression of human wants."

10. Andrew Colvile (1779–1856), known as Andrew Wedderburn before 1814, was progressively deputy governor (1839–52), governor, and director of the Hudson's Bay Company in London. This fort took the place of Spokan House because of its more cental location near the Kettle Falls fishery.

11. Paul Kane, Canadian artist, traveled along the Oregon Trail and stayed at the Whitman mission during 18–22 July 1847. He also repeatedly visited the Eells-Walker mission and Fort Colville. He arrived at the fort on 20 November 1846 after portaging around the falls. His hosts for three days were John Lewis and his Cree wife. The visit consisted of alternately eating and sleeping, which improved his looks and the spirits of his crew. After he left in the July heat, his meat and fish became infested with maggots, and the men joked about tying the fish down so it would not leave of its own accord. He came back to the fort on 8 August, noting, "Ft. Col-

ville stands in a small prairie, about one mile and a half wide by about three miles long, surrounded by high hills . . . an island of fertility, surrounded by barren rocks, sandy plains, and arid mountains, the distance of three or four hundred miles along the river, the Spokan valley to the south being the nearest land fit for cultivation" (Kane 1859, 1971:122).

Kane went on to Walker's Prairie on 9 September and came back to the Colvile village on 17 September 1848. He was a careful recorder in both ink and oils. His pictures of Kettle Falls and portraits of Allummak-hum, Chief of the Earth, and of See-pays, Chief of the Waters (the salmon chief) are important sources of information. The former has to be related to Martin Ilemux-solux, chief of the Arrow Lakes people, as mentioned by Mourning Dove. Similar views of the falls were also painted by John Mix Stanley.

12. After founding the Flathead mission of St. Mary, De Smet went to Fort Colville 15–18 November 1841 for winter provisions, spring seeds, tools for his converts, and cattle to establish a Jesuit-style reduction. Archibald MacDonald was in charge of the fort, and Skoyelpi, an intelligent man, was chief of the Kettles (Chittenden and Richardson 1905:356).

13. The story of Old Ignace La Mousse Saxa and the three missions to St. Louis to ask for Black Robes with the Great Prayer is well told by Palladino (1922:8–19) and McNickle (1978). Josephy (1979:88, 119, 163) discusses Nez Perce treks to St. Louis in 1831, 1835, and 1837.

14. Anthony Ravalli came to the Northwest with De Smet in 1844. He was at the falls during September of 1845 and built St. Paul's Chapel then. The second church was built by Joseph Joset in 1847. Ravalli was trained in Western medicine, designed Sacred Heart Mission for the Coeur d'Alenes, and made the first local mill saw from a discarded wagon-wheel rim. He was sent to California in 1857 but returned in 1865. He died at St. Mary's Mission on 2 October 1884 (Schoenberg 1962:546).

15. Peter De Vos was active in Montana and Oregon during 1844. Primarily known as an administrator, De Vos supervised the Vicariate Apostolic in 1844, when Francis Norbert Blanchet went to Montreal to be consecrated a bishop, and became the first resident missionary at St. Paul's in 1848, staying there for three years.

16. Difficulties often revive faith, as was the case with the earthquake of 14 December 1872. The Sanpoil prophet Kwolaskin had warned people previously that something would happen, and when his prediction came true many joined his community at White Stone, where he had them

building an ark during the next several years in preparation for another disaster. His charisma was such that many Sanpoils became practicing Catholics only after his death, although he became a Catholic convert at the Corpus Christi celebration of 30 May 1918. His remains were moved to the Keller cemetery and his log church to the Nespelem agency campus just before the water rose behind Grand Coulee Dam.

Other prophets are also recalled, only some of whom have been mentioned in print. The Plateau was a hotbed of prophetic movements and cults (Spier 1935; Ray 1936b; Walker 1969; Schultz 1971; C. Miller 1985).

17. Angus McDonald, nephew of the famous Archibald McDonald, was the last trader in charge of Fort Colville, 1852–72. When it closed, he moved the goods to Kamloops and settled down on his Montana ranch, where he died 1 February 1889. He was married to Catherine, a sister of the Nez Perce leader Eagle from the Light, and they had thirteen children. While Mourning Dove mentions only the meal served to Stevens and Mc-Clellan (see below), the men's consumption of fifty imperial gallons of grog during and after dinner has also been recorded (Howay, Lewis, and Meyers 1917; Williams 1922).

18. Isaac Stevens and Joel Palmer, Indian superintendent for Oregon, reached the Walla Walla treaty grounds on Mill Creek near the old Whitman mission on 21 May 1855. The council met for thirteen days, and three treaties were signed, establishing reservations for the Yakimas, for the Nez Perces, and for the Cayuses, Walla Wallas, and Umatillas. Treaties with the Spokans and Colvilles were postponed to allow him time to make Fort Benton by midsummer for the treaty with the Blackfeet (Richards 1979:215–26). On his return, Stevens met with the Colvilles on 22 December 1855 to discuss the possibility of a treaty and to plead for their neutrality during the Yakima War.

19. McClellan, later commander of the Union Army, was selected by Isaac Stevens to explore possible passes through the Cascade Mountains as a route for the northern transcontinental railroad. During this 1853 survey, the Yakimas became extremely suspicious, correctly viewing McClellan as an omen of impending land loss. Some have said that his presence helped instigate the 1855 Treaty War (Ruby and Brown 1965: 27–29).

In his harsh assessment of McClellan's survey for a railroad route through Washington Territory, Overmeyer (1941:59) concluded that he had a "splendid capacity for superficiality," since he missed no fewer than eleven passes and apparently was terrified of snow. Abiel Tinkham earned the gratitude of Stevens by showing that it was possible to travel through Snoqualmie Pass during 20–27 January, after McClellan refused to make the attempt.

As had many other soldiers starting their careers at this time, Stevens and McClellan served together during the Mexican-American War (Richards 1979).

20. The Colville Salish reservation was created and changed three times by executive orders. The first reservation was created by President Ulysses S. Grant on 9 April 1872. An order of 2 July 1872 moved it across the Columbia River, opening the prime Colville Valley to white settlement. The Columbias, Peskwaws, Chelans, and Entiats were assigned to the Moses Reservation, created 19 April 1879 and expanded 6 March 1880. The Spokan Reservation was separated from that of the Colvilles in 1881. On 7 July 1883 Chief Moses signed away the Moses Reservation and agreed to move everyone to Colville, except for some Chelans who decided to take 640-acre allotments at Wapato Point along their beloved lake. As a result of the 1887 General Allotment Act, nearly all Indian reservations were eventually divided up into individual allotments, with the "surplus land" being opened for homesteading. The Colvilles shared this fate when the North Half was lost to them. On 1 July 1892 the North Half reverted to public domain except for the allotments of 660 Indians. On 1 July 1898 the South Half or reduced reservation was opened for prospecting and mining.

The McLaughlin Agreement, signed 1 December 1905, stipulated that the South Half be allotted in eighty-acre parcels, but this was not completed until 1914. On 10 October 1910 whites were allowed to homestead, and on 3 May 1916 the unallotted land was made available. Eventually such abuse of land and other rights led to the Indian Reorganization Act of 1934.

The tribe was governed by its traditional chiefs until a business council was instituted on 26 February 1938. The Colvilles entered another black period in the 1950s when termination was threatened. By 1970 the tribal council decided to develop the reservation economically for the benefit of all members (Colville Confederated Tribes 1981). Although the Colville Reservation was created by executive orders, some of those enrolled at Colville belong to tribes that are "successors in interest" to the 1855 Walla Walla treaty. They include members whose ancestors were Nez Perce, Palus, Wenatchi, Columbia, Chelan, or Entiat.

21. The vitality of traditional beliefs about mythic time and events is such that Colvilles still frequently remind each other that someday Coyote will return from the East and break up the sixteen dams along the Columbia, restoring their ancient traditions, waterways, and foods. At present the salmon can reach upriver only as far as Chief Joseph Dam. Their belief rests on the account of how Coyote initially broke up the first fish trap impounding salmon near the mouth of the Columbia, releasing the primordial Salmon in the days when the world was young. The size and quantity of the salmon in each of the tributary rivers is said to be proportional with the beauty of the wife each village let him have. Those who refused him ended up with waterfalls blocking any salmon runs into their rivers.

22. Timentwa acted as a source for the 1930 field school under the auspices of the Santa Fe Laboratory of Anthropology among the southern Okanogans. The students said of him that he was forty-eight, chief of the Kartar band, Moses-Columbia and Kartar on his mother's side, Chelan on that of his father, and overall an "intelligent person with mystical tendencies; prone to formalize everything into a cosmic scheme centering around his religious ideas" (Spier 1938:4). All in all, this is the hallmark of an effective leader. Later he became a forceful advocate for the traditionalists, spearheading the opposition to the Indian Reorganization Act. In a letter, Mourning Dove says he was writing a Bible, probably an Okanogan account of Creation.

23. This is an invaluable bit of information. When Alexander Ross moved to the Red River settlement, Sarah (Sally), his wife, went with him and lost contact with her people. Except for Mourning Dove's saying she was the great-aunt of Timentwa, we would probably never know her family connections (see Van Kirk 1985 and note 22 above).

24. Curiously missing from this historical sketch is any mention of the Wilkes expedition. An exploring and scientific expedition sent around the world by the American government, it spent considerable time in the Northwest. Lieutenant Johnson of the *Porpoise* reached Fort Okanogan on 8 June 1841 and Fort Colvile on 15–19 June 1841. He marveled that the basket trap was raised three times a day, each haul filled with three hundred fine salmon, which were shared among all. He also approved of the two hundred acres of level land nearby and the large herds of live-

stock. Horatio Hale, expedition philologist, disembarked in Oregon and went home across the county. He visited the Whitman mission, Walker's Prairie, and Fort Colville, collecting a set of month names (cf. chap. 1, n. 12) (Wilkes 1845, 4:433–45, 441–474).

CHAPTER 14: THE BIG SNOW AND FLOOD RAMPAGE

1. After much research, I established that Mourning Dove was describing the winter of 1892–93. Buckland (1966:93, 94) said a mild November and December were succeeded by subzero temperatures in the New Year. By April most of the cattle were dead of cold and starvation. Ruby and Brown (1965:307) said that winter was very severe and mentioned great loss of livestock. The temperature fell to −22°F on 8 February. Fries (1951:231) was most explicit: "The summer of 1890 was cool, so that the greater portion of snow in the mountains did not melt, and the rivers had only a normal runoff. The following winters were severe, followed again by cool summers. The winter of 1892–3 was marked by fierce blizzards and very deep snow. Mr. French, a ferryman between Brewster and Pateros, reported snow six feet deep in a sheltered place where it had not drifted. And again, the summer of 1893 was not warm enough to cause any unusual runoff."

2. Other bad winters are also recalled by Colville elders. In the winter of 1907, many animals froze to death. The carcasses of horses and cattle had to be left until spring, when only their hides were of any use. Hardest hit was Coxit George, who lost most of his herd. A prominent man in the Kartar Valley, he was married to Christine, the daughter of Chief Seattle. He was often on horseback because it was easier for him than walking, since he was slightly crippled after breaking a leg falling from a horse. Coxit means "broken" in Chinook jargon, the Northwest trade language. He died in his sleep at St. Mary's Mission near Omak, waiting to celebrate the 1922 Corpus Christi (Raufer 1966:230).

   In February of 1907 a man died at Goose Lake, and it took all day for the body to be moved from there to the home of Coxit George. After a rest, seven horsemen broke trail by bucking their horses through the snow. That night people made a sled, and the next day they took the body to Father De Rouge, who had another sled waiting by prearrangement to take the remains to the mission for burial.

3. As an example of how bad conditions can get in this region, Toole

(1959:144–45) describes the conditions of the bad winter of 1885–86 in Montana. Although the weather itself was mild, without strong winds or heavy snow, there was a three-month combination of factors that proved devastating. It became the most famous of the bad winters of the West, with heavy losses throughout the region.

The summer had been hot, and the northern ranges were crammed with cattle. Grass was thin, and the rains did not come. A series of violent storms came one after another all during November. This snow began to melt during a mid-December thaw, only to be frozen into a firm sheet of ice by low temperatures and bitter winds over the succeeding months. Stock cut their noses and legs trying to break through the ice. The bitter cold of January was followed by severe blizzards in February. Finally, in March, the warm "chinook" wind came to thaw the land, but by then stock losses were staggering and the cattle industry was in a shambles.

4. This chapter dates the birth of this sister to March 1893; the census rolls indicate early 1892.

5. Balsamroot famine food is discussed in chapter 4, note 3.

6. Direct questioning or anything that appears to be prying into the affairs of someone else is bad manners and still has not been accepted into Salish etiquette despite years of interacting with whites. As some old people are still fond of telling too-eager children, "Don't ask. When I think you're ready or you need to know something, then I'll tell you. Not before." When instruction does take place, many tribes prefer to do it while the child is eating so that everything gets swallowed together and nourishes the child.

7. Although this chapter is full of high drama, Charles Quintasket described it as "the Hollywood version." Actually, during the 1892–93 winter, his father Joseph kept his stock close to home. Pete Pierre Arcasa had plenty of hay and generously offered part of it to Joseph. As the winter got more and more severe, however, Pete looked increasingly unhappy. Joseph correctly guessed that the hay was being used more quickly than anticipated. To spare Arcasa's supply, Joseph and Henry Martin drove their herds north of the Laurier border station, between Cascade and Grand Forks, British Columbia. They left the stock and went home to Pia, where four feet of snow built up during the winter. The endless bad weather broke on Easter Sunday, and the snow was gone a week later. When Joseph and Henry went for their herds, expecting to

find only bones and bodies, they were delighted to find them healthy and well fed. Mourning Dove probably chose a tragic version because it was more dramatic, made a better story, and saved her father from possible envy by neighbors who were not as wise or lucky.

CHAPTER 15: EARLY FARMING

1. Pia is actually the term for the red-tailed hawk. As Mourning Dove remarked in a June 1930 letter, although she was well versed in the Salishan names for species, she was not always sure of their proper English identifications. This is a case in point. See also Bouchard and Kennedy (1979:308, #328).

2. The third site for the St. Regis Mission was on land provided by Chief Kinkanawah under the stipulation that as long as the fathers maintained a church and school there, they could use the land. Should they abandon missionary activities, however, the locale was to revert to its original owners, if any survived. Otherwise it was to pass to the Colvilles (Raufer 1966:94–95).

3. Ridiculing laughter acts as a very effective deterrent throughout native America. Colvilles and others learn it as a means of social control from infancy. In any such close, supportive society, it assumes the character of a rejection, albeit a psychological rather than a physical one.

4. Edna Ferber (1963:56) describes a stone boat as a flat sled made of heavy timbers, used for hauling stones and such.

5. The Adolph family among the Colvilles is closely identified with the Lakes and their traditions. Lake and Kootenay canoes are distinctive for their sturgeon-nosed bow and stern.

6. Cusick, Washington, is the site of a small Kalispel reservation.

7. Moya is actually Moyie, the name of a river, lake, and town in south-eastern British Columbia. This trek took the family southeast to Cusick, northeast to Bonner's Ferry, then north along the Moyie River and Moyie Lake.

8. During the 1864 gold fever resulting from rich placer finds on Wild Horse Creek in southeastern British Columbia, John Galbraith started a ferry service. When miners began to move away, other settlers were brought into the area by the construction of the Canadian Pacific Railroad. The new population became increasingly involved in disputes with long-resident Kootenays. In 1887 Superintendent Samuel B. Steele and

seventy-five Mounties built a post at Galbraith's ferry. In 1888 a bridge was built, and the detachment left. The growing town, however, became known as Fort Steele in honor of the man who served so well that there were no hostilities or bloodshed. Another boom came in 1892 after silver and lead were discovered. The town became depopulated when the 1896 route of the British Columbia Southern Railroad went to Cranbrook instead. At present its buildings and land compose a Provincial Park and Heritage Centre.

9. Gold mining claims are registered as placer or quartz, depending on their depositional origins and the extractive techniques needed. Quartz (also called lode) deposits are original, while placer ones are a consequence of erosion.

10. Broken Nose Abraham was one of Mourning Dove's favorite storytellers. Crippled, he rode double with his blind wife on a white horse. He also provided Mourning Dove with war songs (Mourning Dove 1933:11, 1976: 12).

11. The Kootenays' enthusiasm for gambling, especially after missionaries opposed other of their traditional recreations, came to involve some creative social adjustments. There was a practical rule that siblings never gamble against each other. However, since sibling terms also applied to cousins, Kootenays sometimes shifted from kin terms to first names so that teams could be organized, even if it meant that collateral relatives were playing against each other (Turney-High 1941:143).

12. Palmer (1980) provides a fine study of a comparable situation among Coeur d'Alene farmers.

CHAPTER 16: THE INVASIONS OF MINERS AND SETTLERS

1. Elders recall other stage lines that went through the Sanpoil Valley. A buggy went from Wilbur to Republic regularly, stopping for passengers at the Keller post office and store. In 1918 its driver had long hair parted on the right, according to a Sanpoil elder who saw him when she was a girl. Edwin Harrison McCuen ran a stage line from Wilbur to Republic, stopping at Nespelem and Grand Coulee. Before 1900 he had the mail run between the same destinations, using the crest line of Central Peak for part of his route.

2. Albert M. Anderson (1862–1928) was born and orphaned in Wisconsin. He came to Spokane Falls in 1877 looking for work and found several

jobs, including those of clerk at Forts Colville and Spokane and of clerk and chief assistant to the agent of the Colville Reservation in 1889–93. He moved to Olympia but returned as Colville agent in 1897, when he assumed the title of major, as did most agents (cf. Wissler 1971:13). In 1903, the same year he married, Anderson was removed from his post for gross irregularities in his account records. According to Gidley (1979:57), "both John W. Bubb, in 1896, and Albert M. Anderson, in 1904, were removed from their posts after discoveries of financial irregularities. Anderson had gone so far, it was alleged, as to claim guardianship over Indian children and then take the monies from leasing their allotments." Similar abuses were conducted on a grand scale in Oklahoma by court-appointed white guardians, especially when native children had lucrative oil leases (Debo 1972).

3. The best known of these early policemen at the Colville agency was Poker Joe. So fond of this game that it provided his nickname, he learned to play cards at Fort Spokane, perhaps while on rotation guarding the jail inmates. He came from an important Columbian family and spent his entire adult life in service. His homestead was near Belvidere or Wide Spot between Nespelem and Grand Coulee Dam.

4. According to Indian agent William Winans, when Chief Kinkanawah became too old in the estimation of the Jesuits, they advised the tribe to have him resign. He did so, and in his place the tribe elected Joseph Cotolegu, who "checked gambling, drinking, and other disorders and broke up illicit connections among the Indians. Two subchiefs, Chief Orphan [Aropaghan, also Arophan, Urpaghan] and Chief Bernard [the policeman], aspired for a time to leadership after Chief Kin-ka-nowha died. After Chief Orphan's death, Chief Bernard proved himself a fine Christian leader. Bernard was the nephew of Chief Kin-ka-nowha." Later in life Bernard organized the Colville Indian Association to fight for the legal rights of natives (Raufer 1966:224).

5. As anthropologists have been slow to realize, this particular closeness between alternating generations of grandparents and grandchildren has the advantage of placing the young in the care of knowledgeable teachers. Thus, native traditions can be passed on despite the efforts of schools, churches, and government to turn self-reliant natives into impoverished whites.

6. More needs to be known about Clair Hunt, Peter Alex, Charley Brown,

and their respective roles in the survey. This allotment survey is the context for Mourning Dove's first menstruation as described in chapter 2.

7. Except for fishing and hunting rights, the North Half of the reservation was lost on 1 July 1892, save for the allotted lands. As Yanan writes, "The North Half, a land of high valleys, mountains and many lakes and streams, was prized by the Indians for its game and shelter. White miners found gold in the region and mines operate there to this day" (1971:17). It was bought by the government in the aftermath of the Dawes Severalty Act of 1887 and a May 1891 agreement to allot the land. These allotments had not been approved in 1896 when the area was opened for settlement, and some people were forced off land where they had lived for countless generations because they did not then have clear title. For a comparable experience during the opening of Oklahoma for homesteading, see Alford (1979).

8. See the reference to cow's milk in chapter 5, note 5.

Glossary of Colville-Okanogan Terms

Included in this list are all the Indian words used by Mourning Dove in her writings that make up this book. These forms are listed as found in the text, along with translations and comments. Transliterations into present-day standard Colville-Okanogan orthography are offered as certain (unmarked), hypothetical (prefixed by an asterisk), or unavailable (?). The format of the entries is as follows: The form found in the text is given first, followed by the page number in parentheses. AS = alternate spellings; RF = related form; TC = textual comment and/or translation; * = reconstructed or inferred, therefore uncertain form; TL: transliteration; CM = comments and/or literal translation. The hyphens used by Mourning Dove were probably intended to mark syllable boundaries; hyphens (-) in the transliteration mark word-internal morpheme boundaries; = marks a lexical affix (concludes a lexical prefix and introduces a lexical suffix); √ introduces a root; < means derived from. The single reference cited herein is Verne F. Ray, *The Sanpoil and Nespelem, Salishan Peoples of Northeastern Washington*, University of Washington Publications in Anthropology, vol. 5 (1933). This glossary is the joint work of Clara Jack and Anthony Mattina to match his dictionary.

Allum-mak-hum (p. 224). TC: chief of the earth. TL: ilmíxʷm.
Arapaghan (pp. 130, 232). AS: Aropaghan, Arpoghan, Urpaghan. TC: chief's name. TL: arp=áxǝn.
Arsell (p. 112). TC: woman's name. TL: ʕasál. CM: < Angela and/or Ethel.
Cone-quah (p. 132). TC: shaman's name. TL: *qʷǝnɬqʷáʔ.
Coosta (p. 132). TC: shaman's name. TL: *kʷǝstá.
En-am-tues (p. 20). TC: sitting on the summit, placename. TL: n-ʔamt=ús. CM: landmark near Molson, Wash., Hee Hee Stone.
En-hwx-kwas-t'nun (p. 4). TC: arrow scraper; an Okanagan village. TL: *n-x̣ʷq'ʷ=aʔst-nú-n CM: This form would mean 'I managed to scrape the arrow.'

En-koh-tu-me-whoh (pp. 4, 148). TC: Nicola people. TL: nk'ʷ-t-mixʷ. CM: This form usually refers to the Thompson people.

En-we-num (p. 126). TC: gift at give-aways. TL: nwínəm.

En-yas (p. 151). TC: Ignace. TL: nyas.

E-ya-ya-ya Taa-to-pa (p. 218). TC: to refer to Sweatlodge. *yayàm t'at'úpaʔ. CM: ya-yám, 'sweatlodge chanting,' t'at'úpaʔ, 'great-grandparent.'

Ha-ah-pecha (p. 16). TC: striped blanket, woman's name. TL: ʔaxəxp=íc'aʔ.

Hu-mi-shu-ma (p. xvii). TC: mourning dove. TL: ham'ís-ham'ís.

Ilemux-solix (p. 151). AS: Ilemux-solux. TC: chief of Arrow Lakes people. TL: ilmxʷ ... CM: apparent compound, only the first part of which is clear.

Ilthkoyape, Ilthkoyope (p. 149). TC: Explorer and surveyor David Thompson's term for Kettle Falls. TL: *s-xʷyʔ=iłp-x. CM: Thompson's intended form is unclear. Cf. *Skoyelpi, Swhy-ayl-puh* for comments that pertain.

Inisiscachin (p. 121). TC: little canyon, placename. TL: ?.

In-kla-whin-whe-ten (p. 20). TC: battling place, Midway, B.C. (placename). TL: ?.

In-sil-whu-eet-qu (p. 20). TC: Pacific Ocean. TL: n-slxʷaʔ=ítkʷ. CM: 'ocean,' 'big river,' 'big water.'

In-ya-tin-k (p. 91). TC: walking in front, man's name. TL: nyaʕtínk. CM: the reference is to walking from lodge to lodge as when searching for a person.

Ka-atqhu (p. 16). AS: Ka-at-qhu TC: big beside water, woman's name. TL: ...atkʷ. CM: only the final suffix can be inferred.

Kalalen (p. 113). TC: Caroline. TL: kaləlín.

Kanatal (p. 107). TC: name of whipper and chief's aide at Kettle Falls. TL: ?.

kee-su (p. 20). TC: dog salmon. TC: kísuʔ. CM: Coho salmon.

Kee-ten (p. 6). TC: pet name for Christine. TL: *kitín. CM: the expected and occurring form < Christine is klistín.

Keleta (p. 160). TC: Mourning Dove's sister's name. TL: ?.

Kel-yel-pas (p. 177). TC: tree in the center of the land; Camp Eureka, later Republic (placename). TL: ... yəl ... CM: The root √yul(t), 'large tree' is recognizable.

Ken-kin-awah (p. 105). AS: Kinkanawah, Kin-ka-nowha. TC: Chief's name. TL: kən-kanáxʷaʔ.

klek-chin (p. 150). TC: kettles, cooking baskets. TL: lək=cín. CM: The initial *k* remains unclear.

Kolaskin (p. xxix). AS: Kwolaskin. TC: Kolaskin, Joe Skolaskin; Sanpoil prophet. TL: q'ʷlás=qən.

Kutene-us (p. 201). AS: T-quit-na-wis. TC: big fat man; Fr. Caruana. TL: ? CM: may be a Kalispel form; cf. kʷtun-t, 'big.'

kwas-peet-za (p. 146). TC: curly-haired; buffalo (robe). TL: qʷsp=íc'aʔ. CM: Cf. qʷisp 'buffalo.'

kwat-zee (p. 4). AS: qua-zee'ah. TC: pit dwelling. TL: qʷc'iʔ.

Kwolaskin (p. 224). AS: Kolaskin. TC: Kolaskin, Joe Skolaskin; Sanpoil prophet. TL: q'ʷlás=qən.

kwy-lux (p. 151). TC: black robe-gown; form used to refer to Fr. De Smet. TL: q'ʷ$ʕ$ay=lqs. CM: 'black robe,' 'priest,' Jesuit.

La-chin (p. 100). TC: woven kettle or bucket, placename. TL: ?.

Mock-tsin (p. 20). TC: knoll between a divide. TL: *mq'ʷ=cin. CM: 'lump on the edge.'

Mook-mook-t'ku-nalx (p. 11). TC: snow dress, woman's name. TL: *mkʷ-mkʷ=t=qn=alqs or *mk'ʷ-mk'ʷ=t=qn=alqs. CM: Cf. √mkʷ 'snow mounds;' −mk'ʷ 'be snowed in;' =t=qn unclear sequence.

Moses (p. xxix). TC: man's name. TL: muwís.

Mus-aia (p. 102). TC: valerian, stink root. TL: ms$ʕ$ay'.

Okanagans (p. xxvii). TL: uqna=qín-x.

Pah-tah-heet-sa (p. 4). TC: woman's name. TL: ?.

Pak-kum-kin (p. 82). TC: white top; Mt. Baldy (placename). TL: páq-əm=qən.

Patee (p. 8). TC: baby name for Mourning Dove's grandmother. TL: ?.

pee-cha (p. 19). TC: digging stick. TL: píca?. CM: 'root digger.'

pen-pen-nox (p. 18). TC: folded at the ends; Indian trunks. TL: pn-pn=aqs.

Pep-pa-la-wh (p. 29). TC: cream color; horse's name. TL: *pa$ʕ$-pá$ʕ$=lxʷ or *pə-pá$ʕ$=lxʷ. CM: Cf. kɬ-p$ʕ$a=lxʷ, 'cream colored horse.'

Pia (pp. 4, 21). TC: red-tailed hawk; Pia (placename). TL: piyá$ʕ$', pya$ʕ$'. 'Pia Mission,' 'Kelly Hill.'

qua-zee'ah (p. 148). AS: kwat-zee. TC: pit houses. TL: qʷc'i?.

quh-kam (p. 103). TC: tanning rocks. TL: ?. CM: Cf. √xʷikʷ-m, 'scrape.'

Quintasket (pp. ix, 4). TC: Mourning Dove's surname. TL: qʷən-t=ásq'ət. CM: 'blue/green sky.' Mourning Dove suggests that the name was originally T-quin-task-et.

Sanpo-i-il (p. 145). TC: Sanpoil. TL: s-n-p$ʕ$ʷil-x.

Saxa (p. 151). TC: En-yas Saxa, Ignace Saxa; man's name. TL: ?.

S-calm-achin (p. 100). TC: dug ground; placename. TL: ?.

Schwankoo (p. 150). TC: Kettle Falls. AS: Schwan-ate-koo, Sionetkwu, Swah-netk-qhu. TL: ʼs-x̣ʷn=itkʷ. CM: Mourning Dove's orthography suggests she had in mind a different form.

Schwan-ate-koo (p. 6). AS: Schwankoo, Sionetkwu, Swah-netk-qhu. TC: Kettle Falls. TL: x-x̣ʷn=itkʷ. CM: This orthography suggests ʼs-x̣ʷn=atkʷ possible, but not attested.

See-pas (p. 101). AS (?): See-pays TC: salmon divider's name. CM: This and the following entry represent a single word.

See-pays (p. 101). AS (?): See-pas (q.v.).

See-whelh-ken (p. 6). TC: man's name, chief at Kettle Falls. TL: s-yxʷ-ilx=qn. CM: 'dropped, shed horns.'

shumix (p. xxix). TS: power. TL: sumíx. CM: 'guardian spirit,' 'spirit power.' Possibly analyzable √sw-mix.

Similkameen (p. 6). TC: placename. TL: s-məlqʼ-míx. CM: Mourning Dove says the term refers to swans.

Sin-na-aich-kis-tu (p. 6). AS: Sinschirst. TC: Trout Lake band of the Lakes people, Arrow Lakes people. TL: s-n-ʕic=kst-x.

Sinschirst (p. 145). AS: Sin-na-aich-kis-tu (q.v.).

Sionetkwu (p. 150). AS: Schwankoo, Schwan-ate-koo, Swah-netk-qhu. TC: Kettle Falls. TL: s-x̣ʷn=itkʷ.

Ska-ch-cist (pp. 105, 214). TC: flag hung up day, Sunday. TL: ʼs-kʕac=íwʼs. CM: The suffix of the present-day form is probably not what Mourning Dove intended.

Skoyelpi (p. 224). TC: chief of the Kettles (man's name). TL: ʼs-x̣ʷyʔ=iłp-x. CM: 'Kettle people.' This reconstruction is suspect because Mourning Dove gives a form *Swhy-ayl-puh* (q.v.). Cf. also *Ilthkoyape*.

skwant (p. 212). AS: squant. TC: waterfall; placename. TL: skʷant.

Snee-wh-am (p. 126). TC: drop in; give-away at winter dance. TL: s-n-yxʷ-am. CM: 'winter dance.'

Soma-how-atqhu (p. 6). TC: she got her power from water, woman's name. TL: swmax̣-átkʷ.

spit-lum (p. 19). TC: bitterroot. TL: s-pʼiƛʼ-m.

Spok-letch (p. 133). TC: ling fish. TL: s-pqʷlic.

Squant (p. 100). AS: skwant. TC: waterfall; placename. TL: skʷant.

Stui-kin (p. 6). TC: beaver head; personal and family name. TL: ?. CM: The form stútikən is known as a man's name; cf. stunx, 'beaver,' =qin, 'head.'

Sulee (p. 11). TC: Julia. TL: sulí. CM: < French Julie.

Su-le-whoo-mah (p. 38). TC: puberty. TL: ?.

Suesteel (p. 170). TC: woman's name. TL: ?.

Swah-netk-qhu (p. 156). AS: Schwan-ate-koo, Schwankoo, Sionetkwu. TC: Kettle Falls, Columbia River. TL: s-x̣ʷn=itkʷ. CM: Kettle Falls. n-x̣ʷn=tkʷ=itkʷ, 'Columbia River.'

Swhy-ayl-puh (p. 3). TC: Colville people. TL: s-x̣ʷyʔ=iɬp-x. CM: For comments that pertain cf. *Ilthkoyape, Skoyelpi.*

Swimptkin (p. 156). TC: Okanagan chief's name. TL: suyímt=qən.

swool-hu (p. 17). TC: tipi. TL: s-xʷul=ɬxʷ.

S'oo-yoos (p. 20). TC: Osoyoos Lake. TL: sw=iw's, sʔúys. CM: 'There is a dry spot.' Reference unclear.

Teequalt (p. 15). TC: woman's name. TL: ?.

toom (p. 7). TC: woman's mother. TL: tum'. CM: Kin term.

T-quin-task-et (p. 4). TC: variant of *Quintasket,* (q.v.).

T-quit-na-wiss (p. 26). TC: big belly; Fr. Caruana. TL: ?. CM: may be a Kalispel form; cf. kʷtun-t 'big.'

Tyee (p. 101). TC: salmon divider. TL: ?. CM: Cf. √t'ilm, 'divide,' sxʷ= t'ilm, 'divider.'

Urpaghan (p. 232). AS: Arapaghan, Arpaghan, Aropaghan, Arpoghan, Urpaghan. TC: chief's name. TL: arp=áx̣ən.

Wal-looks (p. 103). TC: monte (Spanish card game). TL: walúks.

Whoop-chen (p. 152). TC: hair on the chin; Angus McDonald. TL: wp=cin.

References

ABBREVIATIONS USED

GSA
General Series in Anthropology

NARN
Northwest Anthropological Research Notes

PNQ
Pacific Northwest Quarterly

SWJA
Southwestern Journal of Anthropology

UCPAAE
University of California Publications
in American Archaeology and Ethnology

UWPA
University of Washington Publications
in Anthropology

WHQ
Washington Historical Quarterly

Alford, Thomas Wildcat. 1979. *Civilization and the Story of the Absentee Shawnee*. Norman: University of Oklahoma Press. Originally published 1936.

Anastasio, Angelo. 1972. The Southern Plateau: An ecological analysis of intergroup relations. NARN 6(2): 109–229, supplement.

Atkinson, Reginald N. 1952. Burial Grounds of the Okanagan Indians. *Okanagan Historical Society, Annual Report* 16:5–12.

Ault, Nelson. 1959. *The Papers of Lucullus Virgil McWhorter*. Pullman, Wash.: Friends of the Washington State University Library.

Basso, Keith. 1979. *Portraits of the "Whiteman": Linguistic Play and Cultural Symbols among the Western Apache*. Cambridge: Cambridge University Press.

Bataille, Gretchen M., and Kathleen Mullen Sands. 1984. *American Indian Women: Telling Their Lives*. Lincoln: University of Nebraska Press.

Baym, Nina. 1978. *Woman's Fiction: A Guide to Novels by and about Women in America, 1820–1870*. Ithaca: Cornell University Press.

Beckham, Stephen Dow. 1969. George Gibbs, 1815–1873: Historian and Anthropologist. Ph.D. diss., University of California at Los Angeles.

Bennett, Lee. 1979. *Cultural Resources Overview of the Twisp-Winthrop-Conconully Planning Unit*. Okanogan, Wash.: Okanogan National Forest.

Bischoff, William. 1945. *The Jesuits in Old Oregon: A Sketch of Jesuit Activities in the Pacific Northwest*. Caldwell, Idaho: Caxton Printers.

Bloodroot, Jesse. 1959. *Human Resources of the Colville Confederated Tribes*. Washington, D.C.: Government Printing Office.

Boas, Franz, ed. 1917. Folk-Tales of Salishan and Sahaptin Tribes. *American Folklore Society, Memoirs* 11:1–201.

———. 1918. Kutenai Tales. *Bureau of American Ethnology, Bulletin* 5:1–387.

Bone, Robert. 1958. *The Negro Novel in America*. New Haven: Yale University Press.

Bouchard, Randy, and Dorothy Kennedy. 1979. Ethnogeography of the Franklin D. Roosevelt Lake Area. Report to the Bureau of Land Management, Coulee Dam, Washington.

Broderick, Theresa. 1909. *The Brand: A Tale of the Flathead Reservation*. Seattle: Alice Harriman.

Brown, William C. 1911. *Early Okanogan History*. Omak, Wash.: Press of the Okanogan Independent.

———. 1961. *The Indian Side of the Story*. Spokane, Wash.: C. W. Hill.

Brumble, H. David III. 1988. Preliterate Traditions of American Indian Autobiography. In *American Indian Autobiography*, pp. 21–71 Berkeley: University of California Press.

Brunton, Bill. 1968. Ceremonial Integration in the Plateau of Northwestern North America. NARN 2(1): 1–28.

Buckland, Frank. 1966. *Ogopogo's Vigil: A History of Kelowna and the Okanagan*. Kelowna, B.C.: Okanagan Historical Society.

Burns, Robert Ignatius. 1966. *The Jesuits and the Indian Wars of the Northwest*. New Haven: Yale University Press.

Carriker, Eleanor, Robert C. Carriker, Clifford A. Carroll, and W. L. Larson. 1976. *Guide to the Microfilm Edition of the Oregon Province Archives of the Society of Jesus Indian Language Collection: The Pacific Northwest Tribes*. Spokane, Wash.: Gonzaga University.

Carriker, Robert. 1985. Joseph M. Cataldo, S.J.: Courier of Catholicism to the Nez Perces. In *Churchmen and the Western Indians, 1820–1920*, ed. Clyde A. Milner II and Floyd A. O'Neill, pp.109–93, 228–35. Norman: University of Oklahoma Press.

Chalfant, Stuart. 1974a. Material Relative to Aboriginal Land Use and Occupancy by the Columbia Salish of Central Washington. In *American Indian Ethnohistory: Interior Salish and Eastern Washington Indians*, pp.229–313. New York: Garland Press.

———. 1974b. Material Relative to Aboriginal Land Use and Occupancy by the Wenatchi Salish of Central Washington. In *American Indian Ethnohistory: Interior Salish and Eastern Washington Indians*, pp.315–47. New York: Garland Press.

Chance, David. 1973. Influence of the Hudson's Bay Company on the Native Cultures of the Colville District. NARN, Memoir 2.

Chance, David, Jennifer Chance, and John L. Fagan. 1977. *Kettle Falls: 1972*. Anthropological Research Manuscript Series 31. Moscow: University of Idaho.

Chittenden, Hiram Martin, and Alfred Talbot Richardson. 1905. *Life, Letters and Travels of Father Pierre-Jean De Smet, S.J., 1801–1873*. 4 vols. New York: Francis P. Harper.

Clark, Ella. 1955–56. George Gibbs' Account of Indian Mythology in Oregon and Washington Territories. *Oregon Historical Quarterly* 56:293–325, 57:125–67.

Colville Confederated Tribes. 1981. Socio-economic report, Nespelem, Washington.

Coues, Elliott, ed. 1897. *New Light on the Early History of the Greater Northwest: The Manuscript Journals of Alexander Henry and of David Thompson, 1799–1814.* 3 vols. New York: F. P. Harper.

Cox, Ross. 1832. *Adventures on the Columbia River, Including the Narrative of a Residence of Six Years on the Western Side of the Rocky Mountains among various Tribes of Indians hitherto unknown: Together with a Journey Across the American Continent.* New York: J. and J. Harper.

Debo, Angie. 1972. *And Still the Waters Run: The Betrayal of the Five Civilized Tribes.* Princeton: Princeton University Press.

Densmore. Frances. 1932. An Explanation of a Trick Performed by Indian Conjurers. *American Anthropologist* 34(2): 310–14.

Drury, Clifford Merrill. 1940. *Elkanah and Mary Walker, Pioneers among the Spokanes.* Caldwell, Idaho: Caxton Printers.

———. 1976. *Nine Years with the Spokane Indians: The Diary, 1838–1848, of Elkanah Walker.* Glendale, Calif.: Arthur H. Clark.

Du Bois, Cora. 1938. The Feather Cult of the Middle Columbia. GSA 7:1–45.

Eidlitz, Kerstin. 1969. *Food and Emergency Food in the Circumpolar Area.* Studia Ethnographica Uppsaliensis 32. Uppsala: University of Uppsala.

Elmendorf, William. 1961. System Change in Salish Kinship Terminologies. SWJA 17(4): 365–82.

———. 1965. Linguistic and Geographical Relations in the Northern Plateau Area. SWJA 21(1): 63–78.

Ewers, John. 1948. Gustavus Sohon's Portraits of Flathead and Pend D'Oreille Indians, 1854. *Smithsonian Miscellaneous Collections* 110(7): 1–68.

Ferber, Edna. 1963. *A Kind of Magic.* Garden City, N.Y.: Doubleday.

Fisher, Alice Poindexter [Dexter]. 1979. The Transportation of Tradition: A Study of Zitkala Ša and Mourning Dove, Two Transitional American Indian Writers. Ph.D. diss., City College of New York.

———. 1981. Introduction. In *Cogewea*, by Mourning Dove (1981).

Fitting, James E. 1973. *The Development of North American Archaeology: Essays in the History of Regional Traditions.* New York: Anchor Books.

Fries, U. E. 1951. *From Copenhagen to Okanogan: The Autobiography of a Pioneer.* With the assistance of Emil Fries, ed. Grace V. Stearns and Eugene Hoy. Caldwell, Idaho: Caxton Printers.

Garth, Thomas. 1965. The Plateau Whipping Complex and Its Relationship to Plateau-Southwest Contacts. *Ethnohistory* 12(2): 141–70.

Gidley, Mick. 1979. *With One Sky above Us: Life on an Indian Reservation at the Turn of the Century*. New York: G. P. Putnam's Sons.

———. 1981. *Kopet: A Documentary History of Chief Joseph's Last Years*. Seattle: University of Washington Press.

———. 1983. An Author's Rejoinder. PNQ 74(3): 137.

Glover, Richard, ed. 1962. *David Thompson's Narrative, 1784–1812*. Toronto: Champlain Society.

Gould, Marian. 1917. Okanogan Tales and Sanpoil Tales. In Boas (1917), pp.98–100, 101–13.

Grabert, Garland. 1965. Archaeological Excavations at Fort Okanogan (45 Ok 64), 1964. National Park Service Interim Report.

———. 1974. Okanagan Archaeology: 1966–67. *Syesis* 7, supplement 2.

Guie, Heister Dean. 1933. Editing and drawings. In *Coyote Stories*, by Mourning Dove (1933).

———. 1977. *Bugles in the Valley: Garnett's Fort Simcoe*. Portland: Oregon Historical Society.

Gunkel, Alexander. 1978. Culture in Conflict: A Study of Contrasted Interrelations and Reactions between Euro-Americans and the Walla Walla Indians of Washington State. Ph.D. diss., Southern Illinois University.

Gunther, Erna. 1926. An Analysis of the First Salmon Ceremony. *American Anthropologist* 28(4): 605–17.

———. 1928. A Further Analysis of the First Salmon Ceremony. UWPA 2(5): 129–73.

Gwydir, R. D. 1917. A Record of the San Poil Indians. WHQ 8(4): 243–50.

Haeberlin, Herman, James A. Teit, and Helen Roberts. 1928. Coiled Basketry in British Columbia and Surrounding Region. *Bureau of American Ethnology, Annual Report* 41:11–484.

Haines, Francis. 1938. The Northward Spread of Horses among the Plains Indians. *American Anthropologist* 40:429–37.

Hallowell, A. Irving. 1942. *The Role of Conjuring in Salteaux Society*. Publication 2. Philadelphia: Philadelphia Anthropological Society.

Hanzeli, Victor Egon. 1969. *Missionary Linguistics in New France: A Study of Seventeenth- and Eighteenth-Century Descriptions of American Indian Languages*. The Hague: Mouton.

Hill-Tout, Charles. 1907. *The Natives of British North America*. Vol.1. *The*

Far West: The Home of the Salish and Dene. London: Archibald Constable.

————. 1911. Report on the Ethnology of the Okanaken of British Columbia, an Interior Division of the Salish Stock. *Journal of the Royal Anthropological Institute* 41:130–61.

Hines, Donald M. 1976. Foreword. In *Tales of the Okanogans*, by Mourning Dove (1976).

Howay, F. W., William Lewis, and Jacob Meyers. 1917. Angus McDonald: A Few Items of the West. WHQ 8(3): 188–229.

Hoxie, Frederick. 1984. *A Final Promise: The Campaign to Assimilate the Indians, 1880–1920.* Lincoln: University of Nebraska Press.

Hudson, Douglas. 1986. The Okanagan Indians. In *Native Peoples: The Canadian Experience*, ed. R. Bruce Morrison and C. Roderick Wilson, pp.445–66. Toronto: McClelland and Stewart.

Hull, Lindley M., comp. 1929. *A History of Central Washington, Including the Famous Wenatchee, Entiat, Chelan and the Columbia Valleys with an Index and Eighty Scenic-historical Illustrations.* Spokane, Wash.: Shaw and Borden.

Josephy, Alvin M. 1979. *The Nez Perce and the Opening of the Northwest.* Abridged ed. Lincoln: University of Nebraska Press. Originally published 1965.

Kane, Paul. 1859. *Wanderings of an Artist among the Indians of North America from Canada to Vancouver's Island and Oregon through the Hudson's Bay Company Territory and Back Again.* London: Longman, Brown, Green, and Roberts.

————. 1971. *Paul Kane's Frontier.* Ed. J. Russell Harper. Austin: University of Texas Press.

Kinkade, Dale. 1967. On the Identification of the Methows (Salish). *International Journal of American Linguistics* 33(3): 193–97.

————. 1981. *Dictionary of the Moses-Columbia Language.* Nespelem, Wash.: Colville Confederated Tribes.

Larson, Charles. 1978. *American Indian Fiction.* Albuquerque: University of New Mexico Press.

Leechman, J. D., and M. R. Harrington. 1921. *String Records of the Northwest.* Indian Notes and Monographs. New York: Museum of the American Indian, Heye Foundation.

Leonhardy, Frank, and David G. Rice. 1970. A Proposed Culture Typology for the Lower Snake River Region, Southeastern Washington. NARN 4(1): 1–29.

Lerman, Norman. 1952 and 1954. Okanogan Field Notes for 1952 and 1954. Box 78, files 1 and 2. Melville Jacobs Collection. University of Washington Archives, Seattle.

———. 1953–54. An Okanagan Winter Dance. *Anthropology in British Columbia* 4:35–36.

Lewis, William S. 1927. *The Okanogan, Methow, Sanpoils, Nespelem, Colville, and Lakes Indian Tribes or Bands of the State of Washington.* Washington, D.C.: Government Printing Office.

Lopatin, Ivan. 1960. Origin of the Native American Steam Bath. *American Anthropologist* 62(4): 977–93.

McClellan, George. 1855. *General Reports of the Survey of the Cascades, February 25, 1853.* 33d Cong., 2d sess. House Executive Document 91, serial 791, pp.188–201.

M'Dowell, Malcolm. 1920. Report on the Colville Indian Reservation, Washington (appendix 1). *Board of Indian Commissioners, Bulletin* 120:65–72.

McLeod, Norma. 1971. The Semantic Parameter in Music: The Blanket Rite of the Lower Kutenai. *Interamericano de Investigación Musical* 7:83–101.

McNickle, D'Arcy. 1978. *The Surrounded.* Albuquerque: University of New Mexico Press. Originally published 1936.

———. 1978. *Wind from an Enemy Sky.* New York: Harper and Row.

McWhorter, Lucullus Virgil. 1940. *Yellow Wolf: His Own Story.* Caldwell, Idaho: Caxton Printers.

Malouf, Carling, and A. Arline Malouf. 1945. The Effect of Spanish Slavery on the Indians of the Intermountain West. SWJA 1(3): 378–91.

Markowitz, Harvey. 1987. The Catholic Mission and the Sioux: A Crisis in the Early Paradigm. In *Sioux Indian Religion: Tradition and Innovation,* ed. Raymond J. DeMallie and Douglas R. Parks, pp.113–37. Norman: University of Oklahoma Press.

Mattina, Anthony. 1973. Colville Grammatical Structure. Ph.D. diss., University of Hawaii.

———. 1985. *The Golden Woman: The Colville Narrative of Peter J. Seymour.* Tucson: University of Arizona Press.

May, Robert. 1969. Homicide of a Community: Termination This Time for the Colville Indians. In *The Education of the American Indian*, vol.4, *The Organization Question*, pp.817–49. 91st Cong., 1st sess. Washington, D.C.: United States Senate Committee on Labor and Public Welfare.

Merriam, Alan. 1967. *Ethnomusicology of the Flathead Indians*. Publications in Anthropology 44. New York: Viking Fund.

Miller, Christopher. 1985. *Prophetic Worlds: Indians and Whites on the Columbia Plateau*. New Brunswick: Rutgers University Press.

Miller, Jay. 1979. Rock Art on the Amero-Canadian Plateau. Paper delivered at New Directions in Native American Art History, University of New Mexico, Albuquerque.

———. 1980a. Plateau Rock Art as a Professional and Ethical Problem. Paper delivered at the Northwest Anthropological Conference, Western Washington University, Bellingham.

———. 1980b. High-Minded High Gods in North America. *Anthropos* 75: 916–19.

———. 1980c. The Matter of the (Thoughtful) Heart: Centrality, Focality, or Overlap. *Journal of Anthropological Research* 36(3): 338–42.

———. 1983. Review of *Kopet* by M. Gidley. PNQ 74(1): 45.

———. 1989. Mourning Dove: The Author as Cultural Mediator. In *Being and Becoming Indian: Biographical Studies of North American Frontiers*, pp.160–82. Chicago: Dorsey Press.

———. n.d.a. First Report on the Methow Drainage. Prepared for the Colville Confederated Tribes.

———. n.d.b. Cultural Resources of the Mount Tolman Environs: Ethnohistory and Ethnography. Prepared for the Colville Confederated Tribes.

———. n.d.c. Jesus Visits Sweatlodge: Corpus Christi among the Interior Salish on the Colville Reservation. To appear in proposed festschrift for William Elmendorf.

———. n.d.d. Another Plateau for Totemism and Tribalism in Native America: Two Versions. Manuscript.

Mourning Dove [Christine Quintasket]. 1927. *Co-Ge-We-A, the Half-Blood: A Depiction of the Great Montana Cattle Range*. Boston: Four Seas.

———. 1930. Letter: The Comfort Sisters' Corner. *Comfort* 42(5): 11, 17.

———. 1933. *Coyote Stories*. Ed. and illus. Heister Dean Guie, with notes by Lucullus V. McWhorter (Old Wolf) and a foreword by Chief Standing Bear. Caldwell, Idaho: Caxton Printers.

———. 1976. *Tales of the Okanogans*. Ed. Donald M. Hines. Fairfield, Wash.: Ye Galleon Press.

————. 1981. *Cogewea*. With an introduction by Dexter Fisher. Lincoln: University of Nebraska Press.

Otter, Lucille Trosper. 1988. Letter about Hector McCloud, Flathead Allotee 1098 (with cover letter from Dr. Ronald Trosper). (In possession of editor.)

Overmeyer, Philip. 1941. George B. McClellan and the Pacific Northwest. PNQ 32:3–60.

Palladino, L. B. 1922. *Indian and White in the Northwest: A History of Catholicity in Montana, 1831–1891*. 2d ed. Lancaster, Pa.: Wickersham.

Palmer, Gary. 1980. Indian Pioneers: Coeur d'Alene Mission Farming, 1842–1876. Paper presented at the twenty-eighth annual meeting of the American Society of Ethnohistory, San Francisco.

Pettitt, George. 1946. *Primitive Education in North America*. UCPAAE 43(1): 1–182.

Pfaller, Louis. 1978. *James McLaughlin: The Man with an Indian Heart*. New York: Vantage Press.

Point, Nicholas. 1967. *Wilderness Kingdom: Indian Life in the Rocky Mountains, 1840–1847*. Trans. and intro. Joseph Donnelly. New York: Holt, Rinehart and Winston.

Primitive Man. 1944. (Special issue on the Shaking Tent) 17(3–4): 45–86.

Rafert, Stewart. 1982. The Hidden Community: The Miami Indians of Indiana, 1846–1940. Ph.D. diss., University of Delaware.

Randolph, June. 1957. Witness of Indian Religion: Present-Day Concepts of the Guardian Spirit. PNQ 48:139–45.

Raufer, Sister Maria Ilma. 1966. *Black Robes and Indians on the Last Frontier: A Story of Heroism*. Milwaukee: Bruce.

Ray, Verne. 1932. The Sanpoil and Nespelem, Salishan Peoples of Northeastern Washington. UWPA. 5:1–237.

————. 1933. Sanpoil Folk Tales. *Journal of American Folklore* 46:129–87.

————. 1936a. Native Villages and Groupings of the Columbia Basin. PNQ 27:99–152.

————. 1936b. The Kolaskin Cult: A Prophet Movement of 1870 in Northeastern Washington. *American Anthropologist* 38(1): 67–75.

————. 1939. *Cultural Relations in the Plateau of Northwestern America*. Publications of the Frederick Webb Hodge Anniversary Publication Fund 3. Los Angeles: Southwest Museum.

————. 1941. Historic Backgrounds of the Conjuring Complex in the Plateau and the Plains. In *Language, Culture, and Personality*, ed. Leslie Spier, A.

Irving Hallowell, and Stanley Newman, pp.204–16. Menasha, Wisc.: Sapir Memorial Publication Fund.

———. 1960. The Columbia Indian Confederacy: A League of Central Plateau Tribes. In *Culture in History: Essays in Honor of Paul Radin*, ed. Stanley Diamond, pp.177–89. New York: Columbia University Press.

Relander, Click. 1956. *Drummers and Dreamers: The Story of Smowhala the Prophet and His Nephew Puck Hyah Toot, the Last Prophet of the Nearly Extinct River People, the Last Wanapums*. Caldwell, Idaho: Caxton Printers.

Richards, Kent. 1979. *Isaac I. Stevens: Young Man in a Hurry*. Provo, Utah: Brigham Young University Press.

Rooney, Daniel. 1973. A preliminary inventory of the records of the Bureau of Indian Affairs, Colville Indian Agency, including the Spokane Agency, 1865–1952. Federal Archives and Records Center, Seattle.

Ross, Alexander. 1856. *The Red River Settlement: Its Rise, Progress, and Present State, with Some Account of the Native Races and Its General History to the Present Day*. London: Smith, Elder.

———. 1923. *Adventures of the First Settlers on the Oregon or Columbia River*. Ed. Milo Milton Quaife. Chicago: Lakeside Press. Originally published 1849.

———. 1924. *The Fur Traders of the Far West*. Ed. Milo Milton Quaife. Chicago: Lakeside Press. Originally published 1855.

Ross, John Alan. 1968. Political Conflict on the Colville Reservation. NARN 2(1): 29–91.

Ruby, Robert H., and John A. Brown. 1965. *Half-Sun on the Columbia: A Biography of Chief Moses*. Norman: University Of Oklahoma Press.

Ruoff, A. LaVonne Brown. 1986. George Copway: Nineteenth-Century American-Indian Autobiographer. Ed. Robert J. Payne. Multicultural American Autobiography Issue. *Auto/Biography Studies* 3(2): 6–17.

———. 1989. Nineteenth Century American Indian Autobiographers: William Apes, George Copway, and Sarah Winnemucca. In *Redefining American Literary History*, ed. A. LaVonne Brown Ruoff and Jerry W. Ward. New York: Modern Language Association.

Ryker, Lois. 1962. Hu-mi-shu-ma: Mourning Dove Was the Sweet Voice of the Indians of Eastern Washington. *Seattle Times*, 18 February.

Sample, L. L., and Albert Mohr. 1980. Wishram Birth and Obstetrics. *Ethnology* 19(4): 427–45.

Schaeffer, Claude. 1969. *The Blackfoot Shaking Tent*. Occasional Paper 5. Calgary: Glenbow-Alberta Institute.

———. n.d. The Curtained Stage: A Study of Kutenai Conjuring Practices. Manuscript filed at the Glenbow-Alberta Institute, Calgary.

Scheuerman, Richard, ed. 1982. *The Wenatchi Indians: Guardians of the Valley*. Fairfield, Wash.: Ye Galleon Press.

Schoenberg, Wilfred P. 1962. *A Chronicle of the Catholic History of the Pacific Northwest, 1743–1960, Arranged after the Manner of Certain Medieval Chronicles and Annotated with Copious Notes for Future Reference*. Portland: Catholic Sentinel Press.

Schultz, John L. 1968. Deprivation, Revitalization, and the Development of the Shaker Religion. NARN 2(1): 92–119.

———. 1971. Acculturation and Religion on the Colville Indian Reservation. Ph.D. diss., Washington State University.

Seiler, Vesta, Chair. 1976. *From Pioneers to Power: Historical Sketches of the Grand Coulee Dam Area*. Nespelem, Wash.: Rima Printing and Graphics.

Showalter, Elaine. 1977. *A Literature of Their Own: British Women Novelists from Brontë to Lessing*. Princeton: Princeton University Press.

Sperlin, Ottis Bedney. 1934. *The Heart Of the Skyloo*. Portland: Metropolitan Press.

Spier, Leslie. 1925. An Analysis of Plains Indian Parflêche Decoration. UWPA 1(3): 89–112.

———. 1935. The Prophet Dance of the Northwest and Its Derivatives: The Source of the Ghost Dance. GSA 1:1–74.

———, ed. 1936. Tribal Distributions in Washington. GSA 3:1–43.

———, ed. 1938. The Sinkaietk or Southern Okanogan of Washington. GSA 6:1–262.

Splawn, Andrew Jackson. 1917. *Ka-mi-akin: The Last Hero of the Yakimas*. Portland: Kilham Stationery and Printing.

Spokesman Review. 1936. Obituary of Mourning Dove. 15 August, p.3.

Sprague, Roderick, and Jay Miller. 1979. Chief Joseph Dam, Ancestral Burial Relocation Survey, Rufus Woods Lake, Washington. Anthropological Research Manuscript Series 51. Moscow: University of Idaho.

Straus, Anne Sawyier. 1976. Being Human in the Cheyenne Way. Ph.D. diss., University of Chicago.

Strong, William Duncan, W. Egbert Schenck, and Julian Steward. 1930. Archaeology of the Dalles-Deschutes Region. UCPAAE 29(1): 1–154.

Suttles, Wayne. 1957. The Plateau Prophet Dance among the Coast Salish. SWJA 13(4): 352–96.

Swanson, Earl. 1959. Archaeological Survey of the Methow Valley, Washington. *Tebiwa* 2(1): 72–82.

Symons, Thomas Wm. 1967. *The Symons Report on the Upper Columbia River and the Great Plain of the Columbia*. Fairfield, Wash.: Ye Galleon Press. Originally published 1882.

Teit, James. 1917. Okanogan Tales. In Boas (1917), pp.65–97.

———. 1928. The Middle Columbia Salish. UWPA 2(4): 83–128.

———. 1930. The Salishan Tribes of the Western Plateaus. *Bureau of American Ethnology, Annual Report* 45:23–396.

Thwaites, Reuben Gold. 1904. *Original Journals of the Lewis and Clark Expedition, 1804–1806*. 7 vols. New York: Dodd, Mead.

Toole, K. Ross. 1959. *Montana: An Uncommon Land*. Norman: University of Oklahoma Press.

Touhy, Patrick J. 1983. *Finding a Way Home: Indian and Catholic Spiritual Paths of the Plateau Tribes*. Spokane, Wash.: University Press.

Turnbull, Christopher. 1977. *Archaeology and Ethnohistory in the Arrow Lakes, Southeastern British Columbia*. Ottawa: Archaeological Survey of Canada 65.

Turner, Nancy. 1978. *Food Plants of British Columbia Indians: Part 2. Interior Peoples*. Handbook 36. Victoria: British Columbia Provincial Museum.

Turner, Nancy J., Randy Bouchard, and Dorothy I. D. Kennedy. 1980. *Ethnobotany of the Okanagan-Colville Indians of British Columbia and Washington*. Occasional Paper Series 21. Victoria: British Columbia Provincial Museum.

Turney-High, Harry Holbert. 1937. The Flathead Indians of Montana. *American Anthropological Association, Memoirs* 48:1–161.

———. 1941. Ethnography of the Kutenai. *American Anthropological Association, Memoirs* 56:1–210.

Uebelacker, Morris. 1978. *Cultural Resource Overview of the Tonasket Planning Unit*. Okanogan, Wash.: Okanogan National Forest.

Underhill, Ruth. 1938. A Papago Calendar Record. *University of New Mexico Bulletin* 322, Anthropological ser. 2(5): 1–66.

United States House of Representatives. 1926. Claims of the Colville and

Okanogan Indians: Hearing before a Subcommittee of the Committee of Indian Affairs, 69th Cong., 1st sess. H.R. 9270.

United States National Archives. 1965. Microfilm of Censuses of the Tribes on the Colville Reservation, 1885–1940. No. 440, reels 49–56.

Van Kirk, Sylvia. 1985. "What if Mama Is an Indian?" The Cultural Ambiguity of the Alexander Ross Family. In *The New Peoples: Being and Becoming Métis in North America,* ed. Jacqueline Peterson and Jennifer S. H. Brown. pp.207–17. Manitoba Studies in Native History 1. Lincoln: University of Nebraska Press.

Walker, Deward. 1968. *Conflict and Schism in Nez Perce Acculturation: A Study in Religion and Acculturation.* Pullman: Washington State University Press.

———. 1969. New Light on the Prophet Dance Controversy. *Ethnohistory* 16(3): 245–55.

Warren, Claude. 1968. The View from Wenas: A Study in Plateau Prehistory. *Occasional Papers of the Idaho State University Museum* 24:1–89.

Wilkes, Charles. 1845. *Narrative of the United States Exploring Expedition, during the Years 1838, 1839, 1840, 1841, 1842.* 5 vols. Philadephia: Lea and Blanchard.

Williams, Christina MacDonald McKenzie. 1922. Reminiscences. whq 13: 107–17.

Wilson, Charles. 1865. Report on the Indian Tribes Inhabiting the Country in the Vicinity of the 49th Parallel of North Latitude. *Transactions of the Ethnological Society* (London) 4:275–332.

———. 1970. *Mapping the Frontier between British Columbia and Washington: Charles Wilson's Diary of the Survey of the 49th Parallel, 1858–1862, while Secretary of the British Boundary Commission.* Ed. George F. G. Stanley. Toronto: Macmillan of Canada.

Wissler, Clark. 1971. *Red Man Reservations.* New York: Collier Books.

Wong, Bertha D. 1987. Pre-literate Native American Autobiography: Forms of Personal Narrative. Special issue, Ethnic Autobiography, *Melus* 14(1): 17–32.

Woody, Ozro. 1983. *Glimpses of Pioneer Life of Okanogan County, Washington.* Okanogan, Wash.: Okanogan Historical Society.

Yanan, Eileen, comp. 1971. *Coyote and the Colville.* Omak, Wash.: St. Mary's Mission.

Index

Abraham. *See* Broken Nose Abraham

Adolph (Lakes canoeman), 170

Adultery, 57, 107

Alex, Peter (Brother of Aropaghan), 183, 232 n6

American Fur Company, 150

Anderson, Major Albert, 4, 180, 231 n2

Andrew (Uncle), 175

Arcasa, Isabel, ix

Arcasa, Pete Pierre, 229 n7

Aropaghan, Andrew, 94, 181, 187, 232 n4; and Medicine Dancing, 130

Arrow Lakes Tribe. *See* Lakes Tribe

Arrow Scraper (Lake Okanagan village), 4, 195 n2

Astor, John Jacob, 150

Babies: betrothal of, 52; care of, 70–78; language of, 209 n9

Baily, Bob (ferryman), 172

Balsamroot, 65, 207 n3

Baskets, 64, 207 n2

Bataille, Gretchen, xxxvii

Bathing, 78, 87

Baym, Nina, xxxvii

Bearcub, Matilde, ix

Bear grease (cosmetic), 67

Beaverhead (father of Mourning Dove's mother), 6

Bench, defined, 200 n22

Bernard, James, 25, 181, 232 n4

Berries, 65, 80

Biles-Coleman Company, xxv

Birth: customs observed in, 72–73; labor as sacrifice, 208 n3

Bitterroot (food), 19, 65

Bitterroot River, 151

Bitterroot Valley, 153

Blackfoot (as enemies), 146

Blanchet, Augustine (Bishop of Walla Walla), 196 n3

Blanchet, Frances Norbert, 224 n15

Bluejay, 73; spirit of, 32

Bone, Robert, xxxviii

Bone game (Slahal), 102

Bonner's Ferry, Idaho, 10, 170

Bossburg, Washington, 170

Boulder Creek, 118

Brewster, Washington, 228 n1

Broderick, Theresa, 193 n5

Broken Nose Abraham, 173, 231 n10

Brown, Charley, 41, 183, 232 n6

Browning Rule, xiii

Brumble, H. David, xxxvi

Bubb, John W., 231 n2

Buffalo (bison): hunts, 220 n3; roundup at Flathead, xvi; used for artifacts, 146

Bureau of Indian Affairs, 182

Burial customs, 93–94

Butte, Montana, 186

Caldi, Fr. Celestine (Salista), 27, 201 n38

Calendar strings, xxviii, 207 n7
Calgary, Alberta, xvii
Camp Eureka (Republic), Washington, 178
Canada, border survey of, 154
Canadian Pacific Railroad, 230 n8
Cards. *See* Monte; Wal-looks
Caruana, Giuseppe (Big Belly), 26, 201 n26
Cascade, British Columbia, 229 n7
Catherine (Nez Perce wife of Angus McDonald), 225 n17
Cayuse, 153, 157
Central Peak, 231 n1
Chantilly, Battle of, 154
Chaperon, 49
Charlie, T. B., ix
Charms, 79–90; ingredients of, 87
Chastity, 49–50
Chelan Tribe, xxvii
Cherries, 114
Chesaw, Washington, 20
Chesnin-Bernstein family, ix
Chewelah, Washington, 29; Metis Cree settlement, 197 n11
Chewelah Valley, 154
Chief Joseph (Wallowa Nez Perce), xxx, 193 n14
Chief Joseph Dam, xxvi
Chinook Jargon, 94
Chinook Tribe, xxvi
Chipmunk, 46
Chirouse, Fr. Eugene, 195 n3
Christine (child of Chief Seattle, wife of Coxit George), 228 n2
Christmas (First Shoot Day), 130; and heavy snow of 1892, 158
Clothing styles, 64, 74, 175
Coal, discovery of, 171
Coeur d'Alene Tribe, xxvii; camp at Kettle Falls, 100
Coffin, Geraldine. *See* Guie, Geraldine

Collet, Emily, 185
Collier, John, xxx
Columbian Tribe, xxvii
Columbia River (Swanetka), 146, 155, 192
Columbine, 87, 210 n4
Colvile, Andrew (Andrew Wedderburn), 150, 223 n10
Colville Indian Association, 155
Colville National Forest, 118
Colville Reservation, xi, xxvi, 226 n20; executive orders concerning, 226 n20; history of, xxx; North Half, xxvi, xxx, 184, 233 n7, 226 n20
Colville Tribe, xiii, xxvii, xxxiv, 3, 99, 145
Conception, 70
Conequah (shaman with Lingfish power), 133
Contests (at Kettle Falls), 102
Cooking, 63
Coosta (shaman at Northport), 132
Corona, British Columbia, 196 n3
Corpus Christi (Catholic feastday), 30, 228 n2, 225 n16
Cotolegu, Joseph (Colvile leader), 232 n4
Cougars, 83
Covington, Lucy, ix
Cox, Ross (at Fort Okanogan), 222 n9
Coxit George (at Kartar), 228 n2
Coyote: and fog, xxiv; smashes dams, 227 n21
Cranbrook, British Columbia, 171, 231 n8
Curlew, Billy, 205 n3
Curlew, Washington, 119, 121
Cusick, Washington, 170

Dancing, Winter, 123–29
Day names, 214 n11

Debo, Angie, 231 n2

Deer, 117; starve in droves, 159, 174

Delaware, 209 n10

De Rouge, Stephen (Entienne), 26, 44, 130, 201 n28

De Smet, Pierre Jean, 4, 105, 151, 200 n24; visits Fort Colville, 224 n12

De Vos, Fr. Peter, 151, 224 n15

Diapers, 74

Diet: neglected, 192; restrictions, 67, 117

Digging stick (dibble), 80

Diseases, 68, 192, 207 n6. *See also* Influenza; Measles; Scarlet Fever

Dogs, 115, 135; carcass cure, 223 n9; whipped, 73

Douglas Lake, 149

Dover, Harriet Shelton, 200 n20

Eagle Feather Club, xxv

Earthquake of 1872, 152

East Omak, Washington, xxii, xxv

Education, 182; about spiritual powers, 37, 39

Edwards, Bridgett, 25

Eells, Rev. Cushing, 117; with Spokan at Tshimakain, 216 n2

Ellisford, 26

Elopement, 52

Emblem-token, 217 n2

Enchelium (Inchelium), Washington, 190

Entiat Tribe, xxvii

Epithets, 189, 219 n5

Etiquette, 78, 118, 229 n6

Farming, 167–69

Fasting, 38

February (Spakt), 125

Fernie, British Columbia, 171

Fir boughs and needles, 87, 219 n4

First Food feasts, 213 n5

Fishing. *See* Kettle Falls

Flags, 214 n11

Flathead Lake, xvi

Flathead Tribe, xvi, 100, 146, 151

Flood of 1893, 164

Flowers, 85

Foods, 121, 129, 167, 175, 207 n3; marrow, 117; mussels, 162; sharing of, 122, 126, 166, 179

Fort Benton, 225 n18

Fort Colville, 9, 106, 150, 152; De Smet visits, 224 n12; Lt. Johnson visits, 227 n24

Fort George (Astoria), 107, 223 n.9

Fort Okanogan, 222 n8, 222 n9, 227 n24

Fort Shaw, xiii, xvi

Fort Simcoe, 196 n3

Fort Spokane, xiii, 180

Fort Steele, British Columbia, 8, 10, 91, 166, 171

Fort Vancouver, 151

Fraser River Salishans, xxvii

Fredin family, ix

Friedlander, Herman, ix

Frye, Dick (husband of Suesteel), 170

Funerals, 89, 94, 210–11 n2. *See also* Burial customs; Mourning

Galbraith, Major John, 8, 230 n8

Galler, Fred (second husband), xxii, 31, 203 n33

Gambling, 102

Gardens, 168

Gender equality, 208 n1

General Allotment Act, 226 n20

Gerome brothers, 218 n2

Gibbs, Marceline and Margaret, 119

Gidley, Mick, 194 n18

Give-Away (at Winter dance), 126, 217 n3
God, Sweatlodge versus Christian, 44, 141
Gold mining, 231 n9
Goodwin Mission, xiii, 10, 54, 119; hymn singing, 106; land given by Kinkanawah, 197 n11; school, xiii, 25–28; Sunday Mass, 105
Goose Lake, 228 n2
Grand Coulee, Washington, 155, 231 n1
Grand Coulee Dam, xxvi, xxx
Grand Forks, British Columbia, 229 n7
Grant, U. S., xxx
Great Falls, Montana, xvi
Griva, Edward, 27, 202 n30
Grizzly bears, 83, 210 n1
Groundhog, eaten, 116
Guie, Geraldine, x, xxxii
Guie, Hester Dean, xxxi; edits Mourning Dove, xxiii
Gunther, Erna, x, xxxii, xxxv

Ha-ah-pecha (Okanogan shaman), 16
Hair, 67, 77; puberty taboo, 42; during mourning, 92
Hale, Horatio, 228 n24
Harelip, 76
Harney's Depot (Fort Colville), 197 n11
Harpoon, 100
Hayes family, 185
Herbs, 68
Hide tanning, 103–4
Hilbert, Vi, ix
Homestead Act, 173
Homesteading, 180
Hoop game, 102

Horses, 115; carcass cure, 223 n9; cayuse, 157, 201 n29; enables buffalo hunts, 146
Household goods, 62
Housing, 192, 199 n.17
Hudson's Bay Company, 152
Hunt, Clair, 42, 182, 232 n6
Hunting: fall, 66; luck, 67
Hymns (Catholic), 93, 94, 102, 213 n7

Ignace (Old Ignace La Mousse Saxa; Iroquois) 224 n13
Ilemux-solux, Martin (Arrow Lakes chief), 151
Illegitimacy, 75
Inchelium, Washington, 26, 190
Influenza, 68, 189
Ingram, Jack (butcher), 121
Inkameep Reserve, British Columbia, xx, 191
In-y-tink (husband of Ka-at-qhu), 91

Jesuits, xxix, 224 n12; change burial customs, 93
Joseph, Mary Rose, 25
Julia (Sulee; Snow Dress), 11

Ka-at-qhu (Big Lips), 16, 95, 121, 216 n5; wife of In-ya-tink, 91
Kala'len (Caroline), 112
Kalispel Tribe, xxvii, 170; at Pend d'Oreille, 145; at Kettle Falls, 100; hunting camp, 116; odor of herb, 102
Kamiakin (Yakima leader), 196 n3
Kamloops, British Columbia, 225 n17
Kanatal (whipper, divider), 106, 112
Kane, Paul, 223 n11
Kartar Valley, 227 n22
Kelawna, British Columbia, 4, 195 n2

Keleta (Mourning Dove's sister), 115, 121, 160

Keller, Washington, 26

Kelly family, takes claim at Pia, 187

Kelly Hill (Pia), Washington, 4, 190

Kel-yel-pas (Lone Tree), 178

Kentucky, 186

Kettle Falls, xiii, xxx, 21, 223 n9; Colvile camp, 100; division of food, 101; hides tanned, 103; housing, 100; other names of, 149, 150; prime fishery, 9, 99, 145; recreation, 102–3; regulations governing women, 104; Skoyelpi, 224 n12; Suicide Cliffs, 104; Sunday observed, 105; swimming, 105; tribal camps, 99; women's sweatlodges, 105

Kettle River, 118, 157

Kinkade, Dale, ix

Kinkanawah, (Colvile chief), 130, 151, 232 n4; orders Sunday observance, 105; introduces whipping for crimes, 107; nephew of See-whelh-ken, 8; prayer at Goodwin Mission, 106

Kissing, 89

Klickitat Tribe, 64, 153

Kolaskin (Kwolaskin, Sanpoil prophet), xxix, 224 n16

Kootenay Pelly, 156

Kootenay River, xii, 10

Kootenay Tribe, xvi, xxvii, 146; at Tobacco Plains, 7; gamblers, 174, 231 n11; Lower, 217 n1

Lake Osoyoos, 121, 157

Lakes (Arrow Lakes) Tribe, xiii, xxvii, 132

Lane, Sheriff John (at Marcus), 190

Latham, Dr. Edward (at Nespelem), 194 n18

Latin, 94, 151

Laughter, as insult, 89

Lemere, Annie, 29, 54

Lemere, Bridgett, 29

Lemere, Eva (musician at Pia church), 29

Lenape, 209 n.10

Lerman, Norman, 209 n11

Levirate, 206 n11

Lewis, John, 223 n11

Lewis and Clark, 149

Lieber family, ix

Ling spirit (Oldman), 133, 218 n3

Little Canyon, 121

Little Rock (Shaman), 132, 135

Lodge, 131, 199 n17

Long Alex (boatman), 119

Louie, Caroline (Kala'ten), 112

Love charm, 87; use of, 88–90

McClellan, George, 153, 226 n19

McCuen, Edwin Harrison (with stageline), 231 n1

McDonald, Angus (Whoop-chen), 106, 152, 225 n17

McDonald, Archibald, 224 n12

McDonald, Catherine, 152

McDougal, Johnny (Husband of Antoinette Somday), 120

McLaughlin, James, 194 n15

McLaughlin Agreement of 1905, xxx, 194 n15, 226 n20

McLeod, Hector (first husband), xvi

McLoughlin Canyon, 120

McNickle, D'Arcy, 215 n16

McWhorter, Lucullus Virgil, xx, xxiii, xxxi

Mallot, Washington, 212 n3

Malta, 201 n26

Manson cemetery, 212 n2

Marchand, Old Lady, 151

Marcus, Washington, 29, 53, 93, 95,
163, 172, 190
Marcus Flat, 106
Maria (Soma-how-atqu; Mourning
Doves mother's mother), xiii, 6,
8; herbalist, 79; moves to Win-
demere, 215 n16
Marriage, 51–59; and desertion, 56;
during Prophet Dance, 205 n7;
feast, 55; half-marriage of native
California, 206 n8; mortgage
right, 58
Martin, Henry, 229 n7
Mary, Aunt (herbalist), 53, 81
Mary Ann (schoolchild), 25
Massage, 208 n4
Mattina, Anthony, ix, 219 n2
Meals, 63, 199 n17
Measles, 68
Medicines, 88
Memorial feast, 95
Menstrual hut, 49, 204 n7; as ref-
uge, 67
Merritt, British Columbia, 8
Methow Tribe, xxvii, xxx
Meyers Falls, Washington, 29
Midway, British Columbia, 121
Milk, cow's, 74, 185, 208 n5
Miller, Jay, xxxiv
Miller, William (first allotee), 183
Miller family, ix
Milwaukee, Wisconsin, xvii
Mineral Law, 177
Moccasins, 66
Modesta (aged Okanogan woman),
148
Modesty, 50, 208 n2, 215 n15
Monse, Washington, 128
Monte (card game), 103
Month names, 198 n12
Montreal, 149
Moon: High Water, 65; Buttercup,
65, 159; Chokeberry, 99; of
Leaves, 65; White, 121

Morrison, Edwin (with stageline),
178
Moses (chief), xxix, xxx, 206 n10,
216 n4, 220 n3
Moses Treaty (1883), 120
Mother-in-law, 56; Retirement of,
61
Mount Baldy, 82, 210 n1
Mount Chopaka, 148
Mount Sinai, 44
Mourning, 58, 91–92
Mourning Dove: active in Colville
Indian Association, 155; advantages as Indian, 12; born, 10;
buys typewriter, xxi; childhood
attire, 32; club activities, xxv;
collects "folklores," xxii;
Cogewea, xxiii; *Coyote Stories*,
xxxi; death of, xxvi; drafts of
"Tipi Life" and "Educating the
Indian," xxxiii; edits Indian legends, xxiii–xxiv; emotional
stresses, xxiv; female bias, xxiv;
fiction and melodrama used by,
xiii, xxiv, xxxviii; first communion, 30; first menstruation,
42–44; at Goodwin Mission, 24,
27; "History of the Okanogan,"
xxxvi; infant betrothal, 52; in-
terviewed, xx; learns sewing, 41;
learns alphabet, 186; manuscript for autobiography, xii,
xxxii; marriage proposals, 54,
88; as migrant laborer, xi; mus-
ing on her future, 32; other
names of, xi, xxvii, xx, xxv, 16,
96; political activities, xxv; pronoun usage of, xxxiv; public lec-
tures, xxv; receives love charm,
87; refuses love magic, 79; re-
jects marriage, 53, 81; religious
search, 202 n.32; and reservation officials, xi, xxv; siblings,
10; as teacher, xxi

Moyie, British Columbia, 171, 230n7
Mus-aia (Valerian plant), 102

Nachumchin, Chief Antoine, 191
Naming, 74, 96
Native American Religious Freedom Act, 202n31
Nellie (at Marcus), shows charity, 164
Nespelem Tribe, xxvii, 26
Nettles, 219n4
Newberry Library, x
Newport, Washington, 190
New Year's Day (Last Shoot Day, Baby Year), 130, 158
Nez Perce, 153; as enemies, 147; of Wallowa Valley, 194n14; sorcery of, 128
Nicola Tribe, xvi, 4, 195n2, 207n7, 220n4; source for pithouses, 147
Northport, Washington, 130
Northwest Company, 149

Oblates, 195n3
Ojibwa Shaking Tent, 218n1
Okanogan (Lake, Canadian, Upper) Tribe, xxvii, 81
Okanogan (River, American, Lower) Tribe, xvi, xxvii, 99, 145; camp at Kettle Falls, 100; Chief Red Fox, 222n9
Oliver, British Columbia, xx
Olympia, Washington, 152
Omak cemetery, 211n2
Openheimer, Marcus (namesake of Marcus, Wa), 179
Oregon grape, 219n4
Oregon Trail, 196n3
Oroville, Washington, 191
Osoyoos Lake, British Columbia, 20, 53, 99
Otter, Lucille Trosper, 193n4

Owhi (Yakima leader), 196n3

Pacific Fur Company, 150
Page, Jennie, 25
Pah-tah-heet-sa (Nicola woman), 4; Fights grizzly bear, 5
Paints, 18, 199n18
Palmer, Joel (Oregon Indian superintendent), 225n18
Pandosy, Fr. Charles, 4, 195n3
Papago, 208n7
Parfleches, 18
Pascal Sherman Indian School, 201n27
Patee, 91. *See also* Maria
Pateros, Washington, 228n1
Pattern numbers: fire, 139; twelve, 219n.3
Paul, Pierre (betrothed infant), 52, 54
Pejoratives, 219n5
Penticton, British Columbia, 191
Peone, Emily, ix
Peskwaws Tribe, xvii, 146, 193n9. *See also* Wenatchi Tribe
Pia (Kelly Hill), xxiv, 4, 21, 130, 229n7; homesteading, 167; Meaning of, 230n1; noted for wild cherries, 114
Pichette, Agatha, 25
Pichette, Louise, 25
Pictographs, 47; at questing sites, 204n10
Pierre, Maggie (wife of Pete Pierre), 185
Pierre, Pete (part-Iroquois innkeeper), 178
Pierre, Mrs. Sam, 112
Pinkley City (Fort Colville), 197n11; early name of Colville, Washington, 4. *See also* Fort Colville
Pipe, 55; at seancing rite, 131; used by See-whehl-ken, 112

Pithouses, 148

Plants: as men, 86, 210n3; chief, 86

Plateau traditions, xxix

Point, Nicholas (artist and Jesuit), 200n24

Poke, John (Wasco elder), 149

Poker Joe (Colville policeman), 232n3

Pole (as world axis), 123, 131, 216n1

Polson, Montana, xvi, xx

Polygyny, 57, 206n10

Population figures, 145, 220n2

Power: emblem of, 217n2; sources of, 47; spirit, 123

Prayer leader (Catholic woman), 93

Pregnancy, 70–72

Protestantism, Spokan converts to, 117

Puberty, 38–39, 204n.1

Purification, 88

Purpose of existence, 69

Questing, 35

Quetasket, Alex (Black Cloud), 25

Quintasket, Charles, ix; on whipping, 215n16

Quintasket, Johnny (Mourning Dove's brother), 30

Quintasket, Joseph (Dark Cloud; Mourning Dove's father), xvi, 4; ancestry of, 4; attempts waystation, 178; endangers baby, 76; gambles with Kootenay, 174; harvests bunchgrass, oats, wheat, 114; hunting success, 116, 122; objects to questing, 45; recalls 1872 earthquake, 152; Works at Fort Steele, 169

Quintasket, Louis Eneas (Mourning Dove's brother), 186

Rains, Major Gabriel, 196n3

Raufer, Sr. Maria Ilma, 201n28

Ravalli, Fr. Anthony, 9, 151, 224n14

Red Cross, 189

Red Fox (Okanogan chief), 222n9

Red River settlement, 156

Relatives, bride, 60; children, 78; grandparents, 35; groom, 51; mother-in-law, 56, 67; multiple wives, 57; husband, 66

Republic, Washington (Camp Eureka), 178

Restaurant, 179

Richard, Fr. Pascal, 196n3

Riverside, Washington, 120

Rock Creek, 121

Rockcut, Washington, 185

Ross, Alexander (marries Sarah Timentwa), 156

Ross, Sally (Sara), 156, 227n23

Ruoff, A. LaVonne Brown, xxxvii

Ryan, Jimmy, xvi, 30, 183; joins Quintasket family, 186

Sacred Heart Academy, 197n11

Saddles (handmade), 115

Sahaptians, xxvi

Saint Francis Regis Mission, 93; made only of wood, 151

Saint Ignatius, Montana, xvii

Saint Mary's Mission, 26, 197n11

Saint Paul's Mission, 9, 105, 151

Salishan dialect chains, 219n1

Salmon, 20; fishing, 99–104, 213–14nn.3, 4, 5

Sands, Kay, xxxvii

Sanpoil Tribe, xxvii, 145; camp at Kettle Falls, 100; steal horses, 222n9

Sauna, 219n6

Scarlet Fever, 68

Seancing (conjuring), 130–35, 217 n1

Seashells, as trade goods, 65

See-pas (Seepays; Salmon Tyee at Kettle Falls), 101; Paul Kane portrait, 224 n11

See-whelh-ken (Colvile chief), 6, 150; father of Maria, 8; meets David Thompson, 149; pipe, 112; served by Kanatal, 112

Seymour, Eneas, marries Annie Lemere, 54

Seymour, Joseph, 25, 178

Seymour, Rosalie, 25

Shamans (native doctors), 34; angered by girl, 127; at Winter dance, 124; healing of sick by, 126; danger to pregnant women of, 71; and duels, 217 n4; gifts given by, 135; initiation of, 126; and seancing, 131–35; red hem of, 207 n1; modesty of, 125

Sharks, 222 n9

Sharp-Against motif, 219 n4

Shoshoni (enemies), 147

Showalter, Elaine, xxxvii

Shurz, Nevada, xvii

Shuswap Tribe, 64, 146

Similkameen Valley, British Columbia, 31; as Nicola colony, 148

Sisters of Charity, 197 n11

Skiuhushu, Rev. Red Fox, xxxviii

Skoyelpi (Kettle Falls leader), 224 n12

Slahal (bone game), 102

Slavery, Spanish, 215 n13

Slocum, Frances (Lost Sister of the Wyoming), xxxviii

Smallpox, xxix, 15, 68

Snowshoes, 21

Social distinctions, indicated by head gear, 204 n.1

Soma-how-atqhu (Maria), 6. *See also* Maria

Somday, Antoinette (wife of Tonasket), 120

Song: of the herb, 80; spirit, 123, 125, 126

Sorcery, xiii; to separate lovers, 85

Sororate, 206 n11

Spider (in Nicola story), 149

Spinsters, 51

Spirits, 32; as "pardners," 203 n3; emblem of, 217 n2; Ling, 133, 218 n.3

Spokane, Washington, 172

Spokan Garry, 156

Spokan House, 223 n9

Spokan Tribe, xxvii; camp at Kettle Falls, 100; hunting beliefs, 117; pregnant girl violates taboos, 118; protestants, 117; shaman, 135

Sportsmanship, 103

Squant Tribe, 212 n2; camp at Kettle Falls, 100

Stanley, John Mix, 224 n11

Stealing, 168

Steele, Major Samuel, 230 n8. *See also* Fort Steele

Stevens, Isaac Ingalls, 152, 225 n10; promises Colvilles their land, 153

Stones, birthing magic of, 43, 70

Stories, told in winter, 157

Stove, 172

Stuart, David (at Fort Okanogan), 222 n8

Stui-kin, Louis (Mourning Dove's mother's brother), 6

Stui-kin, Lucy (Mourning Dove's mother), 6; cooks groundhog, 116; copes with famine, 161; death of, xiii, xvi; labors at Kettle Falls, 104; makes dolls, 23;

Stui-kin, Lucy (*cont.*)
   papers walls with a novel, 186;
   sets up tipi, 22
Sturgeon, 222 n9
Suesteel (wife of Dick Frye), 171
Suicide, 206 n9
Suicide Cliffs (at Kettle Falls), 104
Suitors, 51
Sulee (Julia; Mourning Dove's sis-
   ter), 7, 11, 91, 115, 121, 157
Sunday (Flag Hung Up Day), 105; at
   Kettle Falls, 105; observance of,
   214 n10
Sun power, 85
Suquamish, 209 n10
Survival by sharing, 166
Swansen (Kootenay canoeman), 10
Sweatlodge, 83, 88, 136–42; five
   powers, 36; gender specific, 103;
   prayers, 84; deity, 218 n2
Swimming (at Kettle Falls), 105
Swimptin (Okanogan chief), 156
Syolm (Methow shaman), 203 n5

Taboos, 67
Teequalt (Long Theresa), xvi; as
   puberty trainer, 40; has a bird
   spirit, 45; lives in tipi, 186
Teeth, baby, 209 n11
Thompson, David, 149; describes
   Kettle Falls, 220 n6
Thompson Tribe, 64
Timentwa, C. B. Suzen, 155; writ-
   ing an Indian Bible, 227 n22
Timentwa, Julianne, ix
Tobacco, 82, 222 n9
Tobacco Plains (Kootenay center),
   xvi, 196 n9; home of Maria, 7
Tombstones, introduced, 95
Tonasket, Batise, 178
Tonasket, Joseph (Okanogan
   leader), 128, 178, 216 n4
Tonasket, Washington, 120

Tonasket Indian School, 30
Tools, 62; baskets, 64, 207 n2;
   beamer, 104; bone awl, 115; cra-
   dleboard, 74; dibble, 80; granite
   at Kettle Falls, 103; harpoon,
   100; parfleches, 18; saddles,
   115; scrapers, 103; snowshoes,
   21; wagon, 172
Totems, 205 n5
Toulou Creek, 46
Trade, 64
Transvestite, 223 n.9
Treaty War of 1855 (Yakima War),
   xxix, 152
Trout Lake, xiii, 6, 196 n6
Tuberculosis, 68, 73
Tulalip Reservation, 196 n3
Tyee (salmon fishing leader), 101

Umatilla Reservation, xxvii, 153
Uncleanliness of women, 101
Upchurch, O. C. (Colville superin-
   tendent), xiii

Valerian (stinkroot), 213 n6
Vantage, Washington, xxvii
Vermillion, British Columbia, 18
Vernon, British Columbia, xiii, 120
Village layouts, 199 n17
Virginity, protection of: bloomers,
   49; cape, 49, 55, 204 n1

Wagon, 172
Waiilatpu Mission (Whitman Mis-
   sion), 216 n2
Walker, Rev. Elkanah, 117, 216 n2
Walker's Prairie, 216 n2
Walla Walla, Washington, 10, 90,
   201 n29
Walla Walla Frontier Days, xx
Walla Walla Indian Days, 210 n6
Wal-looks (Monte, card game), 103
Wapato Point, 226 n20

Warm Springs Reservation, xxvii

War stories (bogus), 23, 200 n23

Wasco-Wishram, 148

Wenatchi (Peskwaws) Tribe, xxii; camp at Kettle Falls, 100; shaman challenged, 31

Wheeler-Howard Act, xxx

Whipper: disciplines children, 35, 78, 209 n.12

Whipping, 73, 215 n13, 215 n16; introduced by Kinkanawah, 107

White Stone, Washington, 224 n16

Whitman, Rev. Marcus, 201 n29, 216 n2

Whitman, Narcissa, 216 n2

Wilbur, Washington, 231 n1

Wild Sunflower Club, xxv

Wilkes expedition, 227 n24

Williams, Cecilia (step-mother), xvi

Williams family, ix

Winans, William (Colville agent), 232 n4

Winter: crafts, 67; hard, 228 n3; village sites, 147

Winter Dance (medicine dance), 123–29, 131–35

Wolves, 222 n9

Women's powers, 124; with salmon, 212 n3; as chiefs, 193 n11

Yakima, Washington, xx, xxxii

Yakima Reservation, xxvii, 90, 128, 149, 207 n7

Yuwipi, 218 n1

Zuni, 208 n4

In the American Indian Lives series

I Stand in the Center of the Good
Interviews with Contemporary Native
American Artists
Edited by Lawrence Abbott

Authentic Alaska
Voices of Its Native Writers
Edited by Susan B. Andrews and
John Creed

Dreaming the Dawn
Conversations with Native Artists
and Activists
By E. K. Caldwell
Introduction by Elizabeth Woody

Chief
The Life History of Eugene Delorme,
Imprisoned Santee Sioux
Edited by Inéz Cardozo-Freeman

Chevato
The Story of the Apache Warrior Who
Captured Herman Lehmann
By William Chebahtah and
Nancy McGown Minor

Winged Words
American Indian Writers Speak
Edited by Laura Coltelli

Life, Letters and Speeches
By George Copway (Kahgegagahbowh)
Edited by A. LaVonne Brown Ruoff
and Donald B. Smith

Life Lived Like a Story
Life Stories of Three Yukon Native Elders
By Julie Cruikshank in collaboration
with Angela Sidney, Kitty Smith, and
Annie Ned

LaDonna Harris
A Comanche Life
By LaDonna Harris
Edited by H. Henrietta Stockel

Rock, Ghost, Willow, Deer
A Story of Survival
By Allison Adelle Hedge Coke

Essie's Story
The Life and Legacy of a Shoshone Teacher
By Esther Burnett Horne and
Sally McBeth

Song of Rita Joe
Autobiography of a Mi'kmaq Poet
By Rita Joe

Viet Cong at Wounded Knee
The Trail of a Blackfeet Activist
By Woody Kipp

Catch Colt
By Sidner J. Larson

Alanis Obomsawin: The Vision
of a Native Filmmaker
By Randolph Lewis

Alex Posey
Creek Poet, Journalist, and Humorist
By Daniel F. Littlefield Jr.

First to Fight
By Henry Mihesuah
Edited by Devon Abbott Mihesuah

Mourning Dove
A Salishan Autobiography
Edited by Jay Miller

I'll Go and Do More
Annie Dodge Wauneka, Navajo Leader
and Activist
By Carolyn Niethammer

Elias Cornelius Boudinot
A Life on the Cherokee Border
By James W. Parins

John Rollin Ridge
His Life and Works
By James W. Parins

Singing an Indian Song
A Biography of D'Arcy McNickle
By Dorothy R. Parker

Crashing Thunder
The Autobiography of an American Indian
Edited by Paul Radin

Turtle Lung Woman's Granddaughter
By Delphine Red Shirt and Lone Woman

Telling a Good One
The Process of a Native American
Collaborative Biography
By Theodore Rios and
Kathleen Mullen Sands

William W. Warren
The Life, Letters, and Times
of an Ojibwe Leader
By Theresa M. Schenck

Sacred Feathers
The Reverend Peter Jones (Kahkewaquonaby)
and the Mississauga Indians
By Donald B. Smith

Grandmother's Grandchild
My Crow Indian Life
By Alma Hogan Snell
Edited by Becky Matthews
Foreword by Peter Nabokov

No One Ever Asked Me
The World War II Memoirs
of an Omaha Indian Soldier
By Hollis D. Stabler
Edited by Victoria Smith

Blue Jacket
Warrior of the Shawnees
By John Sugden

I Tell You Now
Autobiographical Essays by Native
American Writers
Edited by Brian Swann and Arnold
Krupat

Postindian Conversations
By Gerald Vizenor and A. Robert Lee

Chainbreaker
The Revolutionary War Memoirs
of Governor Blacksnake
As told to Benjamin Williams
Edited by Thomas S. Abler

Standing in the Light
A Lakota Way of Seeing
By Severt Young Bear and R. D. Theisz

Sarah Winnemucca
By Sally Zanjani

CPSIA information can be obtained
at www.ICGtesting.com
Printed in the USA
LVHW041730200220
647650LV00013B/225